The Cost-Conscious Cruiser

Champagne Cruising on a Beer Budget

FOREWORD – AND ONWARD

MOST PEOPLE, with a new book by the Pardeys in their hands, will skip the foreword. They will be keen to press on, for they know what value is in store for them. Well, let us say that most sailing people will know: there can be few who are not familiar with the writings of an outstanding cruising couple, in both books and magazines. They know that they can expect good seamanship, and sound practical sense from a couple who have thirty years of sail cruising behind them, who have built and maintained their own boat, and who have sailed more than 150,000 miles in almost all the world's waters, including a circumnavigation.

Yes, sailing people will pick up a new Pardey book with pleasurable anticipation, and they will not be disappointed. Once again, they have produced a first-rate work. The primary concern of the present volume is for those who dream of long distance voyaging, with the monetary cost and the emotional costs; with route-planning and seamanship; with equipment and catering. As we have come to expect from this couple, it is both sensible and thorough. Subjects which are rarely treated elsewhere, such as the risky business of hauling-out in unfamiliar foreign yards, or the merits of buying a secondhand boat rather than a new one, are given very thoughtful treatment. Every opinion, every suggestion is backed by examples from real life, from the cruising experiences of other crews, as well as their own.

Though this is a book which will help dreamers to make their bluewater dreams come true, it has great value for those of us who stay in home waters. Good, practical, seamanship is good everywhere. What is good for long-distance, long term voyaging is equally good for shorter cruises. More money does not make it better.

If this modest couple can sail the oceans without VHF, or a diesel, or all the other fancy gadgets that are pressed upon us nowadays, others can take heart. It need not be so costly after all. That hope is justified by this book - after all, Lin and Larry have been proving it for many years past, and now they tell us just how it can be managed.

Denny Desoutter - Founding Editor, *Practical Boat Owner*, UK

ACKNOWLEDGMENTS

OF ALL THE PAGES in the books we have written, this has always been our favorite. When it is time to thank everyone who has helped us, it means our book is near completion. We can sit back and think of friends as well as people we have never actually met, who have so generously offered us information, assistance, or encouragement. Now, as both authors and publishers of this book, our list seems to have grown. We hope all who have helped are included here.

Joey and Terry Marullo, Niki Perryman and Jamie Morrison, John Neal, Barbara Marrett, Steve Callahan, Jack Bakken, and Peter French provided written material and information especially for this project. Paul Gelder, Tom Linskey, Andrew Simpson, Ted Brewer, Bob Perry, Chuck Paine, Greg Matzat of Sparkman and Stephens yacht designs, Barry Van Geffin of Laurent Giles yacht designs, Hal Roth, Totch Hartge, Des MacWilliams, Dave Spargo and Colin Bennett all submitted to interviews. We hope we have used the information they provided to give readers an accurate assessment of their subjects.

The editors of several yachting magazines have given us information and encouragement, plus permission to use diagrams from their publications. They include (but are not limited to) Nick Compton at *Classic Boat magazine*, Dick Everitt and Rodger Witt at *Practical Boat Owner*, Anne Hammick at *Flying Fish* the journal of the O.C.C., Neil Rusch of *South African Yachting*, and Robert Keeley of *Cruising Helmsman*. Denny Desoutter, editor of *Practical Boat Owner*, has given us extra assistance and emotional support. Patience Wales, editor of *Sail* magazine, was with us all the way on the project. On those days when the paper mountain (aka book manuscript) threatened to overwhelm us, her help as a sounding board meant more than she may realize.

People who have been of special help in keeping us on track as new publishers include Jon Eaton, Peter Coles, Joyce Hunsucker, Bernadette Brennan, Matt Morehouse, Oscar Lind and the crew at Robert Hale Co., and Mike Schubel at Thomson-Shore.

Scott Kennedy is responsible for the lovely pen-and-ink drawings that grace the first page of each section. Rob Johnson, cover designer, Peter Phelan of *Photomedia*, and Laura Martin of *Martin Associates* all assisted us. Mike and Pat Miller of *Miller's Maritime Bookstore* in Falmouth, England, let us use their wonderful store as a research center, mail drop, and almost second home. Kathleen Brandes, Pilar Wyman, Adrian Singer, and John Vigor – the editors, indexer, designer, and final editor – have all put up with our wandering ways and worked with the pressure of never knowing where they could contact us. Couldn't have pulled it together without these people.

But the most important extra players in this game have been Brian and Maddy Kerslake of *Topologika Software*, in Falmouth, England. Thanks go to them for putting this all on disk, for reorganizing some chapters time and again, for doing all the copying, and for becoming special friends as we worked together.

A final note of thanks goes to a young man you will meet in this book, a person who came to be almost like a son, Max Elstein. Max and his wife, Danielle remind us all that cost-conscious cruising is still possible, still enjoyable. And Max, you owe your mom a letter!

INTRODUCTION

IT WAS ONE OF THOSE TIMES when we were glad the winds blew fierce and foul. It was early Spring. Porthloo in the Scilly Isles off England's southwest corner offered good protection from the northeasterly gales, good holding for our anchor in a firm, sandy bottom. The ancient, history-laden town of St. Mary's, with an excellent selection of pubs, lay within easy reach. Not a bad place to be. But what really kept us from being restless when our goal was Dublin, Ireland, 300 miles to windward, was that this same gale had forced two other offshore cruising boats and their crews to seek shelter. Without this foul wind, each of us would have gone our own way, never knowing one another. We'd have missed the fine conversations that filled the movable feast, which flowed from one boat to the other and then ashore to include local sailmaker Keith Buchanan and his wife, Carol, who had just returned from three years of cruising the Caribbean on their 30 footer.

Lori Lawson and Carl Henger, two Americans aboard 28-foot *Bijou*, had been wandering under sail through Mexican and Central American waters for five years before making the dash across to Europe. Graham and Hillary Innard, an English couple with two small boys, were just home from two years in the Mediterranean on board their 32-footer, *Fluca*. We had recently returned from three months of speaking at cruising seminars in New Zealand and the United States. Now we were glad to be home, back on board *Taleisin* and this serendipitous gathering of people who shared so many similar experiences was to us a real treat.

As we all came to know each other during those days of strong winds, as we got past showing off our favorite boat improvements, finished exchanging stories of places we'd been, places we'd like to go, friends we had in common or hoped to meet, our conversation turned to the question most often asked by potential cruisers. We all agreed that the vast majority of people ask each of us, "What does it really cost? Dollars and cents, pounds and pence."

At first we discussed how much money each of us needed to continue our cruises. But soon the word *cost* itself became the topic. "Too many people are talking about cash budgets when they should be talking about all of the costs," someone mentioned.

The dictionary we carry on board has two primary definitions for the

The Cost-Conscious Cruiser

Champagne Cruising on a Beer Budget

Lin and Larry Pardey

PARDEY BOOKS
Arcata, California, USA

Copyright 1998 Mary Lin and Lawrence F Pardey

Library of Congress number 98-65766

Printed in the United States of America.

Published in the United States by Pardey Books.

WORD PROCESSING: Maddy Kerslake/Topologika Software

EDITING: Kathleen Brandes

FINAL COPY EDIT: John Vigor

INDEX: Wyman Indexing

COVER DESIGN: Rob Johnson

BOOK DESIGN AND COMPOSITION: Adrian Singer Design

MANUFACTURING: Thomson-Shore Inc.

PHOTO CREDITS: Bob Greiser pages 81, 87; Steinar Johnson pages 87, 89

ILLUSTRATION CREDITS: Vignettes – Scott Kennedy

DISTRIBUTED BY: Paradise Cay Publishing, P O Box 29, Arcata, California 95518-0029, USA. Telephone: 800-736-4509, Fax: 707-822-9163

TRADE DISTRIBUTION: Midpoint Trade Books, 27 West 20th Street, Suite 1102, New York, NY 10011. E-mail: midpointny@aol.com

NEW ZEALAND DISTRIBUTION: Boat Books, 22 Westhaven Drive, Auckland, New Zealand. E-mail: crew@boatbooks.co.nz

UK DISTRIBUTION: Kelvin Hughes Ltd., New North Road, Hainault, Ilford, Essex 1G6 2UR, United Kingdom. E-mail: marketing@kelvinhughes.co.uk

ISBN10: 0-9646036-5-9
ISBN13: 978-09646036-5-3

10 9 8 7 6

CONTENTS

CONTENTS

for

JOEY AND TERRY MARULLO
NIKI PERRYMAN AND JAMIE MORRISON
ASHLEY BUTLER –
the new generation of adventurers

And for all of you who yearn to be
"out there" cruising - to give you food
for thought, to encourage you to use
low-cost, renewable energy resources
(your own skills and the wind), instead of
costly, non-renewable resources such as
your checkbook and fossil fuels.

word *cost* - "amount paid" and "loss." Both definitions can relate to physical and emotional costs as readily as they can to cash.

The eight of us at Porthloo began recalling stories of potential cruisers who had carefully considered how to budget their cash and get their cruising boat, then either did not get away or returned home sooner than planned, dissatisfied or downright disillusioned. In the majority of cases, it was not lack of cash that aborted their cruise, but rather the emotional costs that proved too high: the skipper's loss of confidence in his own abilities, a partner or crew's loss of confidence and trust in the skipper's skills, the crew's worry about taking control if something happened to the skipper. We had all heard stories of gear failures, leaks, and steering breakdowns that began to weaken the feeling of trust in the boat and its equipment. Stories recurred about repairs and maintenance becoming a grind and a time-robber. People who went cruising to gain time and space began to feel that the necessary discomforts and stresses of the cruising life were just not worthwhile, that the whole idea had been pure folly.

Then we eight analysed those who considered their cruises successful - whether a three-month summer sojourn in the Rias of northern Spain, two years in the Med, a Pacific circuit, or an unlimited wander around the edges of the world. These cruisers all seemed to have achieved careful cost control - not only of their finances but also of their getaway plans and boat and equipment choices. Their expectations were more realistic and they had done a lot of mental preparation. They had practiced sailing and cruising before they set off, and they had been more willing to be flexible and try new things once they were "out there."

Preparation is the most important part of cruising. Gaining knowledge - not only from reading but also from hands-on experience - is vital. Only by getting out and gaining sea time can you accurately assess all of the costs you will encounter. Articles we have written over the past 10 years spell out the whole range of costs, along with the potential gains, of cruising. We have collected many of these articles here and added several completely new chapters to answer even more of the questions that potential cruisers ask. We feel that our 30 years of cruising on an earn-as-you-go budget puts us in a good position to provide these answers. This budget is within the reach of most Americans and most British and European people we met - a yearly sum equal to one third of that earned by a third-year schoolteacher, a postal worker, or a carpenter. This is equivalent to the official poverty level for an American couple living in the continental United States ($10,250 in 1996). In previous books, *The Self-Sufficient Sailor,* and *The Capable Cruiser,* we wrote about ways to control cash expenditures. We hope this new book will help you to think about the skills you'll need just as much as it encourages you to save cash for your departure. For you'll definitely need both.

All eight of us gathered at Porthloo were in full agreement. If we considered the time and effort we had put in to go cruising, and if we looked at the ties we had had to break, the cost of reaching that special anchorage was considerable. But we'd willingly pay it again, because we'd found a wondrous sense of freedom, the feeling we were in control of our own fates. Best of all, we knew we'd each set our sights on an achievable dream.

Authors' Notes

This book, like our previous books and our lives, has been a totally joint effort. Our thoughts and experiences are so entwined that sometimes we don't even remember which one of us wrote what! However, at certain times, one of us has a particular story to relate, so the narrative point of view switches from first-person plural to first-person singular. Rather than create awkward editorial parentheses, or cute typographical devices, we've made every effort to establish the context, so you should be able to grasp quickly which one of us is speaking as "I."

To avoid confusion that could be caused by fluctuating currency rates, we have used U.S. dollars throughout this book. For measurements and weights, we have shown both metric and imperial whenever possible. For those diagrams where this could have led to confusion, we have used imperial measurements: a conversion table follows this introduction.

Conversion Tables

	IMPERIAL	METRIC
Sq. inches to sq. millimeters multiply by 645.20	645.20	1
Inches to millimeters multiply by 25.40	25.40	1
Sq. feet to sq. meters multiply by 0.093	0.09	1
Inches to centimeters multiply by 2.54	2.54	1
Feet to meters multiply by 0.305	0.31	1
Nautical miles to kilometers multiply by 1.852	1.85	1
Miles to kilometers multiply by 1.609	1.61	1
Miles to nautical miles multiply by 0.8684	0.87	1
HP to metric HP multiply by 1.014	1.01	1
Pounds per sq. inch to kg per sq. centimeter multiply by 0.0703	0.07	1
HP to kilowatts multiply by 0.746	0.75	1
Cu inches to cu centimeters multiply by 16.39	16.39	1
Gallons to liters multiply by 4.54	4.54	1
Pints to liters multiply by 0.568	0.57	1
Pounds to kilograms multiply by 0.4536	0.45	1

	METRIC	IMPERIAL
Sq. millimeters to sq. inches multiply by 0.0016	0.002	1
Millimeters to inches multiply by 0.0394	0.04	1
Sq. meters to sq. feet multiply by 10.7640	10.76	1
Centimeters to inches multiply by 0.3937	0.39	1
Meters to feet multiply by 3.2810	3.28	1
Kilometers to nautical miles multiply by 0.54	0.54	1
Kilometers to miles multiply by 0.6214	0.62	1
Nautical miles to miles multiply by 1.1515	1.15	1
Metric HP to HP multiply by 0.9862	0.99	1
Kg per sq. centimeter to pounds per sq. inch multiply by 14.22	14.22	1
Kilowatts to HP multiply by 1.341	1.34	1
Cu centimeters to cu inches multiply by 0.061	0.06	1
Liters to gallons multiply by 0.22	0.22	1
Liters to pints multiply by 1.76	1.76	1
Kilograms to pounds multiply by 2.205	2.21	1

YOUR DREAM, YOUR DREAM SHIP, AND THE REALITIES OF COST

WHEN DOES IT MAKE SENSE for me to go cruising? Should I sell my assets? What is a logical financial plan? What size boat do I really need? Do I buy a new or used boat, or should I build my own?

Careful consideration of each of these questions is vital if you want to keep your dream on track. If you are realistic about your budget, your own social comfort levels, if you understand the relationship of boat size to cruising success and boat size to cruising costs, you create a sound plan. And what is a sound plan? One that will lead to a getaway while your dream is still alive (and so are you), yet leaves you many options when you have savored that dream.

CHAPTER

1

ADVENTURESOME DECISIONS: CONSIDERING YOUR GAME PLAN

Life is about more than just maintaining oneself, it is about extending oneself. Otherwise living is only not dying

- SIMONE DE BEAUVOIR (1908-1986)

What do most long-term cruising people have in common? They got "out there" by developing a taste for adventuresome decisions long before they set sail. It wasn't easy to cut the ties, to figure out the best financial course, to find the perfect time to leave. But there are some windows that seem to offer an easier entry to the cruising life than others.

It's easier for young people who haven't yet started a family, or become firmly entrenched in graduate studies, a career, a business, to get out cruising even with quite limited funds. Usually their parents are still healthy and don't need them at home. Young people can explain away this "crazy idea" by saying, "I want to get it out of my system before I settle into a career." Because their egos are less measured by their possessions and their physical comforts, they are likely to be more willing to set off in a smaller, less elegant boat. Some have even bought a modest boat as a first home, gone off exploring for a fulfilling year or two, come back, sold the boat to pay the down payment on a shore base, then started a family. Not a bad game plan. It's people like this we met out in the Indian Ocean and in the South Atlantic in the early to mid-1990s. They were on 25-foot (7.6m) Folkboats, on Triton 28s, 28-year-old Rawson 30s, 28-foot Twisters - all bought pre-owned, some in a very rundown state, most fixed up and outfitted for about US$20,000 to

$25,000.[1] Several set off initially for only 10 or 12 months, yet they were still out several years later.

No question, going off before you start a family is easier. But from the large number of families we've met who take off for a year or more to go cruising, it seems their best window was when the children were between 18 months and 12 years old: out of diapers and able to be left alone in a secure place for a few minutes while both parents handled on-deck problems, young enough to find cruising an interesting reason to be away from their social circle for a while. [2]

If you instil a love of sailing in your children as they grow up, you could be as lucky as three sets of parents we know. In each case, their teenage children suggested having a special cruise together before the family was split up by university, careers, and marriages.

The next window to open - and one you should consider grabbing - is as soon as the children leave home (or, as some of our friends have said, as soon as you can push them out of the nest). In fact, more than one of the mid to late 40s cruising couples we have met said that getting away at this time actually helped their children gain a sense of independence. With college fees behind you, it's a more financially feasible time to get away than many others.

Retirement sounds like a perfect time to go off cruising. If you and your cruising partner are both still healthy, it can be. Age is not a major factor in ocean voyaging. We've seen friends cruising until they were nearing their 80s. They felt that mental and physical activity, the goals and interests, kept them in better health than their shore-based retired friends. But the theme underlying each of these successes is earlier sailing excursions and short cruises that lead to gaining sailing skills well before retirement. Beware, though, the subtle shutter that can make the retirement cruising window close just as you reach it - grandchildren.

We receive annual holiday letters from dozens of cruising friends who have returned "home" to savor each grandchild's early days. The lure of grandchildren seems to be the reason most often stated for ending or putting off cruising - possibly even more often than having young children to consider in the first place. Few parents will let you take your grandchildren cruising with you.

As this brief recap shows, each "window" has caveats. When you are

1. Boat and equipment prices are often higher outside the United States. For example, in the United Kingdom, it would be best to add between 30 and 50 per cent to these figures. So the figure for a similar boat bought and outfitted there would more likely be £18,000 to £23,000.

2. See *The Capable Cruiser*, chapter 4, for more on children and cruising.

young and socially free, you have little money; when you have a career and some money accruing, children are coming into the picture; when the children are grown and you have some more money, grab the chance or grandchildren will raise their cute little heads. After grandchildren (and sometimes before then) come aging parents who may need you. But once again, if you set off when young, or take frequent shorter cruises all through your life, your family, friends, and employers will be less surprised, more prepared, and probably more flexible when you opt for a longer cruise. And so will you. Time is definitely one of the costs you must consider, because it's never recoverable. But what about finances, careers - do you just chuck it all and go? When we look at our friends in their mid-20s to mid-30s who decided to risk their long-term financial success and go cruising, then compare them to friends who stayed on shore to pursue purely financial or career goals, a larger proportion of the cruisers appear emotionally satisfied in the long term. Many of them - ourselves included - actually discovered the careers they wanted just because they *did* go cruising. (Of course, we may be getting a biased view, as a majority of the people we meet on shore are restless would-be cruisers.)

If you want to go cruising now, why wait for retirement? If money is your concern - as it is with most people - don't fall into the trap of trying to get "enough." First, what is enough? Second, if your savings are in one currency and it is devalued, 'enough' can become less than 'enough.' We watched British cruisers go from feeling wealthy to feeling poor in the course of a year when the pound dropped almost 28 per cent against other currencies in the mid 1980s. [3]

Third, there's the problem of finding safe, income-producing long-term investments. If the interest rate drops, as it did in the early 1990's, your reduced income from the "cruise-off forever" fund will force you into an ever more restricted budget. If you have decided you are going to make your funds stretch so you don't have to work along the way, you might find yourself choosing cruising destinations based only on their low cost of living and thus miss out on some very interesting opportunities. That is why we think it is a better idea to plan for shorter cruising breaks between working periods or to look toward working along the way. [4]

---

3. If you have a significant cash fund it could pay to investigate holding it in three or four currencies.

4. See *The Self Sufficient Sailor: 'Go Now, Pay on the Way.'*

Self-employed people of all ages find it relatively easy to break away to go cruising. Since they started their own business once, they can visualize closing it down for a year or two and starting something new and better if and when they return. Surprisingly, when the business climate is poor, we see more self-employed types setting sail. Their rationale often is, "Why keep beating my head against a wall? I'll cruise now on a budget and re-start money-making when the business cycle swings upward again."

From the number of teachers we meet out cruising, it appears the sabbatical system has real rewards. The long summer holidays leading up to the seventh year of teaching give teachers lots of time for trial cruises. Then, when they can take off for a year with either reduced pay or no pay (but a guarantee of a job on their return), they are truly prepared and ready to go. It is amazing how many extend their sabbatical by taking temporary teaching jobs in countries they visit under sail. In less-developed countries, not only teachers but also nurses and others with technical skills are often offered short-term work with no need for additional local credentials.

It is probably hardest for professional people in fast-changing fields to find financially viable windows. Computer specialists, doctors specializing in electronic medicine, advanced research people, lawyers - all must be prepared to compromise career positions if they leave for two or three years. But if the sea calls strongly, there may be another way out. Maybe a break between promotions or projects could work for you. Consider Spencer Langford, a high-powered insurance executive. When his company asked him to transfer from the United States to England, he agreed on the condition that they let him take a break to do research after he had finished the work they needed. Then he and his young family used this break to sail back to the States - a 10-month voyage. His daughter - a 13-year-old when they set sail and now a successful attorney - recalls the trip as the event of a lifetime. Spencer's career was energized when he arrived back fresh and full of different ideas. During later years, he used the same ploy to get several more cruising breaks before he finally retired.

For those who have taken out loans to get through university, then increased the debt to own some of the enticing accouterments of modern life, it is especially difficult to find a good financial window for a year or two of cruising. But waiting until you retire could mean putting off your dream too long. There is no guarantee that your job or business will always be successful, or that a promotion is more likely than a severance, or that you'll have perpetual health. That's why we highly recommend taking time for a six-month limited-area cruise as soon as you can. Rent out your house, then use the boat you have and get out soon. Don't call it a career stopper, but rather a personal-growth and career-assessment break. You could use the time out to consider joining the growing trend toward personal "downsizing." [5]

This idea of downsizing could be especially useful for those in their 40s and 50s, a way of converting a lot of possessions into free time. But there is a caveat we feel is important to consider if you are not self-employed and don't have the qualifications or skills that almost guarantee re-entry to the job market at any time. It is definitely easier to return to the general job market or to retrain for a new career in your early 40s than in your 50s. Once you reach 45 or 50, it becomes especially important to scrutinize your overall financial situation before setting off.

With the arrogance of youth, we ourselves forgot about careers, about building equity. We put everything we had into our cruising plan and decided to semiretire young, work three or four months a year where and when we could, and then go back to work later in life. We now find ourselves (in our mid-50s) working five or six months a year to gather extra funds so we can afford to get someone else to paint the bottom of the boat. We won't have the large government or corporate pensions others may enjoy, so we may have to continue working later in life. But it is a plan we'd definitely choose again, one we'd recommend trying on for a fit if you are under 35. Sell out, get the smallest seaworthy boat you can live in, any way you can. Learn to sail it well, to fix everything on it, and go - with up to 80 per cent of your assets in the boat. But do leave behind at least 20 percent in safe investments, as a personal insurance plan. Then work along the way, or sail for a year and work for a year. You may come back after a few years and have to start at a lower rung on the career ladder than your friends, but you'll have a wealth of great memories and 20 years to save for your dotage.

For younger friends who had started a family and a career, another financial plan that worked well was to buy a real fixer-upper of a house,

---

5. Several interesting books could help as you consider how to add time for some cruising into a career-filled life:
Your Money or Your Life. Penguin, 1992, Joe Dominguez and Vicki Robin.
How Much Is Enough? Earthscan Publications, 1992, Alan Thein Durning.
Voluntary Simplicity: Toward a Life That Is Outwardly Simple, Inwardly Rich.
    William Morrow, 1981, reprinted 1993, Duane Elgin.
Getting a Life - The Downshifters Guide to Happier, Simpler Living,
    Hodder and Stoughton, 1997, Polly Ghazi and Judy Jones.

the worst house in a top-notch neighborhood. They fixed it up until it was rentable, not too fancy or personalized. They bought a modest boat, putting about 50 percent of their assets into the boat and leaving 50 percent in their home. Then they organized their life so they could set off for a year with $10,000 in their cruising kitty, plus six months' mortgage payments in the bank just in case a renter failed to make payments. When they found cruising was for them, they returned, finished fixing up the house, then sold it. The gain produced a solid nest egg to make them feel more comfortable about continuing their cruise for a few years more. (A pitfall here is the difficult-to-control desire to put the gains made by selling the house into a larger, more luxurious cruising boat.)

People near their 40s quite often have a good deal of equity in a home. They speak of selling out, putting all of the money into a boat, using the income from their investments to pay their way, possibly working a bit along the way. This could be a daunting plan for the less-committed sailing member of a couple. A complete cash-out means no place to come home to - sink or swim, so to speak. But the option of renting out a home that is highly personalized could also produce real heartache. Eric and Susan Hiscock acquired and personalized a lovely island home, then rented it out as they cruised around the world for three years. They returned to find many of their favorite belongings roughed up by renters, the painstakingly applied wallpaper scuffed and drawn on by youngsters. "It almost ruined the pleasure of a wonderful voyage," Susan wrote. "We knew we could never rent it again. So instead of letting a house tie us to one place, we sold it to regain our freedom." This was a hard choice, even for two people who both knew cruising was their preferred way of life. Another less-daunting solution is to sell out and then use a large portion of the equity to buy a smaller home with a guest cottage or a garage that could have a small apartment built into it. You could also look for a rundown property, or one with the potential for future development or room for an extra domicile - in other words, a good investment. In this instance, you rent out the existing house, put up a temporary storage unit or use the existing extra apartment as a home base, and set off sailing.

After we suggested this idea at a cruising seminar in Chicago a couple of years back, one of the attendees, a financial planning expert, pointed out the tax benefits. (This could help lower capital gains, if it's set up as a business, but please discuss this all with your tax adviser before making long-term decisions.) The planner also agreed that even for committed cruisers in their middle years, it could be worrisome to put more than 40 to 50 percent of net assets into a boat. It is never a good idea to consider your boat your wealth. Boats and their equipment have far less predictable cash values than homes. The location of the boat, the survey condition of its hull, the current design trends, and popular perceptions of cruising boats could affect its value just when you want to sell it. And you probably won't recoup the money you spent outfitting the boat. We add this somewhat negative note because we witnessed the turmoil of one couple who always assumed their 40-foot (12.2m) boat (a rather unusual but successful design) could be sold whenever they decided to buy a home on shore. So they cruised for 30 years, gathering no nest egg, and at the age of 60 decided to sell their only asset, their boat, in order to move ashore. But no-one was interested. Our friend told us, "I went from feeling rich to feeling poor, pretty quickly."

In 1980, when we decided to build our dream ship - 29-foot 6-inch (9m) *Taleisin* - we considered our age (40) and thought of that story and banked every dollar we received for the sale of 24-foot 4-inch (7.5m) *Seraffyn*. We then built our new boat with wages we earned, just as we had with *Seraffyn*. We felt then, and still do, that being footloose and fancy-free, having only a few thousand dollars plus our boat, was great when we were young - we'd do it the same way again. But few people would have sympathy for us, and we wouldn't feel good about ourselves, if we were broke in our later years. Our streak of financial responsibility gave us $40,000 to pay cash for the ultimate fixer-upper five years later in New Zealand. While we spent two years fixing up that tiny waterfront cottage - with its boatshed and potential to be a small boat-repair yard - we remembered Eric and Susan Hiscock's story and fought our instincts to fancy it up. We kept in mind that this was only a rental unit, one we could personalize if and when we came back to settle. We then went off with a home base to return to, rental income to cover maintenance costs, and a bit extra for savings.

As you near retirement, it's tempting to say, I'll just sell out, buy a boat, and live on my pension. But once again, we have noted that the most successful late-life cruisers used a clever downsizing plan. They reduced the size of the boat they planned to buy, dropping their sights by four or five feet of length, then also bought a small place in a new location on shore and rented it out. This gave them more cash in their cruising kitty, a place to return to during breaks in their cruise, and some extra funds to spice up their cruising life by occasionally "splashing out." Lura and Jack Francis used this scheme. When the dream first took hold, Jack was more "into sailing" than Lura, an artist with a really practical bent. She became more interested when the overall scheme included a place to come home to. After looking at boats in the 37-to-40 foot range, she suggested they save money by buying only a 32-footer (9.8m). They then put the $30,000 they saved in an interest-bearing account, to allow them to do some special side trips during their planned three-year circumnavigation. They sold their home in the city, bought a nice cabin at a nearby ski resort, then set off on a cruise that expanded to cover five years. Their letters detailed extended inland excursions - the French Alps, Romania, the art centers of Italy - all done in style with only the interest from their special downsizing fund.

This scheme has proved to be successful for many of our cruising friends. The existence of a bailout plan, a home base, has relieved the pressure on partners who were less enthusiastic or secure about the whole idea. If the cruising dream didn't work out, they had a place to shelter if the storms of life grew overwhelmingly, if their partner died, or if the boat was shipwrecked. Even insurance doesn't solve the "place to live while we make the next plan" problem. Furthermore, even the most pleasurable cruise has a natural end, a time when you want a change of pace. If you have a bridge of some sort - a place to fix up and keep you occupied while you work your way back into shore life - you'll find the inevitable transition easier. The people who actually go off cruising are often goal-oriented. Having a new goal for "post-cruising years" can be just as important as having that cruising dream years earlier.

The reason we suggest considering a new location for a home base is that people who cruise for more than two or three years change a lot. If they try to return to the community they left, to fit back into the same group of friends, the same activities, they might find their friends also have changed. It could be easier to carry your adventures onward by coming home to a new place on land, with a new project to fill your mind and new people to meet - in other words, a fresh start.

Down to Dollars and Cents, Pounds and Pence

If you feel we are being slightly evasive in putting exact numbers on what cruising will cost - from getting the boat to outfitting to actual monthly expenditures once you set off - you are right. Budget is an extremely flexible term. Each person we meet has a different concept of the word. Bernard Moitessier answered the money question by saying, "It costs as much as you have." In our books on cruising, we've tried to show average prices for people intending to get out there on a limited budget. Nothing has changed. Cruising budgets of $500 to $700 per month are not uncommon among cruisers determined to be out there. There are also a large number of people on boats around 36 feet (11m) living on budgets in the $900-to-$1,200 range. As a realistic guideline, a couple setting out should project a yearly cruising budget of about one-third of one person's annual income on shore. Even though they will be free of many of the shoreside costs of employment, home ownership, insurance, automobiles, and annual holidays, few people will drastically change their spending habits. Don't kid yourself. Twenty-year-olds can laugh off having to eat beans and rice, carry a backpack, and always ride on the least expensive public transport, but it's difficult to convince even the most adventuresome 40 or 50-year-old partners to accept this level of living year-round. If you're accustomed to eating restaurant meals regularly, you'll still want to eat out when you go cruising. If you like buying high-tech equipment now, you'll do the same on your boat, and your costs will reflect this. As Larry succinctly says, "Strict budgets are like strict diets - almost no one can stay on them."

Making the Decision

Interestingly, limited finances do not seem to deter people from going cruising. Nor do unlimited finances seem to help them get away. What keeps people from going off to sample a cruising life is that many of them truthfully do not want to go. Only if you are sure of your goal can you be motivated to overcome all of the obstacles you'll encounter. And there will be an endless list of reasons not to go: children, parents who are growing old, a reluctant partner, a business or job you've worked hard to develop, lack of the perfect boat, limited finances, physical handicaps. But if you're committed to the idea, you'll analyze each of these "problems" and probably discover that each can be solved.

In her book *Journey into my Mind's Eye*, Lesley Blanch listens to her mother's tale of romance with a charming Russian Traveler. Lesley asks her mother why she hadn't run off to Russia with the Traveler, since "she was grown up and free to go anywhere she liked." "One is never really free," was her mother's enigmatic reply. But this didn't satisfy Lesley, for, as she put it, "I had begun to discover that my mother rather enjoyed restrictions. They saved her the strain of making adventurous decisions. Ill health, lack of money, her duty to others - all these things gradually became her allies. She had opted for quiet."

Make your adventuresome decision now and the next decision will be even easier. Make your game plan and stick to it. Begin by learning to enjoy sailing and seamanship challenges as you work toward solving each of the problems you'll encounter, as you acquire your first cruising boat and break the ties that keep you on shore. The amazing variety of people from all walks of life who get out cruising proves this is an affordable dream.

CHAPTER

2

FIRSTHAND ADVENTURES, SECONDHAND BOATS

Her sheer had a jauntiness common to boats built in the 1960s. A seasoned sailor would say, "Not showy, but dependable – a good solid sailing machine."

He was compact, fit, a spring wound just tight enough; intense yet eager to taste life to the full. They were almost the same ages, children of the mid-1960s. They both seemed a good match for their names.

Patience, a 32-foot (9.8m) fiberglass Rhodes sloop, and Max, an ex-Israeli Navy diver, had been together for four years when we met them at Cocos-Keeling atoll, 2,000 miles from Darwin, Australia. Max had fallen for the idea of cruising about the same time that he emigrated to the United States and discovered Marina del Rey at the edge of Los Angeles. Rather than rent a house, he bought a sailboat to live aboard. *Patience* was a logical choice – soundly built but neglected, of a design considered old-fashioned, therefore out of favor, so her price was only $18,000. Using *Patience* as a boat, home, and office, Max earned the funds to outfit and go off cruising by running a bottom-scrubbing service. He tied his Boston Whaler dive boat alongside *Patience* while he searched for low-cost secondhand gear. Two years of intense weekend sailing and $5,000 of outfitting costs later, *Patience* and Max were ready to go. When we met them, they had been out cruising for two years and 17,000 miles without mishap.

Here in the lagoon at this cruiser's crossroads, *Patience* looked rather plain, but she held the distinction of being at the exact mean average length of the boats that sailed into Cocos-Keeling during the three weeks we lay there. The fleet included four crews who were on their second circumnavigations, 11 who had been voyaging for more than two years. If you excluded the one professionally crewed 85-foot (26m) yacht that sailed in (and for a few days generously invited all of us to use their constantly running fresh water to top up our tanks), the fleet ranged in

Patience *lying alongside* Taleisin *at Rodriguez Island, Indian Ocean.*

size from a 24-foot (7.3m) Westerly Centaur sailed by a lone retired Englishman to a 40-foot (12.2m) ferrocement ketch crewed by its Australian owner on his third circumnavigation, and an American woman hitchhiker on her very first voyage. Of 18 boats, more than half were under 30 feet (9.2m) and the majority had been purchased secondhand by people who had modest budgets and no independent incomes. In fact, the majority of these cruisers worked along the way to earn extra cruising funds. Not one of the boats other than the 85-footer had cost its owner more than $85,000 to acquire and outfit.

Such statistics just reinforce our contention that many budget-minded people like Max are getting out cruising today. If you look out into the anchorages of far-flung cruising destinations, you see them lounging in their cockpits or diving for a lobster dinner. We meet enough limited-budget voyagers to know that there definitely are affordable secondhand cruising boats – even ones that could be called bargains, if you are willing to look for them. But how do you find low-cost boats like *Patience* to get you out affordably yet confidently? Which boats should you consider, where do you look? Are there benefits beyond cash savings that make the secondhand boat a more cost-conscious way of getting out cruising?

Some of the benefits of buying secondhand include the fact that you will be inspecting boats that have actually been out cruising, so you will see what construction methods and gear have proven successful, what owners have added to make the boat work. This could be far more instructive than seeing what the manufacturer thinks will look irrresistible at the boat shows. (Ever seen a self-steering vane on a boat-show boat?) Owners of secondhand boats are more likely to take you out on extensive sea trials – not on a one-or-two-hour potter around the bay, but sailing to windward in 18-to-20-knot winds. If there is no wind on the day of the sea trial, private boat sellers are more likely to set up a second test sail on a windier day. You might even be able to arrange to charter the boat for a weekend to see if she suits you and your needs. Each sea trial will teach you more about how different boats perform. You'll see and feel if a boat is tender or stiff, if it has a balanced helm or too much weather helm, if it can back down under power, if you can climb out of the cockpit and up to the foredeck without too much trouble when the boat is heeled.

The mere idea of buying secondhand tends to make all of us think, *caveat emptor* (let the buyer beware). We've watched new-boat buyers so impressed by lovely upholstery, clever drawers and cabinetry, super varnish work, and shiny interior finish that they didn't bother to climb into the less-accessible reaches to check how the bulkheads or chainplates were bonded in place, how the through-hull fittings were plumbed. How many boat buyers do you suppose have had a thorough professional survey done on a factory-fresh $100,000 boat before they signed the final check?

Then there is the pressure, subtle or otherwise, exerted by new boat dealers to get you to buy optional equipment. When you are already spending $80,000 or $120,000, it is easy to be lured into a few little additions that each cost "just another $400, $800, or $1,200." No one will be pressuring you to add options when you buy secondhand. It is easier to be logical about your gear purchases when you are away from the frenzy (and emotional excitement) of buying a new boat, easier to compare prices and decide to install gear yourself to save money for cruising.

Secondhand boat buyers are constantly reminded that compromise is part and parcel of buying, owning, and outfitting a boat. The almost-perfect hull has a cockpit or rig or interior that doesn't quite suit. The vastly lower price helps you accept that you can live with this imperfection until some later date when you might or might not feel like modifying it. New boat buyers do not accept this as willingly, and they often end up buying a semicustom boat, then adding features and making alterations that force the price ever upward.

The secondhand buyer almost always becomes technically and physically involved in bringing the boat up to cruise-ready condition. Those who buy a fixer-upper and contribute sweat equity as much as cash, often find a bonus, gaining skills and technical confidence along the way. Joey Marullo, a young attorney from Louisiana, and his wife, Terry, a paralegal, spent a year upgrading a 20-year-old 37-footer (11.3m) and agree completely (see Fig. 2-1). "I might have been able to earn more money working at my practice and hiring someone to do this work. But I'd have lost out", Joey told us. "Learning to use tools, knowing how everything on board worked, seeing the results of our own labor, was empowering and enabling." In other words, he now felt he could fix most everything on board.

Another advantage of buying secondhand is well stated by Andrew Simpson, a recognized British yacht designer/builder/surveyor who is now editor at *Practical Boat Owner* magazine: "There is the growing feeling amongst informed sailors that with fiberglass-reinforced plastic boats (GRP), older might actually be better. Or to put it another way, that in opting to buy second-hand, you would really be settling for more not less. With certain qualifications, I agree with these sentiments and would put my money on a good quality, mid-1970s yacht – a Nicholson 32, for example – outliving many of the 'plastic fantastics' being built today." [1]

We would feel the same as Andrew Simpson does. Most of the boats called racer/cruisers or cruisers in the years 1970 to 1985 were what is now considered moderate to heavy displacement. Their builders had a healthy skepticism of fiberglass as a boatbuilding material, so with the extra weight allowance of heavy-displacement designs, plus less restrictive material costs, they could and did use heavier layups of glass and resin to make sure the boats were strong. But, over the past 10 years, the economics of boatbuilding has changed drastically. Fiberglass and resin

1. From *Simpson on Secondhand Boats*, published by Waterline Books, 101 Longden Road, Shrewsbury, SY1 9EB, United Kingdom. £9.95. Or from *Motorbooks International*, 729 Prospect Avenue, Osceola, WI 54020, USA.

Figure 2-1. *An example of a 1998 sweat-equity, value-added cruising boat.*

Joey and Terry Marullo supplied the following information regarding their actual costs for buying and outfitting on a limited budget. They have done all of the work themselves, cutting costs by buying wholesale where possible. One example: 300 feet of 5/16-inch 1x19 wire wholesale for $1 per foot, rather than $3 per foot at the local marine store.

THE BOAT: Tayana 37 cutter (11.3m; 1977 model) purchased in cosmetically poor condition; some rigging and hatch damage; headliner damage; mildew throughout interior.

Price paid	**$42,000**

EXPENSES TO REPAIR, UPGRADE AND OUTFIT

general materials	$2,200
tools	500
boatyard charges	800
sewing machine	1,400
windvane	3,200
oil lamps	360
rigger's vice	240
wire	340
turnbuckles, thimbles and rigging	1,200
sails	6,000
sailing dinghy	3,200
EPIRB	800
ground tackle	1,100
inverter	700
miscellaneous	1,000

Total expenses, boat ready to cruise (excluding provisions, spares, and medical/personal gear)	**$23,040**
Total investment for a personalized, ready-to-cruise boat (excluding labor – one and a half year's spare time and probably half a year almost full time)	**$65,040**

The average list price of the same boat in good condition would be $70,000 to $80,000. Even for a well-outfitted boat in that category, an additional 25 percent of the buying price must be added to cover outfitting – or $18,000 to $20,000. **Total price: $88,000 to $100,000.**

prices have gone up, as have the costs to conform to environmental and fire-prevention regulations in boat factories. More reason to cut back on hull materials, more reason for lighter-displacement designs, more reason to convince boat buyers to seek speed, achieved by ever-lighter-displacement boats with extreme fin-keel designs. (Boatbuilding materials cost by the pound, just like beefsteak. Save a pound on materials and you can put the savings into the profit column.) But is this what you, as a prudent cost-conscious cruiser, really want? We think a lightly constructed boat traveling at high speed is a recipe for grounding or collision damage. Serious things happen to spade rudders and extreme fin keels when they hit immovable objects! More risk of structural damage or holing equals less confidence in the boat, less peace of mind - definitely a high emotional price for any benefits of having a "fast, modern" boat. [2]

But the major reason to buy secondhand is that it gives you the most affordable chance to get out cruising. *Affordable* is the operative word. It is rare to find an out-and-out bargain. You must be willing to pay in one way or another, either with money or with labor. A boat that needs sweat equity (i.e., physical labor) beyond your skills or patience level is no bargain; nor is one that requires a large amount of money to make it cruise-ready. But from what we have seen as we wander around the world's boatyards and storage yards, there is a large pool of potentially successful secondhand boats.

The first step toward finding one of these boats is to carefully define your budget – not only what you can spend to buy the boat but also what it will cost you in the medium and long term. Remember that no matter what price you pay for a potential cruising boat, the necessary upgrade to make it voyage-worthy always seems to cost an extra 25 percent (see Section Two). This is true for new boats, secondhand ones, ones you build yourself. Our friend Max figured that *Patience* was a secondhand boat, so secondhand gear was suitable for her refit. If you paid for a newer, fancier boat, you'd probably feel secondhand or lower-cost gear would reduce its resale value or diminish your pride of ownership.

Then there is insurance, an ongoing expense that increases with the value of the boat. Those of us on boats of lower value seem to be less nervous about cruising with either minimal or no insurance at all. But when you invest $80,000 or $120,000, you begin to feel very much "at risk" financially, so you will want to keep your boat well insured.

2. See *'Parameters for Choosing a Cruising Boat,'* Capable Cruiser.

Offshore ocean-crossing coverage costs 6 or 7 percent of replacement value of the boat. Six percent of $100,000 is $6,000 per year; 6 percent of $150,000 is $9,000 per year, or $750 per month. Lower your total investment on the boat and you can lower your costs. Or, along with many cruisers including ourselves, say, "the heck with it," and invest instead in preventive insurance, such as another large anchor.

You should also consider the eventual resale of your boat. Carefully chosen boats, carefully maintained, can retain much of their purchase value. They might even gain a bit if, like Joey and Terry, you put in a lot of labor upgrading them. But it is more likely that you will have to sell for about 20 per cent less than you have invested. On a $30,000 boat, that is only a loss of $6,000, easily acceptable as a very low price to pay for the pleasure of living on the boat for two or three years. On a $100,000 boat, it is a more worrisome total of $20,000. And finally, when it comes time to sell your boat, there are far more people who can afford Fords than Mercedeses. A bigger pool of shoppers means a better chance of a quick sale.

With your logical capital-investment limit established, it is time to look at size. Beyond the cost savings associated with outfitting, handling, insuring, and maintaining a boat under 35 feet (10.7m), there is another important factor. In the secondhand market you'll be far more likely to find a good deal in what are today called "smaller boats," simply because far more of them have been built every year. Despite the impression created by dozens of pages of yachting magazine advertisements featuring bigger boats, and the number of larger boats you may see in the Caribbean or Mediterranean, it's a cold, hard fact that between 1991 and 1997, fewer than 3,500 boats over 35 feet (10.7m) were built annually in the United States. This includes race boats, charter boats, and cruising boats. Furthermore, the number of potential cruising boats built and sold in the States is on the average divided one-sixth over 36 feet (11m), five sixths between 24 and 36 feet (7.3-11m) according to *Sail* magazine (1998.) Simply put, this means five or six times the number of under-36-foot boats are out there on the secondhand market: more boats for sale, more chance you will find the right one for you.

As you shop, do not limit your choices to well-known brand names. Certain boats have gained almost legendary reputations and their secondhand prices reflect this. To be cost-conscious, you have to figure out where legend takes over from actual design and engineering value. Some names come immediately to mind – Swan, Hinckley, Rival, Rustler 28, Island Packet, Pacific Seacraft, Bristol Channel Cutter. All are relatively well-built boats from reputable builders, but they're high-priced on the secondhand market due to the mystique attached to them. Buy these boats and you join clubs of proud owners who feel they have "the best boat." But careful research might help you find used boats that are designed and built just as well for a third of the price, as Max found when he looked for *Patience*. She was one of only 12 boats built by a yard that went bankrupt. Rumor has it that this was from spending too much on the construction of the boats, not enough on marketing. Designed by Philip Rhodes, famed for good sailing boats, *Patience* cost probably one-third of the price of a more immediately recognizable brand of the same vintage and size.

Research is the key. Begin by gathering as much information as possible about each type of boat, so you will be able to evaluate whether you are looking at a bargain or a potential disappointment. The local sailing pundits may be a poor source of information – not only because each has personal prejudices but also because few have had chances to sail on a variety of boats in a variety of conditions. We've heard pretty knowledgeable people condemn an acceptable brand of boat by saying, "She's a dog to windward." But with more or better-quality ballast (i.e., solid lead instead of iron punchings), added sail area, better sails, feathering propellers instead of fixed ones, we've even seen boats such as the Westsail 32 become better sailing boats! So try to talk to delivery skippers, yacht surveyors, boatyard owners; get out and sail as many different boats as you can so you can base your choices on fact, not opinion or popular perception.

Find out about the construction flaws and advantages of various boats by consulting consumer influenced reviews. *Practical Sailor,* [3] an American publication, has published two volumes of reviews of secondhand boats, not only evaluating sailing qualities, but also listing the problems previous owners have found and solved through the years. *Practical Boat Owner* [4] magazine is a good source for reviews of secondhand boats sold in Europe. *Cruising World, USA* [5]

3. *Practical Sailor*, 14 Regatta Way, Portsmouth, RI 02871, USA. For individual boat reports, write to this address or call 203-661-6111. For the two volume set of *Practical Boat Buying – 140 Boat Reviews*, write: *Practical Sailor* Boat Division, 75 Holly Hill Lane, P.O. Box 2626, Greenwich, CT. 06836, USA.

4. *Practical Boat Owner*, Westover House, West Quay Road, Poole, Dorset, United Kingdom. Tel: 01202-680593, Fax: 01202-674335.

5. *Cruising World*, 5 John Clark Road, Newport, R.I, 02840-0992, USA. Tel: 401-847-1588, Fax: 401-848-5048.

with its "Another Opinion" column, helps you get in touch with previous owners of boats you might be considering. If you use their service, try to contact several owners who have already sold their boats, as people are more likely to be open and forthcoming about the flaws of a boat they no longer own.

With your list narrowing, it could pay to consult a surveyor who has a long history of surveying the type of boats you are considering. Offer the professional an hourly consultation fee to sit down and go over the pros and cons of each one. Andrew Simpson, the British surveyor, says he prefers talking to potential buyers before they set their sights on a particular brand of boat, or a specific boat within that brand. He feels he can turn them into better shoppers by pointing out potential defects, by suggesting other boats worth considering that offer better value but have less mystique. "I'd rather the buyer checked for major flaws and rejected or decided to go forward with the idea of a full survey based on that knowledge," Andrew told us. "Saves both of us time, money, and disappointments." A surveyor consultation will also help you put worries about osmosis into perspective. Many people with whom we have spoken feel that the problem is being exaggerated – not only to sell more services and osmosis cure products, but also to try to turn buyers from the secondhand market toward the new-boat market.

Joey and Terry Marullo found the boat they felt was a good buy when researching through *Practical Sailor*, plus a survey indicated a particular model was prone to problems they felt they could fix. When they found a boat priced at half the going rate because of water damage from major hatch leaks, Joey felt the necessary repair jobs were 'do-able. The same boat had been turned down by several buyers put off by the mildew-covered headliners and interior. (Figure 2.1)

There are times and places for finding better buys. Boat prices do drop at the end of the sailing season. Also, you can often find more bargains where there are more boats. If you are shopping in your local area, don't confine your search to magazines and brokers; look in storage yards or places where mooring is particularly inexpensive. Don't limit your shopping to boats that are listed for sale. Some owners have found just what they were looking for by putting a note on a boat that seemed to fit their needs, especially one that looked slightly down at the heels or neglected. The owner might have wanted to sell the boat but knew he had to spruce it up to fetch a decent price. He doesn't have the time, or feels the repair time would produce little capital gain. Your offer might free him from his dilemma.

We've seen several people out cruising on "insurance write-offs." One of the better known of these is Don Street's famous *Iolaire*, purchased while she was under water. After a hurricane left 250 boats sunk along the Texas coast, one of them, a Baba 30, was written off. A clever sailor then paid $3,500 for a boat with some nasty-looking damage but he was out cruising 18 months later for a total investment of $35,000. But, before you are tempted to save money by buying a fixer-upper, be careful to assess your abilities and patience levels. Refurbishing cosmetically disadvantaged boats is relatively do-able. Structurally damaged boats demand a higher skills level, so some outside assistance and advice may be required.

Traveling to look for a bargain can be part of the adventure of setting off cruising – either in your own country or farther afield. We've seen some definite bargains at downwind cruising destinations. Owners concerned about a trip to windward sometimes offer their boats for sale; others are abandoned by their crew. Some cruisers ready to call it quits find that customs laws complicate resale of their boats to local people, or they may find the local people are not interested in cruising boats. So they will sell to a potential voyager from overseas for a heavily discounted price; the buyer can avoid customs duties by leaving with the boat before taxes become due. If you are willing to be patient and accept the risk of some dead ends, places to consider looking are major landfall ports along traditional downwind sailing routes such as northern Spain, Baja California, Gibraltar, Panama, and New Zealand. Though the boats you see in these locales may look travel-worn, they have been tested in the big tank. With a proper survey, you will be able to spot their weaknesses more easily than you would on a boat that has never been to sea.

Unfortunately, the problem with searching for overseas bargains is that you must be in the right place at the right time. This means traveling with a flexible schedule. If you can consider taking a year off to gain experience and search, there are two options we have seen work. The first is to buy a camper van to live in while you travel and consider the search both a holiday and an adventure. Our best friends from Canada spent eight months roaming by van through Europe. In Spain, they bought a tatty-looking, basically sound Rival 32, spent two months sprucing up and outfitting *Taganita*, then set off for a year of Mediterranean cruising. Goal accomplished, they sold *Taganita* and returned home. Their original investment was intact, and their two years in Europe had cost them less than a third of what they normally spent at home. Another couple invested in a small sailing dinghy, which they carried on top of their van.

This added pleasure and range to their search. It also introduced them to other sailors, who offered not only boat-buying leads but also pleasant afternoons of cockpit lounging and boat talk.

A second option is to consider hitchhiking.[6] Try to find crewing positions along what are called the "Milk Run" or "Rally" routes. Not only will you learn the realities of cruising, you'll be in the right position at the right time if a true bargain appears. If not, good crew are sought for delivery trips to bring cruising boats to windward, and you could earn funds toward maintaining your boat-buying venture.

With any boat you purchase overseas, be sure to factor in some extra costs. Boat gear in the United States is much cheaper than in Europe, so keep in mind that your outfitting costs could increase by up to 25 or 30 percent.

If you are looking for a true "bargain," try not to be dazzled by an impressive array of electronic gear, a two-page long list of gear headed by the statement, "fully outfitted for offshore cruising." Remember that the owner hopes to get back everything he put into his boat. But is the gear what you would want on board? Is it in good working order? Secondhand electronic gear is a very poor investment – and in resale value, it might even be a negative. Replacing it with newer gear might mean modifying or rebuilding the cabinetry. Fancy upholstery, lovely varnished interior joinery and shiny cosmetic features will catch your eye as a buyer. They do *not* add real cruising value to the boat you are seeking. What you are looking for is a sound, collision-resistant hull and excellent, sturdy steering gear and rudder installations. Other hard and true high-cost items to look at are the sails, the spars, the rigging, the wiring system, the engine, and wind-vane self-steering. If you want to go now, affordably, you might be able to make slipcovers to hide worn upholstery; you can't do the same for tired rigging – you must replace it.

On the other hand, if you are looking for a very low-cost way to get a boat, consider ones that have fallen to the bottom of their price range or been withdrawn from sale because of a major problem that has discouraged other buyers. Max got *Patience* for a reduced price because her topsides and deck looked bad – the gelcoat was crazed and horrible. A blown engine could be the beginning of a bargain if you are looking at boats that displace less than 10,000 pounds. Adventurous young sailors have deep-sixed the engine, installed an outboard well or bracket, and added a four-cycle outboard to get out – money in hand. Among other

---

6. See *The Self-Sufficient Sailor*, 'Hitchhiking across Oceans.'

Max (The Winner) and his adopted "Mum" at Mauritius.

problems that shove prices down but are fixable are osmotic blistering, water-damaged interiors, even badly damaged rigs.

But before you jump in and pay for a fixer-upper – or any boat for that matter – get a full survey from a professional surveyor or boatbuilder. Do not let the broker or seller suggest a surveyor; do not accept a survey done "only six months ago;" do not trust yourself. It is too easy to fall in love and blind yourself to defects because you are anxious to finish your quest for a boat. Joey Marullo recently wrote, "We chose a surveyor who a lot of people in our area knew and who was recommended to us by a close friend. As we later found out, the survey was not nearly as detailed as we had hoped. The surveyor later explained that he did a 'general condition' survey, even though we told him what we were planning on doing with the boat. Even worse, the surveyor missed some items which were later discovered quite easily and which would have been important to us. For instance, there were several bulkheads which had rotted away in spots due to leaks. All that was necessary to discover this was to open a couple of small lockers and shine a light inside. I also discovered, when I was below one day while it was raining quite hard, numerous other leaks all over the boat." Joey's suggestions: "Do not casually choose a surveyor, research the surveyor yourself; ask for copies of surveys, ask for the surveyor's checklist, learn as much as you can about surveying boats yourself so that you may intelligently watch the survey being conducted and ask meaningful questions. Either view the boat on a rainy day or have someone run a hose over the entire boat while you are down below looking for leaks!"

To avoid any chance of collusion (intentional or unintentional) between seller and surveyor, get someone from out of town who is completely dedicated to your side of the deal. Your surveyor's job is to show you where any potential problems exist to help you understand the boat's true condition. The boat will not pass or fail a survey. The only time that happens is when a boat is being surveyed to see if it meets governmental regulations, such as charter or passenger-for-hire regulations.

Even surveyors and boatbuilders themselves need independent surveys. We have seen yet another case of a surveyor letting emotion cloud his eyes this past winter. "J" found an apparent bargain. He loved the look and feel of the boat and spent a day going over her, but he did not poke around in hidden corners, as he would have for a client. Result: twice the repair work and cost he had anticipated.

Carry a flash-equipped pocket camera as you shop for boats. As the one you choose is being surveyed, shoot pictures of each part of the boat. This serves two purposes: Not only will it help you remember details of the different boats you have looked at, but it also can serve as an inventory list when you are ready to make your final offer.

Be sure to determine what gear will stay with the boat. If it is equipment that could be removed and replaced with a cheaper substitute, get serial numbers as well as a written or photographic inventory. Then check to make sure all of this gear is still on board when you take possession.

Hand-over time can be tricky; you don't want to part with your money until you are sure everything is in order and the complete inventory of equipment is intact. With a live-aboard boat – especially one you are buying overseas – it could be a temptation for the owner accidentally or intentionally to pack a few bits of gear in his luggage. So, on hand-over day, have the owner move *completely off* the boat. Go over the inventory with a checklist and then – only then – arrange the final transfer of the funds.

Now that you've finally found her, she's yours, she's lovely or scruffy, ready to go or barely usable for weekend cruising. Get her out sailing before you set to work upgrading her. Don't be tempted to lay up the boat immediately so you can make her your "ideal cruiser." Your ideas might be right on, but they could just as well be expensive solutions to inexpensive problems. We've seen people become so bogged down in rebuilding that they forgot the pleasure of using a boat. Make a point of cleaning up every few weeks and going out sailing. Do sea trials. Not only will you be learning more about the boat, gaining sea time (experience), and reminding yourself what this work is all about, but you also will see if your improvements are actually working and maybe find some ways to save money.

If you need to do work that is dependent on good weather, spend the money to get the boat under cover, even in areas with relatively little rain. Find a shipyard with affordable undercover shed space, or build a plastic shed to protect the boat. Plastic dome covers, advertised in magazines such as *WoodenBoat*, cost less than two extra months in a shipyard or marina. The covered working conditions save you time, money, and labor. You'll be able to keep working when the rain, sun, or dew would otherwise threaten your paint and varnish work.

And what about Max? After three years of voyaging, he was slowly heading through the southern Caribbean, bound for California, to finish his circumnavigation and then fulfill his desire to become a boatbuilder. But in Trinidad, a lovely Italian woman sailed in with money in her pocket, looking for a cruising boat of her own. *Patience* suited her budget and her desires, but Max wanted to finish what he had started. Compromise: He sold the boat and she agreed to let him sail with her on *Patience* until they reached Max's starting point in California. They never reached California. Instead we received a letter from the crew of *Patience*, postmarked Taiohae, Marquesas. "What a winner," Larry yelled as he read. "Max got around the world, sold the boat, then married the owner!"

Hull Material Choices for Secondhand Boat Buyers
We've described these in the order of availability:

FIBERGLASS (GRP)
This is far and away the most popular choice of production-built boats, so there is a wide selection available. But you must be careful to distinguish between well-built and poorly constructed boats. Time and

observation have shown where most of the problems lie in fiberglass construction. These include, but are not restricted to, insufficient reinforcing material connecting the mast-step area; poor bonding of floors and bulkheads to the hull; cracking and failure where insufficient strengthening has been added; osmosis; rotting core materials (i.e., the plywood, foam, or balsa used to stiffen decks and coach roofs). If you choose a well -built, solid-glass hull, most of these problems can be removed and repaired for a reasonable price. With waterproof hull coatings, osmosis can be avoided; bulkhead bonding can be beefed up and deck core material can be replaced. But we would avoid any cored fiberglass hulls. Surveys of many older hulls that have been sailed hard to windward and downwind show a definite tendency toward breakdown of the core material or separation at the bond between the core and the glass. Once this happens, water can find its way into the core – which, if it is balsa, will definitely result in rot.

Glass hulls can be neglected for longer than steel or wooden hulls. They can then be polished and waxed or resprayed and restored to fine condition.

STEEL

This material is touted as being great for bumping into reefs. Yet the reefs of the world are dotted with the wrecks of steel yachts and ships that may have survived the collision but are impossible to refloat (or too damaged to be worth the effort). Do not consider the steel-boat option unless you are willing to do the considerable maintenance that it entails (sometimes as much as two or three times more than for a wooden boat, according to Eric and Susan Hiscock, who owned both). Even with the newest of coatings, you must be prepared to do a regular patrol to patch up any scratches or dents caused by dropped winch handles, chafing lines, or general wear and tear. Both of the Hiscocks said steel would be their last choice for a cruising boat – not only because of the maintenance problems but also because of compass deviation. They found some ways around this – mounting their main compass up the mast and using a repeater on deck – but they missed being able to rely on a hand-bearing compass. Furthermore, they were always concerned about the fact that steel boats invariably rust from the inside out. Hidden damp areas, such as those below the marine toilet, under the ice chest or refrigerator, and in the chain locker, are susceptible to serious rusting. This is why most marine brokers consider a 10-year-old steel boat to have a very low resale value. If, on the other hand, you are willing to remove the complete interior and refinish the hidden corners of a steel hull and replate some areas, you could find an affordable secondhand boat at a low price.

ALUMINUM

The French have been using aluminum for many well-built, long-lasting boats. They cut maintenance by simply leaving the topsides bare and letting the metal assume a dull, battleship-grey color – no expensive paints to buy, no fillers, no need to repaint on a regular basis. The trade-off is that alloy is very susceptible to electrolysis caused by any meeting of dissimilar metals, plus leakages from the ship's electrical system. Several of our technocrat, alloy-hull-owning friends have recommended isolating the electrical system from the hull by using an insulated propeller-shaft coupling, plus an isolated starting motor. The starter, according to these people, should not be grounded to the engine block, and the boat should have a complete two-wire, positive-negative electrical system. Since most aluminum yachts are built on a custom-designed, one-off basis, they tend to be more expensive and hold their value, so it is difficult to get bargains in the second-hand market.

WOOD

Timber did not go out of fashion because of any particular fault of the material, but because it is cheaper and faster to build production boats using glass. Because of this, most of the traditionally built timber boats available secondhand are now quite old. In spite of the romance associated with these older boats, it is *very important* to survey them to ensure that they are in sound condition. Remember that softwood hulls (Douglas fir, pine) with iron fastenings were not intended to last more than 25 or 30 years. More recently, wooden boats have been built of wood/epoxy, but they are often sold at discount for two reasons: one, many of them are home-built, or designed to off-standard parameters; two, it's become evident that epoxy adhesives are not waterproof and are sensitive to heat (becoming soft at temperatures as low as 120°F). This has cast doubt on the long-term integrity of epoxy-laminated, multiskinned hulls. Look for well-built traditional boats with solid hardwood hulls. Or look for laminated boats built with rot-resistant timbers such as cedar or teak, using fully waterproof, heatproof, fatigue-resistant resorcinol adhesives (the glue lines will be reddish-brown). In each case be sure that only bronze or copper fastenings were used throughout the boat. To minimize concern about teredo worms, add three coatings of creosote to the bare wood of the underwater areas of any wooden boat before you put on the bottom paint.

FERROCEMENT

Unfortunately, the vast majority of ferro hulls have been amateur-built and therefore are difficult to insure. Ferro is almost as difficult to maintain as steel, and it is far more puncture prone. Because of these concerns, it has a very low resale value, so the original builder loses a lot of his investment. On the other hand, quite a few sailors have gotten out cruising inexpensively on secondhand ferro boats. One of them told us he solved the annoying problem of getting paint to stick to his hull by moving away from conventional paints and using the rubberized paint formulated for the white and yellow lines on highways.

Each hull material has its advantages and disadvantages for the builder, for the owner and for the secondhand buyer. But because of the sheer number of fiberglass boats available, it is probably the best choice if you are after the most affordable, soundest secondhand cruising boat.

CHAPTER

3

THE ECONOMICS OF HOME BOATBUILDING

The laughter of two boisterous boys caught our attention that first day. We had sailed into the deserted anchorage at Bahia Partida, 50 miles north of the noisy anchorage at La Paz, Baja California, Mexico, just after noon. Then, after a leisurely lunch in the cockpit, we'd gone below for a siesta. As we slowly drifted into wakefulness, both of us enjoyed listening to this indication that we had new neighbors. The heat of the day gave way as soon as the sun slipped behind the surrounding mountains. When the two boys finally climbed out of the water, we decided to row across the half mile that separated us to say hello to the crew of *Skye II*.

The small-world syndrome was reinforced as we came to know Cottee and John Ross and their two sons. They were not only Canadians but also friends of Larry's parents. They had built this 38-foot (11.6m) fiberglass cruising cutter only a few miles from the Pardeys' home on North Pender Island, just 30 miles from Victoria, British Columbia. Both of us couples were out cruising for a second time on the second boats we had built for ourselves from the keel up. So for the next week, we spent hours of each day talking of the interesting home-built boats we had seen out cruising, of different materials and methods, the lessons we'd learned. We parted company a week later, to meet again in French Polynesia. There we met Mary and Rudy Kok, who had cruised down from Hawaii on the Cape George 31 cutter they had bought as a bare hull and finished themselves. They came to anchor near *Skye II* and *Taleisin*. Now when all three couples got together for late-afternoon drinks, our discussion broadened to include this bare-hull option – one that opens many of the advantages and savings of home boatbuilding to people who feel building their own hulls is too difficult.

Though cruisers sometimes may be seen as dreamers, those who actually build their own boats are forced to be practical. So all of us were aware of the pitfalls of home building and could relate stories of unfinished dreams – boats started from bare hulls or from the keel up then left to rot in a garden or storage yard, boats sold for materials costs, or worse, just given away. We all agreed the percentage of success seemed to be highest among those people who had been actively involved in sailing before they started building projects. Compared with those who built from the keel up, more of those who started from a bare hull seemed not only to finish their boats in a reasonable length of time, but also to get out cruising. The highest failure rate seemed to be among people who had never owned or maintained a boat over 25 feet (7.6m), those who chose a hull over 35 feet (10.7m) as their first boatbuilding project, and even more so among people lured into building by the promise of a cheap hull material such as ferrocement or steel. Among these latter categories, the success rate (i.e., a finished boat in a reasonable time, then a few years of cruising) is less than 25 percent. What's the difference? It appears that people who have spent time around boats, who have repaired and maintained them, are more able to picture the costs and time they will have to invest in a boat-building project. They recognize that outfitting and finishing the boat costs more than just building the hull.

The allure of boats and the dream of cruising can be irresistible. For the person who could never imagine accumulating $30,000 or $50,000 or $80,000 in one lump sum to buy a ready-to-go cruising boat, the idea of investing a few hundred dollars in a hunk of timber, or a barrel of resin, or some sheets of metal – then using spare time to achieve that dream – can seem not only irresistible but also logical. Careful consideration of the true costs can temper that dream and keep it achievable.

The easiest way to estimate your time and financial involvement in this project is to remember that no matter what design you build, boats cost by the pound. If you call professional boatbuilders and tell them the estimated displacement of the boat you'd like to build, they can often give you an estimate right over the telephone. In 1997-98, quotes of $13.50 to $25 a pound for yacht-quality custom boats were normal in most developed countries. An interesting contrast is that the price per pound of a new production cruising boat in the 30- to 40-foot (9.2-12.2m) range is from $10 to $18. Light-displacement boats tend toward the higher ($25) end of the scale, heavier ones toward the lower ($13.50) end. We have checked these figures with professional builders, high-profile and lesser-known American, British, Norwegian, New Zealand, and South African yards and found that the formula discussed here holds

The skills you learn could help pay your way as you cruise.

true whether you choose wood, glass, aluminum, or steel. The materials component of the price runs about $2.10 to $4 per pound and includes the cost of all hull and deck materials, iron or lead ballast, spars, basic sails, bilge pumps and tanks, a simple engine, wiring for lights, and simple interior appointments. It doesn't allow for electronic gear or sophisticated winch systems. This materials cost is based on the professional discounts available to boatbuilders, who buy at wholesale and in quantity. If you are unable to get these discounts, your estimate should be about 25 percent higher for your future boatbuilding materials.

Part two of this formula divides these materials costs into three parts: one third for materials to build the hull, deck, and cabin, including the ballast keel: one third for the engine, tankage, plumbing, wiring, and interior: one third for rigging, deck hardware, sails, sailing gear, and ground tackle. These numbers have been confirmed by more than a dozen professional builders with whom we have met in the past two years. Unless you are buying an already completed hull, this breakdown will hold true for home construction as well. It is this one-third cost breakdown that makes so-called low-cost hull construction less than a bargain, as we'll discuss in detail later.

Labor is the one category where home builders can save cash. But few first-timers realize that professional builders allow 800 to 1,000 man-hours per 2,000 pounds (900 kg) of displacement for the completion of any custom yacht. Carlo Sciarelli, a well-known Italian yacht designer, has kept charts on the construction times for nearly 200 boats built to his designs. These boats ranged from 20-footers (6.1m) displacing two tons up to a 140-foot (42.7m) 100-tonner. All were built by professional yards; some were cold-molded, some had conventional wood or aluminum construction, about one-third were built of glass. The figures never seemed to vary by more than 5 percent. Light-displacement boats, which tended to be larger and more scientifically built, came closer to the 1,000-hour figure. Carlo added that amateurs building to his designs tended to need 25 to 50 percent more hours to complete their boats. We asked both Lyle Hess (who designed *Taleisin*) and Rod Stephens of Sparkman and Stephens to review Carlo's figures. They both agreed and cautioned that these were estimates for professional builders. (Figure 3-1)

The final part of this formula is a breakdown of the building hours. A bare hull with no deck or ballast keel represents only 20 to 25 percent of the labor figure for a professionally built hull. Add the ballast keel, rudder, deck, and cabin and the average boat is close to 40 percent finished. The second 40 percent of the labor allowance will be spent installing tanks, engine, plumbing, wiring, and the interior. The final 20 percent is for rigging the boat and installing deck hardware, winches, and hatches. These times include an allowance for purchasing parts and supplies and occasionally cleaning up the shop and tools. Not included is

Figure 3-1. *Materials costs and time estimates for the construction of yacht-quality, one-off cruising boats.*

This chart is based on the cost and time estimates discussed in this article. Cost figures are for professional builders as of spring 1998. Displacement and length figures are for average cruising designs available from contemporary designers.

Length on Deck	Displacement	Materials Costs ($)	Average Man-Hours
20 ft. (6.1m)	4,500 lb.	9,450 to 18,000	2,025 hours (1 yr.)
25 ft. (7.6m)	4,800 lb.	10,080 to 19,200	2,200 hours (1.1 yr.)
30 ft. (9.2m)	9,500 lb.	19,950 to 38,000	4,275 hours (2.1 yr.)
33 ft. (10.1m)	13,900 lb.	29,190 to 49,200	5,850 hours (2.75 yr.)
35 ft. (10.7m)	17,000 lb.	35,700 to 68,000	7,200 hours (3.6 yr.)
40 ft. (12.2m)	20,200 lb.	42,420 to 80,800	9,090 hours (4.5 yr.)
40 ft. (12.2m)	29,000 lb.	60,900 to 116,000	12,000 hours (6 yr.)

1 work week = 40 man-hours
1 work month = 160 man-hours
1 work year = 2,000 man-hours, including 2-week holiday.

the time to build a boat shed or set up shop. That could add 200 to 300 hours of labor, depending on your situation. Another factor to add to this section for amateurs is the complexity of lofting and handling the fairing of a hull for the first time. This is likely to add a lot of hours to the hull-construction phase of your project. Probably a fair breakdown of hours for a first-time builder would allocate up to 35 percent of the time to the hull and deck construction.

With the basic information presented in this formula, you can take a careful look at the magnitude of your dream project before you step off the deep end. This is vitally important, because any way you look at it, building yourself a boat is going to be an expensive project. For an average 30-footer (9.2m) displacing 12,000 pounds, you'll need between $25,000 and $48,000 for materials, plus at least 4,800 hours of your time. If you start a 24,000-pound 40-footer (12.2m), your materials cost will range between $50,000 and $96,000, plus 9,000 to 10,000 hours of labor.

We have heard designers, builders, and people who supply materials to home builders say, "Ah, but you are talking about traditional boatbuilding methods. You can build boats a lot faster than that." Or they will say they have found a method that cuts cost, or time. They'll suggest special strip-planked methods, longitudinally framed, ply-covered methods, glass-plank systems, epoxy/wood resin systems – all claiming the low cost will let you build faster and cheaper than the figures formulated here. Unfortunately, we have seen proof time and again that this is untrue. Though each method can produce a potentially good cruising yacht, it will not substantially reduce costs or labor. Either the finished product will not be to real yacht quality or the apparent saving will be only in one aspect of the project. Perhaps the resale value of the finished boat will suffer tremendously. In just one example, a friend who had only about the same earning power as we did was talked into building a boat 48 feet (14.6m) long and displacing about 23,000 pounds, instead of the 38-foot (11.6m), 20,000-pounder he originally wanted. The highly self-publicized designer told him, "I've got this magic new idea – you can get the boat built with only 4,500 hours of labor." We watched sadly as the hull and deck alone took that much time. Our friend then came up against the true cost – the interior finishing, the outfitting. The project proved to be so far beyond his earning power that the boat took almost 10 years to reach completion.

Steel and ferrocement hulls are often suggested as a way of saving substantially on materials costs and some on labor time. But even if everything goes as the advertisements promise, this could be a false economy. When you figure that the hull and deck of a boat represent only one-third of the materials cost, even a 50 percent savings here will only save you 16 percent of the materials costs for the total project. If you save one-third of the time building a steel or ferro hull, this will still only represent about one-eighth of the hours you put into this whole project. So, on the 40-footer (12.2m) we used as an example, this means you could save maybe $9,000 on materials and 1,000 hours on labor. But if you check with yacht brokers, you'll learn that a steel hull will cut the resale value of your finished boat by one-third or more: a ferro hull will cut it by half or more in comparison to a wood, glass, or aluminum hull of similar design. That means your eventual loss could be 10 times the initial savings.

Although it may seem frustrating to pay $400 to $1,000 for six sheets of paper for stock plans (a custom design is 5 to10 percent of total boat cost) from a recognized designer, this is another place where it pays to spend. Not only will a good designer's name help when you eventually go to sell your boat, but the details on the plans will help save hundreds of hours of frustration while you are building. If the plans include good rigging and fastening schedules, you'll save money by being able to purchase parts when they are a bargain, not at the last moment when you have to pay whatever price the market demands. So, please don't try to save money by creating your own boat plans or buying the cheapest plans available. Your designer's fee will probably end up being less than 1 percent of the final value of the boat.

The same mathematics should be applied to materials. Look at the overall finished value of your boat before you skimp on anything. If fir or sheathed decks will only save you $800 over the cost of teak ones, it's not much of a savings in the end when your boat's resale value will drop $10,000.

I know you are saying, "I'd never sell a boat I built!" We said that when we finished building *Seraffyn*. But after she took us around the world, we too succumbed to the 5-foot-longer syndrome. When it came time to put a price on her, we were glad we'd opted for copper and bronze fastenings throughout instead of saving $500 by using galvanized ones.

We do know of some home builders who have scrounged materials and lowered some of their dollar costs. We collected wheel-balancing lead for our own ballast keel and ended up paying 40 percent less than commercial buyers. Other friends have cut their own timber or found excellent buys on fittings and fastenings by haunting waterfront centers. But this means spending extra time, and this scrounging time should be factored into the final analysis of your whole project. Everyone who has to work to earn the money for his boatbuilding project should remember: Time equals money, money equals time.

The cost-and-time formula also applies to the idea of rebuilding an old boat that someone is willing to sell cheaply. Even if the hull is in pretty good shape, interior outfitting and rigging will still cost by the pound, as the formula describes. So before you are bewitched by old photos of the ragged beauty you're shown, get a surveyor to go over the hull in detail and ask him for an estimate of the costs involved in bringing the boat up to cruise-away condition. Check out all of the gear, rig, and sails. Remember that even with a sound hull, deck, and house, you only have one-third of the costs and 40 percent of the labor behind you. The other side of this old-boat coin is that outfitting a boat is one of the biggest expenses. So even if you happen to have access to a well-outfitted cruising boat with fine rigging, a good motor, lots of equipment but a rotten hull, it may pay to consider building a completely new hull, then transferring the old ballast keel, spars, and gear. We've seen this done with great success. But it pays to go over every aspect of the project with the cost-and-time formula in mind to prevent another dream from being shattered.

A careful look at the time aspects of the formula could save you from making the most tragic error of all. There is nothing more depressing than watching a "one-year project" drag on until it is still unfinished four or five years later. Surveys of home builders who actually launched their dream boats show that the average time for amateurs building 30- to 35-footers (9.2-10.7m) was seven years from start to finish. Forty-footers (12.2m) were taking up to 10 years. We ourselves know of several boats that took 14 years to complete. This may seem crazy until you figure that the average working man with a 50-week 8-to-5 job spends 2,000 hours a year at his job. It is difficult to expect this same man to go home and work on his boat more than 20 hours a week. That adds up to 1,000 hours a year for the project. So if the home builder can be as productive as a professional, he will be looking at 10 years to finish the 40-footer. This is the reason Carlo Sciarelli will not sell his plans to amateur builders until he arranges a meeting with the builder and his wife and has them honestly appraise construction times. "A project like this could be a terrible drain on a marriage, and boats are supposed to be happy things," he wrote to us. "I don't want to feel that my work led to the eventual break-up of a good marriage."

If, after looking at this formula and costing out the boat you'd like to have, you still feel you want a boat that is special – one that's really yours, free and clear – there are ways to cut the cost, time, and risk involved. The first, simplest, and hardest to do is to choose a smaller and/or lighter-displacement boat to cut the materials and time cost factors. There are two ways you can do this – either go for a short-ended, heavier boat with bowsprit and boomkin, or choose a longer but more lightly built boat. We personally prefer medium-to-heavy displacement boats for cruising, since they make better cargo carriers and have a comfortable motion at sea. So we've chosen a short, heavy, beamy boat to keep within our affordable displacement range of 17,500 pounds. We built a 30-footer with an immersion factor of close to 900 pounds per inch. That means we are able to load a ton of cargo on board and only sink the boat two and a half inches. That also meant we finished the boat in three and a half years, since Larry could put in close to 2,100 hours a year and I put in another 600 a year.

If you choose to build a larger, lighter-displacement boat to cut your materials costs, remember that your labor hours will increase by close to 20 percent. This is because the larger volume of the boat will mean more interior to build and a larger hull area to finish, and lightweight construction requires more time and care to make it strong.

Another cost-and-time cutting procedure will sound like words from a broken record when we say them. But consider cutting out the frills and build the simplest boat possible. In 1967, we decided against an inboard engine for *Seraffyn* because it would cost $2,600 to $3,000 just for the diesel motor, tanks and through-hull fittings. That represented money for a year of cruising in Mexico. Thirteen years later, a good diesel for *Taleisin* would have cost between $5,000 and $6,000, not including installation labor. Again that represented a year of cruising. So again, we said, "No, we'll buy an outboard for $600 or a nylon drifter if we don't want to sit and wait for the wind." The time-savings factor for engine installation could be as much as 200 hours of work.

If you feel an inboard engine is vital, opt for the simplest hand-start diesel to save both time and money. Eliminate the electric starting system and electronics; choose a cutter or sloop rig instead of a two- masted rig to cut out extra spars, rigging and sails. Go over the design you've chosen and eliminate every possible option without compromising safety. If necessary, the options can be added later. But right now, while you are staggering under the materials costs and time load of a boatbuilding project, these options could ruin your chances of sailing your dream boat within a reasonable period.

The most critical part of boatbuilding is the lofting and construction of your hull. A mistake here could blow the whole project. If this is the first time you've ever built something as large and complicated as a boat, it might be worthwhile considering a production or professionally built hull, or a more complete kit boat. Although your initial costs will be higher, you'll have something with resale value right from the start just in case circumstances get in the way of your boat's completion. You'll be sure of the integrity and sailing qualities of the hull you buy. The eventual cost difference between a totally home-built hull and a kit will probably be less than 25 percent of your total costs. The time savings could run as much as 35 percent. On the 30-foot (9.2m) example used earlier, this could be a savings of up to 2,000 hours, or two years of spare time. On the 40-footer (12.2m), a ready-built hull could save you up to 4,000 hours, or four years. A ready-built hull does mean you'd lose some of the thrill of owning a custom one-off boat. But we've seen people build an all-wood deck and cabin for their production hulls, ending up with a boat that was distinctive and custom-looking.

Carefully considered, logically coordinated home boat building can be very rewarding, especially if you have sailed on lots of different boats and know exactly what you want. If you have a knowledge of basic woodworking skills, there is no more challenging project. If you accept the realities of cost and time, building your own boat is a fine savings account. Each dollar you spend, each hour you put into the project will be yours tax-free. Some people will discourage you by saying, "You could make more money working at a job in your own field, and save the money to hire a real professional. You'd be money ahead." This might be true for people in highly lucrative professions. But they will be looking at boatbuilding as a challenging contrast to their normal working life. Most of us would find we couldn't save every penny we earned at a part-time job. Part of it would go to taxes, part of it to work expenses. Then we would find it hard to put every penny in the bank for five or six years to gather enough to hire someone to do the building for us. Like ourselves, you might find it far easier to gather a few thousand dollars to start the building project, then put $200 or $300 a month into materials to keep it moving along.

When you are finished, you'll own your own boat free and clear – no loans to pay off before you can set sail, no banks calling for their interest. But, most important of all, if you choose good materials and take the time to do a meticulous job as you build, you'll end up with an unexpected bonus. The skills you learned while you built your own boat should help pay your way as you cruise, since there is an acute shortage of skilled craftsmen in many parts of the world. In early 1997, good yacht carpenters in the United States and Europe were charging from $25 to $35 an hour. The boat you lovingly built for yourself will not only provide a floating home to show you the world, but if you maintain it while you sail, it will be the best possible business card – an obvious example of your boatbuilding skills.

If this will be your first attempt at boatbuilding, or at outfitting a bare hull, we suggest you first consider building or finishing a small boat, one that maybe could serve as a tender for your offshore cruiser. This smaller project will help reinforce the formula we have outlined here. It will also give you a chance to get afloat during breaks from your bigger project. This job also will introduce you to the skills and tools you'll need when you start building your own full-size cruiser.

There is no cheap shortcut to getting a good boat you'll be proud to own and sail – one that is safe and seaworthy and will give you a good return if you decide to sell it. But a careful pre-project estimate of your eventual cost and time involvement could cheer you up as you work. It will also help you choose the right boat for your time schedules.

CHAPTER

4

TIPS FOR NEW-BOAT BUYERS

W ho can deny the pleasure of stepping on board a brand-new, purpose-built offshore cruising boat? The special smell and feel of fabrics, finishes, and gear touched only by those who assembled them just for you. Customized features that are exactly what you desired. The respite from maintenance that comes with having all-new equipment. With luck, you should not have to spend a lot of time changing this boat or repairing its gear for three or four years. "New" gives you the feeling that you can set off cruising almost as soon as you load the provisions. If you can afford this luxury, it is important to make sure the purchase goes smoothly and the experience is emotionally rewarding. But it's not everyone who has this opportunity.

To compile advice for fortunate new-boat buyers, we spoke to five well-known yacht designers, and also to several dealers, builders, insurers, and finance people, in the United States and the United Kingdom. Each confirmed that if you have cash limitations, it's difficult to justify buying either a new production boat or a new custom-built boat. Chuck Paine, known for the Morris cruising boats, Cabo Rico 40, and others, states, "The premium you pay for buying new compared to buying a boat a few years old is at least 30 percent – maybe more when you consider the costs for the bits and pieces you'll usually get with your secondhand boat (shackles, fenders, lines, etc.)." Chuck went on to say, "This is probably an appropriate investment for the person who is working long hours, earns good money, and feels he has little time to deal with working up a secondhand boat. But even with a new boat, there is still a lot of work and time involved in bringing it up to snuff."

On the other hand, even though "new" is part of the whole cruising dream for many people, it can be emotionally and financially risky unless you have already owned and sailed several different boats. Each of the designers we spoke with confirmed that a significant number of the buyers who bought an offshore cruiser as their very first sailing boat found the purchasing and commissioning process to be difficult.

Nancy Cann, owner of Crusader Yacht Sales, Annapolis, Maryland, representing Pacific Seacraft, agrees: "People who have never before owned boats, then buy a brand-new 34- to 40-footer (10.4-12.2m), are often distressed at the steep learning curve they face."

Even experienced sailors have more problems than necessary when they decide to get their first brand-new production or custom-built boat. Bob Perry, designer of the Baba 30, Valiant 40, and Tayana boats, says, "I cannot believe the number of successful contractors who will enter into a boat-buying deal they would never consider in their own line of business." We agree. It must be because boats are about dreams, about pleasure and freedom from the pressures of workaday worlds. The majority of people you meet around the waterfront are friendly, warm, and welcoming. In this relaxed atmosphere, it can seem out of character and maybe even a bit rude to come on like a hardnosed businessperson. But there are just as many rogues in the marine business as in any other, just as many salespeople interested more in their commissions than your sailing dreams. But, unlike the mass-market automotive or airplane industries, the sailboat business is virtually a cottage industry, as these figures show:

Figure 4-1. *New cruising/racing sailboats built in the USA in 1996.*	
20 to 29 feet in length	1,833
30 to 35 feet	890
36 to 40 feet	751
41 to 45 feet	385
46 to 60 feet	80
Source: North American Sailing Industry Study	

Bluewater cruisers make up less than 25 percent of these figures in the under-40-foot range. In 1997, Pacific Seacraft built only 18 34-footers (10.4m), Island Packet built 20 35-footers (10.7m). With limited numbers like these, it is easy to understand why there is no funding for a sailboat consumer-protection organization, no pressure for a governmental agency to regulate sailboat construction, and no design and equipment testing agency such as the FAA (Federal Aviation Administration) in the airplane industry or the NHTSA (National

Highway Traffic Safety Administration) that regulates the automotive industry. Anyone can set up a company to build or design boats; no qualifications and financial bonding are required. Two British designers agreed, noting that the situation is similar in the Britain. One went so far as to say, in regard to boat construction, design, and equipment innovations, "It's the Wild West out there!"

Because this is such a small industry, builders cannot afford to spend much money conducting tests on hulls and equipment. So you, the boat buyer, end up doing this free of charge. (Basically, what happens is that if and when things break on board, you have to expedite the repairs or return the gear to the factory. This is only a hassle when you are near the source, but in Fiji or Tahiti, it is a super pain in the transom!)

Then there are the financial arrangements. No standard escrow procedures cover the boat buyer, no bonding company protects your deposit, as in a house purchase. The deals that go wrong are common enough that magazines such as *Practical Sailor* (USA) and *Practical Boat Owner* (UK) and others have devoted major editorial space to stories about dealers absconding with large deposits, about builders using a new customer's payments to complete a previous buyer's boat, about legal battles among buyer, designer, and builder, about companies going broke or raising the prices during construction.

Although we cannot cover every contingency of this very serious and complex transaction, we think the information in chapters 2 and 3, plus the following pointers will give you parameters so you can comfortably heed the important warning, *caveat emptor* (buyer beware).

Production Boats

1. Research and evaluate different designs, different builders, and different dealers, just as you would when buying secondhand. But also ask for the name of five or six recent customers. Nancy Cann warns, "Make sure you speak with people who have dealt with both the broker and the boatbuilders within the past year. Things change fast in the sailboat building industry – sometimes for the better, sometimes for the worse."

2. Don't be lured by prices that look like bargains – i.e., the biggest boat for the least money. Try dividing the base price of the boat by the designed displacement to arrive at the price per pound (Fig. 4-2).
   As explained in chapter 3, this is a more effective measure of a boat's

true construction costs – and far better for comparison than dollars-per-foot-of-length.

If one boat appears significantly lower per pound, be cautious and establish how the cost savings were achieved. Sometimes it could be by cutting quality or by lower labor cost; if you are truly comparing similar-quality boats, built for similar purposes, the prices per pound should be pretty close.

Figure 4-2. *Displacement /price = cost per pound or kilogram*

Example:

A well-known U.S. 34-foot (10.4m) bluewater cruiser, selling price $167,000
Displacing 16,000 lb. (or 7,270 kg)
167,000/16,000 = $10.43 per pound (or $22.97 per kg.)

---

3. Be willing to pay extra for a company's reputation. Simultaneously, though, be sure the same builders and managers are running the company. As Barry Van Geffin, managing director and designer for Laurent Giles, UK, told us, "Just in the 1990s, Westerly Yachts, who build to some of our best-known designs, went bust twice. Then the molds and rights were taken over by new people. Not much we designers can do to ensure the new company builds to the same quality." This is true world-wide. Companies such as Hinckley and Pacific Seacraft in the United States, and Dufour in France, have changed hands in the past few years. This may or may not have affected quality standards.

4. Research the builder's credit standing and financial backing any way you can. Do the same for the dealer who is handling the transaction. Andrew Simpson, editor of *Practical Boat Owner* and a boat designer/builder, cautions that the financial ups and downs of a company can cause variations in the quality of the boats they build: "When things are good, they pay for better help, buy higher quality gear. When things are bad, they can cut down and the customer may not be able to spot the differences."

5. Consider hiring a surveyor or professional boatbuilder to go over the display model you are interested in buying. Check each item on the specifications list with him. This is important even for boats in the top-quality range. If you do not spot problems until after you have signed

the purchase agreement, it will probably cost you to have them put right. At one recent London Boat Show, we went on board the "best of show" bluewater cruiser. There we found ball valves threaded directly onto the through-hull fittings. A surveyor would have demanded the more reliable, stronger arrangement of a through-hull fitting threaded into the body of a proper seacock with a flange bolted securely through the hull.

6. Resist rushing the purchase process. Once you have decided on the boat and basic equipment, spend several days considering the specifications list and the pros and cons of your choices.

7. Resist the urge to change the standard boat. Not only will this drive up the costs, but the complexity and close spaces in any cruising boat mean that each change affects the whole. Unless you actually can mock up the new idea in an existing boat, you might find, for example, that "just moving that bunk a few inches" gives you a more spacious-feeling sleeping area, but it also means engine access becomes impossible.

8. Avoid being the owner of the prototype of any new production boat, either with a start-up company or an established builder. In the first case, the company could go broke before you get your boat. In the second, you will, as we said before, be "doing the testing for future boats." We delivered two different first-off-the-line offshore boats for two different companies and in each case sent back substantial lists of installation and equipment problems. We later learned that one of the companies was building boat numbers four and five using our suggested modifications.

9. Avoid built-for-the-boat-show boats. Dealers and builders may offer you special options at reduced prices if you buy their demo boats. But John Burgreen of Annapolis (Maryland) Yacht Sales warns customers to allow 30 days' leeway for boat deliveries. Boat-show demos must be on site on a specific day, ready or not. So these boats often are rushed to completion, and technical details may have been overlooked, or the installed options may not be what you really wanted or needed.

10. Resist the pressure to buy more gear "at the factory." Ted Brewer, known for his Whitby 42, Niagara 38, and others, says, "Avoid the equipment trap, avoid problems, keep more money to get out sailing sooner." Not only can factory-installed extra equipment push the price of the boat ever upward, but as he cautioned, the yard crew might not be the best people to install the gear. Furthermore, once you get out on sea trials, you might have different ideas about what gear you want and need. This is especially true of electronic gear, for which prices

could drop drastically between the time when you signed a contract for a new boat and actually are ready to set off cruising. The GPS (global positioning system) is only one example of this – changing within three years from bulky, power-consuming $2,000 units to miniature, relatively low-power-consumption units costing less than $200.

11. Hire a surveyor to check the layup of your hull as it is built, then as bulkheads are bonded in place, and again when the deck is being bolted on. Many yards will resist this, as it slows production unless scheduling is arranged beforehand.

12. Have your surveyor check the installation of all of the boat's systems when it is commissioned, and before you hand over final payment. Although the vast majority of new hulls are unlikely to present problems, the complexity of systems on today's boats can mean that even the most competent builders and dealers can overlook poorly installed plumbing, wiring, and sailing gear. We delivered a well-built new 39-footer, commissioned by a well-known broker for a personal friend in Mexico. Halfway down the Baja California coast, the loose engine wiring harness melted when it landed on the engine manifold. Two days later, the pad-eye for the boom vang preventer pulled up, bringing a 4-inch-by-6-inch patch of fiberglass with it. Someone in the factory had neglected to put nuts and washers on the pad-eye bolts. These two details might have been caught by a surveyor, or by a builder who was aware his boat was going to be inspected by the surveyor before the final payment.

13. Arrange to take delivery of your boat at the dealer's location or as close to the factory as possible, and do your sea trials nearby. No firm – not even the most reputable – can be sure of delivering a trouble-free boat. The dealer or factory will be reluctant to pay another yard several hundred miles away to fix an oversight – not only because of the extra cost but also because it could hurt their reputation. One winter several years ago, we delivered three brand-new boats for the same broker. Two were factory-fresh, never seen by the owners until we sailed them from Miami to Puerto Rico. When we arrived, we had a two-page list of problems: some minor glitches such as missing door catches, rusting hose-clamps, blocked drains, but also more serious problems including poorly designed chainplates and bits missing in the rigging. The third boat had been sea-trialed right near the dealer. Then the owner spent a month gunkholing around Miami, returning the boat to the dealer for a few final adjustments before we picked it up to deliver it to his home in New York. The owner commented, "I

saved more than the cost of your delivery fee by being able to work right with the dealer, and this made the whole project a lot of fun!"

14. When you sign the sales contract, arrange to hold back 5 or 10 percent of the boat's price until after you have done all your sea trials. This gives you leverage should there be details that need attention.

15. Spend at least a day going over the boat with the dealer or factory rep before you take it for the first sea trial. Before you go sailing, take photographs of anything you feel could be questionable. Otherwise, it is hard for the dealer to be sure things were not broken during the sea trials.

16. Don't plan to begin your cruise too soon after the delivery date of your boat. John Burgreen of Annapolis Yacht Sales cautions that anything from fires at the factory to trucking disputes can hold up delivery. His firm and Crusader Yacht Sales both offer a 90-day final inspection to catch any last factory bugs. Add to this the time you'll need for familiarizing yourself with your boat and outfitting it properly and you will understand why most people find they should figure at least nine months from the factory delivery date before they can enjoyably set off cruising.

17. Be even more careful about the finances of new-boat buying than you would about home buying. Each dealer, each manufacturer with whom we spoke seemed to offer a different purchase arrangement – from 10 percent at time of order with 85 percent on delivery and the final 5 percent after dealer debugging to three progress payments with the total due before the boat was launched. No one could suggest a secure way to recover your money should the boatbuilder go bankrupt or refuse to deliver your boat for some reason. A letter of credit could offer some protection, but most U.S. and UK boatbuilders are working on such tight margins, such tight production schedules that they would balk at this arrangement. But there are two ways you might protect yourself. First, make sure you are assigned a specific hull number and that all payments and invoices include this number. Next, be sure the number is on the hull at the factory, and get a photograph of it. Then create the legal documentation to be sure that your boat, at every stage of completion, is and remains your property in the event that the builder should go bankrupt. One way to do this in the United States is with a Uniform Commercial Code form (UCC). This document secures ownership of the boat in your name during construction and costs approximately $50 (forms are available from state offices or from most boat finance companies). Second, make sure

your progress payments are designated for the completion of specific building stages, not just specific dates. Link the payments with definable steps, such as layup of the hull, with installation of the bulkheads and deck. Inspect your hull to be sure this stage is satisfactory before you send the next payment. Should the builder go broke, these measures and your UCC form are the best you can do to insure and protect your investment.

The Custom-Built, Custom-Designed Boat

THE BUYER'S VIEWPOINT: "I want a boat that is uniquely mine, filled with all of the qualities and pleasures I missed on my other boats. I want the process of designing and building it to be fun, interesting, trouble-free. I want to enjoy working with the designer and builder." (As witnesses to this scene, we know the buyer also feels that dealing with the designer and builder in hard, cold business terms is the antithesis to the whole dream.)

THE DESIGNER'S VIEWPOINT: "I want to please the buyer, but I would like to end up with a set of stock plans I can sell to other people. I want to get any publicity I can from having a custom design under construction. I also would like to try out a few new ideas and see if they work. And, of course, I need to earn a living."

THE BUILDER'S VIEWPOINT: "I need this job. It will keep the crew going through the winter. If I can persuade the buyer to build it the way we built the last two boats, I can make some extra because I am set up already." Unfortunately, in the custom-boat field, more than in any other, each participant has his or her own agenda – agendas that may or may not be in conflict. Here, more than in any other boat-acquisition scenario, it is vital that the buyer have previous sailing experience and be fully aware of the true costs of boat-building. The costing methods discussed in chapter 3 are similar to the guidelines still used by Sparkman and Stephens to give customers a quick estimate of what a custom boat will cost. If you multiply the construction time in man-hours by the shipyard's normal hourly rates, then add the materials cost plus 10 or 20 percent to cover the yard's profits, you can estimate the total construction costs you will face for a 30- to 45-foot (9.2-13.7m) custom-built cruising boat. Design fees average from 5 to 10 percent of the construction costs (stock plans are less).

Interestingly, four of the five designers with whom we spoke felt it was possible to have a custom-designed, custom-built boat over 35 feet for about 8 percent to 10 percent more than a similar-quality new production boat. The fifth, Chuck Paine, flatly states, "It is more realistic to look at 30 to 50 percent extra, unless you are lucky enough to be on the right side of a foreign-currency deal."

All five designers agree that this is not the place for the buyer with less than $200,000 to spend, nor is it the place for the first-time boat owner. You need serious boating experience to be able to speak 'marine-tech,' the language of designers and builders. A high degree of communication is required to allow you to explain your ideas and desires, to get the boat built strongly so it will sail well, and so it eventually, when the time comes, will have a good resale value. Ted Brewer echoed each of these designers by saying, "A lot of clients are too set on what they want. They don't listen to their designers and they probably should. We've seen the same ideas tried time and again, especially interior design ideas. We know they didn't work, but if the clients won't back up and consider this input, we have to go with what they want." Unfortunately, if you do not have the experience to comprehend the designer's ideas and suggestions, the design that emerges might need to be modified during the building process. This is very expensive, as Greg Matzat of Sparkman and Stephens stresses: "Allow lots of time for the design process and for the selection of a builder." Time spent at this stage means money and hassle saved later. Most cost overruns come from changing the plans partway through the building process. Remember that if you request changes after work commences, the builder will have to charge you time and materials costs above and beyond any contract price. Furthermore, the change might mean double the work, as the builder will have to remove the error, then modify the area around the change, before he can incorporate your new idea.

Barry Van Geffin of Laurent Giles, UK, adds, "People often forget to budget for a project supervisor. Even if they take on the task themselves, they should consider the costs of transportation and accommodation, as few people are lucky enough to live right next to a good boatbuilder."

Additional Points to Consider

1. Avoid being the first client of a new designer (especially if that designer is yourself), unless you have sailed on some of his boats. This does not mean we recommend only the best-known designers. Lyle Hess, who designed our past three boats – *Taleisin, Seraffyn* and *Cheeky* (our faithful dinghy) – was not well known. But we had sailed on two of his

other boats and seen their racing history (and successes). Because Lyle was less famous, he probably did give us a lot more attention than other designers might have. If you choose a well-known designer, be sure that he will be drawing your boat, not letting his apprentice try his wings at your expense.

2. Avoid being avant-garde or faddish if you are building a cruising boat, even a so-called fast cruiser. The sailing world is a highly conservative one. Remember that water ballast and winged keels were touted as wonderful ideas for offshore cruising, and they have proven to be less than perfect in the real world.

3. Think carefully before using composite construction for a cruising boat. It will raise building costs by up to 25 percent and double eventual repair costs. According to the designers we consulted, it only serves the purpose of saving weight. Barry Van Geffin echoed all of the others when he said, "There is little justification for true light displacement in a cruising boat, especially when the vast majority of owners will ruin any speed advantage and possibly stress the hull and rigging by adding all of the gear and provisions they feel are necessary for comfortable cruising." He and Chuck Paine added almost identical statements: "A moderate to heavy cruising boat not only has a better motion at sea and can be safer, but it's also faster because you will be able to carry more sail area and keep the boat driving harder and still feel comfortable."

4. Be careful when choosing a builder, and make a point to speak with several of his previous clients. Bob Perry warns, "If you visit a builder and see one of his clients living in a house trailer right on site, working to get his boat finished, be wary. The owner might be there because it is the only way to goad on the builder. He might also see you as his salvation, because your cash deposit up front could be the money the yard needs to get the current boat finished, so his recommendations might be self-serving."

5. Do not assume that overseas builders will give you a better or lower price. Shop locally and compare. Remember that the cost of freight and customs to import gear, plus hiring an overseas project supervisor, can reduce the savings offered by cheaper labor prices. You will also be missing out on the pleasure of watching your dream come to life. But if an overseas yard specializes in the construction method you prefer, and if you catch the right side of a currency devaluation, overseas could be a good choice.

6. Once your boat is being built, give yourself the pleasure of frequent

visits, but do not interrupt the builder or his crew. A six-pack of beer delivered after working hours (5 o'clock) will possibly speed your boat along. A half-hour chat during working hours stops the whole crew, and to be fair to all concerned, you should be billed for that extra time if the yard is working to a contract price. You *will* be billed for the extra time if your job is being done at 'time and materials.'

The biggest factors that will keep your new boat purchase on track include being experienced enough to know what you want, being fair and realistic about the true costs of new boats, keeping the costs within your means, and finding builders, dealers, and designers who earn and deserve your trust. Then be patient, logical, clever, and alert so that you can enjoy the whole procedure – from planning through purchasing to launching and beyond.

ARE YOU A CRUISER OR A CONSUMER?

IT TAKES A PERSON WITH FIRM RESOLVE to make a plan, get a seaworthy boat, then say, "I am going cruising now – even if it isn't the absolutely perfect time." That person is usually what others call "a real individualist." If that same person wants or needs to be truly cost-conscious, this individualism will be challenged more during oufitting than than at any other time.

But stand firm, because the decisions made here determine how much cash can be left in a good, safe investment fund earning dividends to extend your cruise. Even more important, outfitting – unlike boat buying – is not a one-off expense. Nor is the expense limited only to cash. As you cruise you have to maintain and repair the electronics, machinery, sails. If you are not cautious as you outfit, this could eat up the free time you set sail to find. If you cannot fix the gear yourself, you will have to spend days rushing around to find trained specialists to do the work at prices that can be staggering to your cruising budget in a distant port. In addition, every two or three years, you will have to refit the boat and its pool of accumulated equipment, and then replace the original spare parts.

The chapters in this section describe alternative ways to consider some of the choices you must make. Remember, there is no right way to outfit a boat. Each decision should be based first on seamanship, then on affordability – with affordability meaning the cash you pay to purchase and maintain the gear as well as the costs that will be incurred if the gear breaks down at sea or in a deserted anchorage.

Will you be left feeling immobilized or will you select gear that you can fix yourself? Your decisions will determine whether you return from your cruise feeling more personally empowered or more enslaved to today's consumer society.

CHAPTER

5

COST-EFFECTIVE OUTFITTING

We call them "freedom chips," others call them "funnits." Name them what you will – the dollars, pounds, or euros you save by being cost-conscious as you outfit can get you cruising sooner, or give you more reserve funds to spend on special experiences that can make your voyaging memorable. Just as important, choosing highly dependable, thoroughly tested gear that you can fix on board will give you more time to savor these experiences. The biggest problem we see among cruisers today is that *they seem to spend a disproportionate amount of their time* fixing their conveniences. Most skippers hate this. A few revel in recounting their repair triumphs, oblivious to the boredom of the rest of the crew who would have preferred being off skin diving, daysailing, or sampling the local wines.

It is impossible to create one simple checklist to suit all outfitting needs for all sailors. The choices are influenced by as many factors as the choice of automobiles. Therefore, the idea behind Figure 5-1 is to give you the confidence to consider downsizing your equipment purchases so you can get out cruising now. If, a few thousand miles along the way, you find you really *need* a particular piece of gear, you can still buy it locally or from a mail-order marine store. We guarantee you will make a more clever and appropriate purchase armed with your pool of voyage-acquired experience.

To help you make a list that truly fits your income and repair skills, we have purposely shown the two extremes of the outfitting scale. The four voyagers shown on the right side of this chart might be classified as "cheap and cheerful." They have all had long-term success and, some would say, have continued cruising year after year just because they had low operating costs and avoided the frustration of maintaining superfluous gear. What they did carry and use would, in our opinion, reflect the basic needs for enjoyable, safe, and efficient offshore cruising.

Figure 5-1. OUTFITTING A BLUEWATER CRUISER

STANDARD ITEMS

Assumes crew of 2. Figures in US$ Spring 1998. All but *Taleisin* and *Seraffyn* have inboard engines. HB = Home Built, SH = Secondhand, B = Class B EPIRB

ITEM	Theoretical 35 ft (10.7m) 16,000 lb (7 tons) Minimum	Maximum	Lin and Larry's *Seraffyn* 24 ft (7.3m) 10,500 lb (4.7 tons)	*Taleisin* 30ft (9.2m) 18,000 lb (8 tons)	Eric and Susan Hiscock's *Wanderer III* 30 ft (9.2m) 14,000 lb (7 tons)	Hal Roth's *Whisper* 35 ft (10.7m) 16,500 lb (7.5 tons)	Jamie Morrison/ Niki Perryman's *Siandra* 35 ft (10.7m) 16,000 lb (7 tons)
Global Positioning System (GPS)	250	2,999				220	220
Shortwave receivers	220	2,100	220	220	220	220	399
VHF marine radio, antenna, cable	385	584		205			
Handheld VHF	399	599					600
Dinghy/tender	1,295	3,449	600	1,200	1,200	1,200	500
Dodgers	585	3,000					500
Wind-vane self-steering	1,595	2,995	200 HB	300 HB	800	800	800 SH
Depth Sounder	379	969	50	50	50	20	200 SH
Distance log and knotmeters	639	799	100 SH	100 SH	100	100	200 SH
Bilge pump	679	1,000	150	150	150	150	200
Liferaft	3,800	4,579	200	200 HB			1,200
Emergency watermakers	499	1,349		499			
EPIRB	799	799		239 B			239
Safety harness and tether	70	290	30 HB	30 HB			30 HB
Additional safety gear (2 vests, flares, etc.)	367	1,420	120	120	100	100	150
First aid and medical kit	400	1,200	250	400	200	100	200
Fire extinguishers	218	508	30	56	80	56	56
Handheld 12V spotlight	40	63		30			30
Radar reflector	37	160	5 HB	5 HB	15		15
Tricolor nav lights	47	145				47	47
Batteries (ship's)	742	898		79	79	150	250

Battery condition meter (voltmeter)	34	199		15			34
Foulweather gear	650	2,166	150	250	150	250	250
Tools	200	400	200	200	200	200	200
Lifesling hoisting tackle (man overboard)	345	345					
Whisker or reaching pole	398	890	150 HB	250 HB	300	300	300
Ventilation	150	600		200			
Additional water tanks	60	300	20	30	30	30	30
Water-taste filters	45	45					
Additional fuel tankage	34	278					
Bosun's chair	80	109	34	50	34	34	34
Swim ladders	68	179					
Snorkling gear	200	400	80	80	80	80	80
Additional cabin lamps (solar and oil)	214	535					
Anchor rollers	209	209	209	209	209	209	209
Anchor ready	38	38					
Secondary compass below decks	59	294		20			
Hand-bearing compass	38	350	30	90	90	38	38
Binoculars	90	809	50	330	90	90	49
Dividers, parallel rules, plotting sheet	30	30	30	30	30	30	30
Barometers	56	206	56	356	56	100	100
Chronometers	56	247	56	100	56	56	56
Backup chronometer	30	60	39	39	39	39	39
Primary metal sextant	420	2,640	400	400	400	400	400
Secondary plastic sextant	33	199		60			
Charts, nav tables, cruising guides	1,500	2,500	300 SH	400 SH	400	350	350 SH
Engine and boat spares	500	1,500	200	300	300	300	300
Storm jib, storm trysail and drifters & MPS	3,500	7,000	800	1,800	2,000	2,000	600
Awning, rain catcher, cockpit canvas	600	2,000	500	700	500	500	200 HB
Rigging and canvas spares	300	300	100	500	100	100	100
Flags	100	300	50	100	100	50	50
Anchors (3)	1,165	1,165	900	1,100	1,100	1,100	1,100
Chain: 350 ft. 5/16" on Theoretical 35	808	808	808	1,000	808	808	808

Figure 5-1. OUTFITTING A BLUEWATER CRUISER – continued

STANDARD ITEMS

Assumes crew of 2. Figures in US$ Spring 1998. All but *Taleisin* and *Seraffyn* have inboard engines. HB = Home Built, SH = Secondhand, B = Class B EPIRB

ITEM	Theoretical 35		*Seraffyn* 10,500 lb (4.7 tons)	*Taleisin* 18,000 lb (8 tons)	*Wanderer III* 14,000 lb (7 tons)	*Whisper* 16,500 lb (7.5 tons)	*Siandra* 16,000 lb (7 tons)
	Minimum	Maximum					
Anchor windlass	1,461	1,895	400	1,000		800	1,300
Spare anchor rodes 300 ft. bow + 300 ft. stern	250	250	250	250	250	250	250
Backup nav lamps (oil or sealed battery)	200	200	200	200	200	200	100
Spare foulweather gear	200	200		200			
Abandon-ship bag (panic bag)	150	500	150	150			
Sailing rig for dinghy	-	-	200	200		300	
Backup oil interior lamps	100	100		50		100	100
TOTALS	27,816	60,151	8,317	14,542	10,516	11,657	12,443

OPTIONAL ITEMS

ITEM	Theoretical 35		*Seraffyn* 10,500 lb (4.7 tons)	*Taleisin* 18,000 lb (8 tons)	*Wanderer III* 14,000 lb (7 tons)	*Whisper* 16,500 lb (7.5 tons)	*Siandra* 16,000 lb (7 tons)
	Minimum	Maximum					
Radar	1,579	3,189					
Single sideband	1,849	1,849					
Ham radio	1,399	1,399					
Autopilot	698	3,907					
Fuel Filter	15	149					
High-output alternator w/regulator	443	993					239
Outboard motor	937	2,001					400
Solar panel	259	575		159			300
Electric cabin fan	78	174					78

12V vacuum cleaner	27	49				27	
Watermaker	2,759	7,590					
Refrigeration	1,639	6,000					
Sewing machine	650	2,245					
SCUBA gear	400	1,500					
Weather facsimile	795	1,600					
Inverter	100	795					
Towing generator	595	739					
Notebook computer	1,200	3,729					
Inmar sat - C/GPS	3,990	3,990					
Video camcorder	700	1,695					
Folding bicycle	350	800			400	400	
Roller furling	1,760	4,490		500			
Underwater camera	235	539	300				239
Television	450	450					
Fully battened mainsail and batt-cars	2,000	2,800					
TOTALS	**24,907**	**53,247**	**300**	**1,086**	**400**	**0**	**1,256**

OUTFITTING A BLUEWATER CRUISER – *note*

Theoretical 35 – From the outline used by John Neal for West Marine-sponsored cruising seminars. John has voyaged around the Pacific on two boats named *Mahina*, a Vega 27 and a Halberg-Rassy 31. He now runs Mahina Expeditions, offering sail/navigation training and adventure charters on a 46-footer.

Wanderer III – a Laurent Giles 30 used by Eric and Susan Hiscock for three circumnavigations. She is still out making passages. Under her new owner, Theis Matsen, *Wanderer III* has now completed two more circumnavigations carrying essentially the same equipment as she did when the Hiscocks owned her.

Whisper – a Spencer 35. This boat took Hal and Margaret Roth around the Pacific, to Cape Horn, and then around the world.

Siandra – a 35-foot Lion-class sloop. Niki Perryman and Jamie Morrison left Australia when the boat was near her 40th birthday and they had not yet reached their 30th. Six years of sailing on a minimal budget has taken them to many corners of the Indian Ocean, Red Sea, Mediterranean, and on to Norway's far northwest. They earn their cruising funds as they go by doing yacht deliveries, boat repairs, writing, and house carpentry.

Somewhere between the "cheap and cheerful" and the Theoretical 35 lies your personal comfort zone.

To give a fair comparison of the cost to outfit each boat, we have priced the gear for all six using the 1997/98 marine catalogue from a well-known American company. The chart does not include an allowance for harder-to-quantify, highly personal choices, such as galley gear, sleepwear, entertainment items, and spare mooring gear. Nor does it include the cost of installation, from wiring to special brackets or extra labor. This could add from $2,000 to $15,000 over and above the purchase prices shown on the chart.

As you find your place on this chart, remember that any money you save by downsizing your desires could be put to potentially better uses. As Figure 5-2 shows, if you budget $800 to $1,200 a month for two years away from home, and outfit your boat using gear similar to the cheap and cheerful voyagers, you could have money for an extra three months of cruising. Or it could cover the cost of a month-long inland excursion for two – to ride on horseback across the Pyrenees or ski the Alps or raft the wild waters of New Zealand's South Island. For other people, the savings could mean the difference between going cruising now or putting it off for "someday when......."

But how do you reduce this outfitting list to fit your budget yet cover your personal needs and preferences? The first step is to prioritize among items that are truly necessary, those that provide comfort, and others that fall into the luxury category. (A priority list is discussed in detail in *The Self-Sufficient Sailor*, chapter 21.) Then, once you have made this list, stick to it and avoid these potential traps: advertising pressures, untested gear, just-introduced gear, complex laborsaving devices, hard-to-maintain-but-might-be-handy-in-a-one-off-emergency gear, and peer pressure.

Unfortunately, it's very difficult to stick to this priority list. Almost everyone you encounter as you make your choices would like to have some of your $18,000 to $48,000 worth of "freedom chips" in their bank account, compounding interest and dividends to finance their particular schemes or dreams. Manufacturers, outfitters, and sailmakers will use all of the tools of marketing to convince you, "This widget or magic box will make you safer, more comfortable, save labor." So, as you proceed, be aware!

The world of advertising well understands human nature, and ruthlessly exploits human frailty. It generates new needs so that it may endlessly sell us new products. Advertising fuels our wants and desires. For it to succeed, it must

Figure 5-2. *Potential investment gains from cost-conscious outfitting (comparison of "cheap and cheerful" long-term voyagers to the Theoretical 35).*

	Theoretical 35 *low cost*	Theoretical 35 *high cost*
Standard items only	$27,816	$60,151
"Cheap & cheerful" average costs	11,495	11,495
Reserve principal [1]	$16,321	$48,656

Dividends and interest if compounded for 2 years at 9.5% per annum with an average cruising cost of $1,000 per month: [2]

$3,248 = 3.2 months extra cruising time	$9,713 = 9.7 months extra cruising time

[1] This principal amount could become your personal cruising fund, or emergency reserve. Remember that all of the extra gear you put on board will need repairs and continue to depreciate and lose value. Roll over the interest in this cruising fund and it will probably keep ahead of inflation.

[2] This assumes a relatively low-risk investment such as Fidelity GNMA fund, with no tax liability. Since most cruisers have little other income once they set off, this would probably all be tax-free gain.

persuade large numbers of people that enough can never be enough. It works by making us feel unhappy or insecure about our diet, appearance, and possessions, in other words, every aspect of our lives. Nine times out of ten it is selling us something we don't really need. But it proves irresistible nevertheless. – from Getting a Life, *by Ghazi and Jones. Hodder and Stoughton, 1997.*

As you begin to outfit your boat, new gear will be coming onto the market all of the time. Almost everyone you speak with will urge you to add them to your list. The pressure they exert will be difficult to resist, especially since cruising sailors are always eager to extol the virtues of gear they have on board. If you say, "Well, I am getting by okay without it," you are implying they bought something they didn't really need, or that they did not have the basic seamanship skills to do without. Even when it may be the main reason for resisting or deciding against a purchase, few of us are comfortable saying, "I can't afford it."

So, rather than look only at your monetary budget as a reason to control your outfitting desires, consider the most valuable commodity any of us have – *time*. Once you head offshore, the maintenance of your hull, rig, and each piece of gear on board will become a very personal and pressing problem. To be assured of pleasurable cruising and peace of mind, all of your gear must be kept in top working order – which requires regular inspections, maintenance, and upgrading. If you do the work yourself, it is often less time-consuming, less frustrating than trying to find dependable, skilled people to do it for you, especially in a foreign port or isolated anchorage. Even cruisers with *unlimited* budgets cannot avoid this frustration and loss of time. That is why we suggest that if you can't fix it or maintain it yourself, maybe you shouldn't have it on board. In either case, few people realize the time involved in maintenance. Since 1965, we have been totally immersed with cruisers and their problems, so we can *confidently* provide the following estimates.

Figure 5-3 indicates the time each aspect of maintenance would take a reasonably handy person who does his own work.

If, as many cruisers do, you plan to voyage 9,000 miles during the year on a boat that can average 130 to 150 miles per day on a downwind passage, you will need at least 100 days for provisioning, fueling, passage planning, chart organization, dealing with officials, and sailing time. You will need 55 to 60 days per year for simple crew care, buying and preparing food, doing the laundry, and writing necessary letters, plus 30 days for simple cleaning chores and housekeeping, such as scrubbing decks, cleaning the dinghy and the interior, wiping up oil leaks, sorting out lockers and bilges. Add all this to the absolute minimum of 46 days of basic maintenance time shown in Figure 5-3. Now, assuming you have

no gear breakdowns, you have accounted for 231 days of your precious voyaging year. That leaves you 134 days to explore ashore, make new friends, and savor the other reasons you decided to go cruising. Compare this to the free time you had when you worked onshore – 52 weekends plus 19 paid holidays, or 123 days each year – and you will see why some people feel they have less free time while cruising than they did before. To

Avoid being a yacht-chandlery display boat. This will cut costs and keep your decks clear for easier sailing and easier boat handling.

Figure 5-3.

Maintenance time required to keep a straight-forward 35-foot (10.7m), 16,000-lb (7.5-ton) fiberglass cruiser in good condition, ready to go to sea. This assumes no gear failures or breakdowns and is based on an assumed passage of approximately 9,000 miles per year. Estimated engine usage, 600 hours per year.

Hull, steering, and rigging maintenance and inspection, including four-day haulout, through-hull inspection and greasing, anode replacement, hull waxing and polishing, bottom painting, not including varnishwork	20 days
Sails, running rigging, canvaswork inspection and maintenance, including going aloft twice a year, adding chafe patches, repairing worn sail stitching, servicing winches and blocks	8 days
Routine engine inspection and maintenance, including oil changes, fuel-filter service	4 days
Electrics – checking batteries and alternator, tightening and inspecting all connections for corrosion	2 days
Ground tackle, regalvanizing chain, marking lines, checking rodes and anchors, servicing windlass	4 days
Tender and outboard, oars, sailing rig Refrigeration, pumps (bilge, water, shower), plus total water system	4 days
Life-raft service	2 days
Total time needed for basic maintenance	**46 days per year**

avoid this feeling, it is imperative to be conservative and resist buying extra gear that requires more of your personal time for maintenance.

Think twice before choosing the newest ideas, the latest equipment. Otherwise, you could unwittingly find yourself doing the research and development for the manufacturer. Unfortunately, it is almost impossible for the manufacturer to simulate all of the possible ways gear will be used (and abused). No amount of testing can show all of the possible stresses or the problems created by poor installation and wear and tear. Even the automotive and aerospace industries which have huge budgets for engineering aviation and test-to-destruction facilities, still find it necessary to issue recalls on a regular basis. In our world of marine and sailboat equipment, from the simplest sailhandling ideas to the most sophisticated of electronics, innovation is constant. The big difference , as we mentioned earlier, is that there is no Federal Administration or National Highway Traffic Safety Administration to assist and protect the marine consumer. Manufacturers are always incorporating minor and major changes influenced by what they learn from customers as well as from "price war" pressures exerted by their competitors. Some of these changes are definite improvements, others may not prove advantageous for the sailor. Offshore, far from repair facilities, is not the place to learn this.

Therefore we suggest being sure that any gear you buy has had several years of use by active cruising sailors. Talk to repair specialists who work on all brands of the gear you are considering, not the dealer's repair personnel. Before you part with your freedom chips, find out whether improvements have been incorporated and tested. (See *The Capable Cruiser*, chapter 7, for more ideas on how to determine which gear will be more dependable.)

Sails – the simplest yet most important component of your boat – often are victims of performance-oriented innovations that not only may make them less durable but also can make offshore cruisers feel like they are doing the sea testing for the manufacturer. Fully battened performance-oriented mainsails have had heavy promotion lately. Unfortunately they are the antithesis of cost-consciousness and reliability. Just think of what happens when the battens press against the shrouds on a reach or when running downwind. Not only does the sail get chafed through, but even the battens develop grooves. In the Round-the-World Rally, almost all of the 15 owners who chose this option expressed disappointment. John Rose, who sailed on *Midnight Stroller*, a Trintella 53, stated he had several broken travelers and tremendous amounts of chafe not only at the ends of the battens, but also where the shackles on the batten holders rested against the aluminum mast. They eventually chafed holes right through the wall of the mast. Brad Bernardo, who sailed his Hinckley 42 in the rally, stated, "It might be okay for racing, but it's no good for our kind of sailing. Though we have done everything to prevent chafe such as putting on leather patches, it hasn't helped. I only went for a fully battened mainsail because three years ago that was the fashion and *I was simply talked into it.*" (From *Round-the-World-Rally*, by Jimmy Cornell, p. 36. Adlard Coles, 1993).

Des MacWilliams, head of MacWilliams UK Sails, agreed about the chafe and recommends *no battens* for offshore cruising. Des says, "Battens of any sort make it difficult to pull the mainsail down unless the boat is headed into the wind. Full-length battens can act just like a ratchet to jam the sail partway up, partway down if the aft end of the sail comes down more quickly than the forward end." His conclusion: "Fully battened mainsails are a triumph of advertising over engineering." So, to save

Figure 5-4. *The batten question.*

Battenless Mainsail	Short Battened Mainsail	Fully Battened Mainsail
300 sq.ft.	300 sq.ft.	300 sq.ft.
28 sq.m.	28 sq.m.	28 sq.m.
$1,100 (£700)	$1,440 (£900)	$1,920 (£1,200)
No extra gear	Battens $110 (£70)	Battens $400 (£250)
		Batt-car system, including track and cars, $1,440 (£900)
Total $1,100 (£700)	**Total $1,550 (£970)**	**Total $3,760 (£2,350)**

Prices courtesy of SKB Sails, Falmouth, England, and MacWilliams UK Sails, Cork, Ireland.

money right now and as you cruise, consider the actual pricing for a brand-new bluewater cruising-quality mainsail, with and without battens.

In *The Self-Sufficient Sailor*, we discuss the advantages of using the lean, tough battenless option. This option may not be "currently fashionable," but it definitely is an alternative worth considering, as is the choice of hanked-on headsails instead of the roller-furling headsails recommended by so many people today.

We, too, have been impressed by the ease of setting and shortening sail using roller-furling gear. Yet when we step back and consider the furler side of the option – from cost to poor sail shape to windage when furled in an anchorage or hove-to, to the all-too-real risk of breakdown, especially in strong winds – we reconsider. John Neal and Barbara Marrett told us how they helped cruising pals recover from a furler-caused dismasting just south of Alaska. During an 80-knot summer storm, the owners of the 45-footer (13.7m) decided to heave-to. They were riding well for more than an hour when the lock on their roller-furler drum let go. The sail broke free and began to flog violently. Within 10 minutes, the whole rig came crashing down. This is only one of literally dozens of furler-caused, domino-like disasters we have heard of directly and secondhand. We have experienced problems with this gear while delivering other people's boats, as well as at anchor in strong winds near furler-outfitted boats. Out at sea in a sudden fierce squall is no place to find that you cannot get a sail to furl away. It is like finding that the brakes on your car fail to work halfway down a steep hill. *We demand that brakes work all of the time, and it is just as important that all*

Figure 5-5. *Survey of roller-furling gear used during the Round-the-World Rally.*

During this 18-month rally, the majority of the sailing was downwind in light to moderate conditions. The fleet experienced no gales. Murphy's law becomes rampant when the winds blow gale force. Courtesy Jimmy Cornell, *Round- the-World Rally*. Adlard Coles,1993.

JIB FURLING GEARS

MAKE	NUMBER	PERFORMANCE	RELIABILITY
Manual			
Hood	7	8.3	9.2
Profurl	5	9.6	8.4
Harken	5	9.6	9.6
Reckmann	3	9.7	9.7
Plastimo	1	10	10
Furlex	1	10	10
Goïot	1	7	8
Focmar	1	8	7
Elvstrom	1	8	8
Canglini	1	6	8
Electric			
Reckmann	1	10	5
Profurl	1	9	9
Hydraulic			
Rondal	1	10	10
TOTAL:	29		

sails come down when you need them down. Yet a poll of the 29 (out of 32) people who carried a roller-furling headsail on the Round-the-World rally showed that *only three* gave their gear top (10 out of 10) marks for reliability (Fig. 5-5). This is among a wealthy group of people who could afford to join such a rally in the first place and who used and bought "the best" brands.

A look at the actual prices for roller furling shows that it is the far more expensive option. As not only do you need the furling gear, but the basic roller-furling sail needs to have a cigar-shaped foam insert along the luff, plus a sun-protection cover. You then need at least one other jib (in case the primary sail's clew pulls out) plus a storm staysail that can be set on its own stay inboard of the working jib. But "modern thinking" downplays these costs and adds the emotion-laden statement: "Roller-furling gear keeps the crew where they belong, safely in the cockpit." This is misleading and potentially dangerous. Think of the realities of offshore cruising. Most cruising boats are handled by couples. We feel safety lies in knowing that both of these partners can work confidently and

Above: *Keep in mind that offshore you want sails that come down when you want them down, that do not cause extra windage when you are hove-to, and that are reliable and easy to maintain.*

Below: *Not only can roller furling become an expensive convenience, but incidents such as this have frightened many novice sailors and put them off sailing permanently.*

competently in almost every possible weather condition on all areas of the ship – from the foredeck to the side deck to the mast area, and even aloft if necessary. If you and your mate have not practiced getting out of the cockpit to hoist a small jib or put a reef in the mainsail, how are you going to deal with the realities of life offshore? These realities include setting a small staysail, hoisting the trysail, getting out and streaming a para-anchor, inspecting all of the foredeck gear for chafe on a windy tradewind passage, and attending to the less frequent but potentially vital job of going aloft to replace a halyard or fix a loose spreader. (Neither one of us would feel good about going to sea with a sailing partner who was afraid to leave the cockpit!)

Start from the premise that you cannot buy safety; you must learn and practice safety techniques to gain confidence and efficiency. If you do this, you will save a tremendous amount as you outfit, because the list of available safety gear is endless. The whole topic of offshore safety is as emotionally charged as the sanctity of motherhood or patriotism. It's hard to argue the ideal of safety. Marketing executives know and exploit this to sell an ever-growing array of safety gear. But it is sad to watch a timid wife walking through a boat show with her enthusiastic, "gung-ho" husband. First, she sees videos of hurricane-swept Caribbean anchorages with boats dragging anchor and ending up on the rocks being pounded to destruction – followed by the message, "Buy our insurance or risk losing everything." Then she sees storm photos overlain with messages to buy inflatable life rafts, harnesses, survival packs, flares. This is reinforced by messages urging you to attend safety-at-sea seminars where you have to watch demonstrations of ready-made safety gear, such as Lifeslings and inflatable flotation vests. All are *supposed to reassure* sailors that if they buy just one more item, they will be safe. But we feel it has just the opposite effect. It convinces people (timid partners included) that sailing is a very unsafe pastime. This worries us, as ours is the only pastime where this seems to be the case. Skiing, motorcycling, mountain climbing and horseback riding are far more risk-prone, yet you don't hear an endless litany about safety. The industry leaders in these sports know it would scare people. As a potential cruiser, you have to remember that no matter how many safety features you add to any mode of transportation, *security depends on the driver's skill.* And to reassure your mate, remember that you will rarely be traveling over 6 knots at sea, so you will have time to react to changing situations.

Another way to save money, now and as you cruise, is to avoid interconnected systems. Keep as many onboard items separate from engine and electrical supplies as possible. If vital gear – from your anchor windlass to anchor lights, nav lights, cooking and navigation gear – can be hand-operated, run on its own self-contained fuel supply, or backed up by solar or kerosene (paraffin) power, you will not end up trapped in an isolated anchorage unable to sail onward. While you are outfitting, if you go along with the idea of integrated systems, you may be buying gear with more functions than you need. You'll also find it hard to mix and match different brands of components to save money.

Electronics – from VHF to radar to chart plotters – are costly additions that can be skipped now to get you out cruising sooner. You can safely sail without any electrical gear other than a dry-cell-battery-operated quartz watch, shortwave receiver, and, if you wish, a GPS – especially if you are determined to go now using your own skills. In the 66 countries we've visited, we have never been required to have a transmitting radio. Despite what many people say, no one will or can refuse you entry if your radio stops working or if you don't have one.

A favorite story of ours occurred the time we arrived at Santa Barbara harbor, admittedly a small port, and tacked up to the almost-empty 200-foot-long floating pontoon. We tied alongside, then went up to the harbormaster's office where we were told we could stay right there for as long as we liked. Then his radio came on and another yacht called in to ask, "Is there a berth for the night?" The harbormaster looked at the clock, saw it was only 10 minutes until he could leave for home, then answered, "Sorry, we're full; you'll have to go on to the next harbor."

Electronic gear can be handy; if it keeps working, it can add pleasure to your life (we love our stereo, 12V vacuum cleaner, and our video cameras), but it's all extremely difficult to maintain in the damp, harsh salt laden environment of a sailing boat. As a rough rule of thumb, figure on spending twice the original purchase price on maintaining and repairing electronic gear you carry for a voyage of two or three years.

As you outfit, avoid being seduced by brand names, and look beyond marine stores for potentially lower prices. Foulweather gear is a major purchase if you buy highly visible brand names. As a cruiser, you will spend very little time sitting on the weather rail, so you don't need "the ultimate" gear. We have found that store-brand "coastal style" foulweather gear, at one-third the cost of brand-name "voyager" items, has worked quite well, even in the cold sailing waters of Scotland and Norway. We back up this gear with even less expensive rugged fisherman's gear, so our total outlay for four sets (i.e., two each) was less than the cost of one set of high-tech gear. When one of our foulweather jackets was blown overboard and lost during a visit to another sailor's boat near Hobart, Tasmania, it was annoying but not budget-crushing. For other sailing clothes, such as rainproof jackets or wool socks, sun-protection hats, consider camping stores, where you'll save money and can buy potentially more rugged clothing and gear.

If you are outfitting your boat in a marina where several other friends are also preparing for a voyage, it is important to resist adding their desires to your list of necessities. We watched six couples in Fremantle, Australia, as they met at the Monday night barbecue after spending the day shopping, making decisions, stowing gear and provisions on board. As we all shared our bring-a-plate potluck dinners, and turned our sausages or burgers on the barbie, each couple would talk of another item they'd bought – an extra guidebook, a propane barbecue, a watermaker, a ship's stamp. Then the other new cruisers would become concerned and wonder if they should have this latest item. The local chandler told us that he had had a rush on "ship's stamps" after one such evening, and he asked us if they really were "absolutely necessary." He was surprised to hear that the one time we were asked to add our ship's stamp to a document, the customs official said, "Don't have one? Just sign your name and write, 'no ship's stamp.' "

Keep your desire to go cruising uppermost in your mind and pare your outfitting list to the bones. It is not easy when today's marine stores are filled with mouthwatering "gotta-have" choices; a chandlery is even called "the candy store" by wannabe cruisers. As members of the "cheap and cheerful" faction (Fig. 5-1), we know it was less difficult to decide 30 years ago just because there was less gear available. Since we started off this way, we have been able to resist complicating our boat and our lives by remembering that we got along fine without this or that. We'd rather have less gear to maintain, more money in the bank.

Fortunately and wisely, some of the cost-conscious cruisers who start off today are learning to evaluate their needs, to choose multipurpose, well-tested *essentials* that they can make themselves or acquire affordably. To downsize your outfitting list, resist *all* gear temptations until you have sailed your boat a lot. Then consider emulating Jamie and Niki who acquired *Siandra*, a simple, standard 35-foot (10.7m) cruiser/racer, and started off from Sydney to cruise locally along the east coast of Australia. As they began to taste the first golden fruits of freedom, they decided to acquire only what they absolutely needed, one item at a time: an anchor windlass, better ground tackle, an Aries wind-vane self-steering gear. Interestingly, like Max on *Patience* (see chapter 2), Niki and Jamie told us they didn't add much extra gear as they voyaged across oceans to England, and they actually discarded several convenience items that proved unreliable and expensive to maintain.

They are out there now. If you can resist being a consumer, you, too, could be a "right now" cruiser.

Three crews who have chosen to cruise cost-consciously. On the east coast of Norway, we had a delightful rendezvous with Niki and Jamie from 35-foot (10.5m) Siandra and Frank and Wendy Mulville of 28-foot (8.6m) Iskra.

CHAPTER

6

THE BONNETED JIB

*S*eraffyn had been anchored at the port of Manfredonia on Italy's southeast coast for almost a week, while I waited for Lin to rejoin me after a 3 week break. Just after noon each day, a little pulpero (octopus boat), one of the last Italian sailing/fishing boats, would come winging through the breakwater entrance. I rowed over and asked the owners about their lateen rig. They put up with my awful Spanish-cum-Italian for a few minutes until, in polite desperation, they invited me to go out sailing at 3 the next morning. I immediately accepted.

During our return from the fishing grounds, we had a light offshore breeze, which gave us a reach back to port. The surprisingly weatherly lateen mainsail had four rows of normal reef points, plus several small grommets along the foot. Since the two brothers who owned the boat were keen to get back for lunch, I wasn't surprised to see them tie a rectangular addition to the foot of the mainsail, using the grommets as lashing points. This increased the little hooker's speed by about a knot. The shape of the bonnet [1] did not impress me much, as the lashings caused wrinkles to radiate out from the lacings along the foot of the sail. But the bonnet did seem like an easy, inexpensive way to add area to the sail.

Several years later, when Lin and I were sailing our new cutter (*Taleisin*), we found we were not completely satisfied with the reef points we used to transform our 100-percent lapper down to a working jib. Though this reef-point system had worked well on *Seraffyn's* 257-square-foot lapper, *Taleisin's* 430-square- foot reefing lapper was harder for Lin to handle. She found it difficult just to drag the heavier sail along the deck and hank it onto the headstay.

The stiffer, heavier cloth (7 ounces compared with 5.5 ounces) was harder for both of us to roll in order to tie in a tidy reef. The reef on this larger sail left a bulky roll that sometimes came untied when we short-

---

1. Laced-on sail additions, used by sailors for centuries, are called bonnets. If an additional section is attached to the bonnet, it is called a drabbler.

Photo 6-1. *On* Seraffyn *we used reefing headsails. But with* Taleisin's *larger sails, we found we needed a more performance orientated solution.*

Photo 6-2. Taleisin's *two-part bonneted jib. We call this 100 percent sail our lapper, as it overlaps the mast.*

tacked in heavy winds. So at times, we would drop *Taleisin's* lapper and sail undercanvased, using just the staysail and main instead of going to the trouble of reefing the lapper into the ideal working jib size.

After a year of sailing with our reef-pointed jib, I recalled my magic sail on that little pulpero, with its brightly painted bow eyes and its wrinkled bonnet laced onto the foot of the mainsail. If only I could get a bonneted jib to set smoothly along the connection, I felt we could have the best of all worlds. We'd have a nice, clean working jib without the inefficient, bulky reef bundle at its foot and we could store the sail in two individual parts so it would be lighter for Lin to handle. If we could make it work, this bonneted jib would give the same advantages as the reef-pointed sail – i.e., two sails for the price of one, a savings in storage space below decks plus faster sail reductions and increases. In addition, the foot of the working jib minus the bonnet would not scoop up and hold water like the bundle of the reef-pointed jib sometimes did. Nor would there be any reef points to come untied as we short-tacked.

When we discussed this problem with various sailmakers, they suggested roller reefing. But, as we've already discussed, we wanted to keep away from the high cost and complexity of roller furling, even though it has the seductive lure of easy, quick sail stowing.

By good fortune, the 1986 challenge for the America's Cup was underway when we sailed into New Zealand. Sail design and development projects were on, full speed ahead, and one spin-off was the heavy-duty YKK zipper. This spirally interlocking, all-synthetic zipper, with its parting-strain resistance of 90 pounds per linear inch, was used successfully on the New Zealand 12-meter's mainsail at the Fremantle heavy-weather eliminations to flatten the mainsail luff for the windward leg of each race. This zipper looked just like the thing to solve our problem and produce a wrinkle-free connection for a bonneted jib.

With this possible solution in mind, the second (and probably most difficult) step in obtaining this two-part sail was to convince the sailmaker to build it. The loft manager, reluctant to build "a flyer," recommended that we stay with the well-proven reef-point jib. He was worried that the zipper would fill up with salt and jam and he was concerned about how long it would last out cruising and wondered how we could hold the zipper together at the high-load areas at the tack and clew.

But with our promise to accept full responsibility for any failures, he gave the go-ahead. The sail designer produced an excellent shape, using 6.7-ounce fabric for the bonneted lapper/working jib combination.

Photo 6-3. *The working jib – i.e., the lapper without the bonnet.*

Once the sail was started, the loft personnel became very interested in the project. The crew at North Sails, New Zealand (Kent Luxton, Monica Collins, Haven Collins and Carol Tremain) had lots of positive input and suggestions at each step of the construction. The one fact we all knew was that the zipper had to be supported so that an even strain was exerted all along its length, with no undue point loading or extreme wrinkles to force open the zipper.

To accomplish this, the sail panels were sewn together and finished without the bolt-rope or leech lines. The sail was then laid out on the floor and reef patches were put on, along with a 3-inch-wide band of Dacron running between the tack and clew patches to support the zipper. (The reef was laid out at an angle so that not only would the sheet lead remain the same when the sail was bonneted or unbonneted, but the luff would stay as long as possible on the working jib for maximum windward drive.) The leech and tack of the sail-to-bonnet connection were then joined with snap-shackles seized onto one side of the bonnet. This seizing can be adjusted to take the initial strain so that the zipper is not overstressed.

Photo 6-4.

The severed bolt-rope at the tack is eyespliced around two rope thimbles; these in turn are seized to the sewn rings on both the bonnet and the jib (Photo 6-4). To spread the strains further the clew area was fastened together using flaps sewn onto both the jib and the bonnet (Photo 6-5). The lacing line connecting the eyelets on these flaps is adjusted so the leech strains are spread evenly onto the patches, and little or no strain is exerted on the zipper in this area. To keep the working-jib part of the sail as clean and free of hardware as possible, the leather flaps, snap-shackles, and zipper car are on the bonnet itself.

Photo 6-5. *The lower or bonnet part of the zipper has a limiting stop sewn onto it so the zipper car cannot fall off. The snapshackle is adjusted with the seizing lanyard so it takes the initial leech strain (The zipper should take little strain at this point.) The felt-pen marks on the zipper tape indicate correct fore-and-aft alignment.*
The arrow points to the hand-sewn car stop on the bonnet side of the zipper.

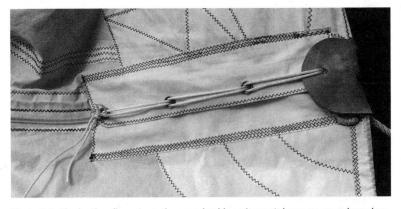

Photo 6-6. *The leather flap covers the snapshackle so it won't hang up on a shroud or dent the mast when we tack.*

The severed bolt-rope inside its luff tape had to be stitched securely to the reef patches on both bonnet and jib (Photo 6-5). A separate tack thimble had to be spliced to the bolt-rope, as shown in the photo, to produce a wrinkle-free tack on the working jib.

The working jib has a foot-line led to the port side of the tack, and a leech-control line is led to the starboard side of the tack, where there is a jam cleat on both the working-jib tack and the bonnet tack (Photo 6-4). These control lines are best led to the tack area because they are easier to reach than if they were positioned on the high-cut clew. The leech line runs up from the tack through its own luff tape and is led onto a small single block at the head of the sail, where the line enters the leech tape, travels down the leech, and is finally sewn to the working-jib clew patch. (Other specialized details of the construction of this sail are explained in the captions for Photos 6-4 through 6-6.)

Once the bonneted jib was completed, we tested it by going off for short cruises and also by racing the two-handed winter series in Auckland, New Zealand. After that, we realized we needed to add a separate leech line to the bonnet. This done, we used the first of our bonneted jibs with complete confidence and sailed with it for seven years, including a midwinter passage across the Tasman Sea, a beat against 20-to-25-knot southeast trades inside the Great Barrier Reef, two subsequent voyages across the Tasman and through the Cook Strait between New Zealand's two islands, and on across the Indian and Atlantic Oceans. The zipper continued to work perfectly and never once jammed or became sticky from salt.

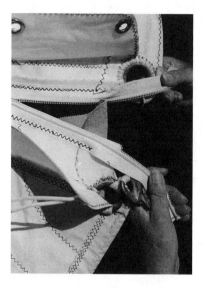

Photo 6-7. *The zipper peels apart easily once the clew attachment shackle and retaining line are released.*

Eventually we became curious to know just what strains the zipper would be able to take, and to find out whether it would work without the clew-reinforcing flap. So we tried the full-size sail in an 18-knot breeze and had the boat rail-down without the flap laced. The zipper held fine, even though we were bucking into a three-foot head sea. We felt that was a good test, but we still use the clew flap to protect the high-load leech area.

We feel this jib has been a complete success, especially since it is so easy to shorten down. Reefing can be done in less than two minutes, even singlehanded, so we have less tendency to sail overcanvased. Here's how we reef the sail:

1. Drop the sail, untie the flap lacing line from the clew flaps (Photo 6-6).
2. Disconnect the snapshackle.
3. Peel the zipper apart right up to the tack, and disconnect the tack snapshackle.
4. Unhank the bonnet from the headstay and fasten the working-jib tack in place.
5. Transfer one of the sheets to the working-jib clew (leaving one of the sheets attached so that the bonnet cannot get blown overboard).
6. Tie down the bonnet and remove the sheet, then attach it to the working-jib clew.
7. Hoist the jib.

Though we still recommend reef points for some headsails, the following considerations might make the zipper jib a better choice than either a roller-reefing or a reef-pointed jib:

1. It is faster and easier to remove the bonnet than to tie in a normal reef or to change one headsail for another, especially with large headsails such as *Taleisin* carries.

2. By using the zipper jib, we have two sails with a smooth, fast sail shape (Photos 6-2, 6-3).
3. If the zipper should pull apart, it's probably time to reef anyway. So we would just lower the sail and remove the bonnet. It is unlikely any harm could be done to the sail, as the strong clew and tack snapshackles would hold it together until lowered.
4. If the zipper or bonnet connectors do fail at sea, the worst case would be that we would have to make do with just the working jib until we reached port.
5. Major repairs can be done anywhere there is a sewing machine and a person with sailmaking skills.
6. The cost of a bonneted jib is much less than that of roller-furling gear with its foam luff and leech and foot UV-protection patches, but it is a bit more than a reef-pointed jib of the same size.
7. In common with reef-pointed jibs, a bonneted jib damaged along its bonneted section can still be used as a working jib. On the other hand a roller-reefing jib badly damaged anywhere in its lower sections is out of business until repairs can be made.

On the negative side, it will be difficult to persuade your sailmaker to experiment with a bonneted jib. Also, you will find it takes a bit more time to attach the bonnet to the working jib to increase sail area than it is to shake out the reef points in a reefing headsail or to unroll your furling jib. Since a replacement zipper could be hard to buy in some countries, it might be prudent to carry a spare. On racing boats with a foil headstay, the crew would need to make one extra move: They would have to start the luff tape of the bonnet into the foil groove as the sail is hoisted.

Bearing in mind all these points, we and some of the staff at both of the sail lofts we've worked with feel a bonneted jib could be used to good advantage for:

1. **CRUISING SLOOP** – storm/working jib combo, number 1 and 2 genoa combo.
2. **CRUISING CUTTER** – working jib/lapper combo.
3. **RACING SLOOP** – storm jib/blade combo. Working jib/number 3 combo, number 2/heavy number 1 combo. Also handy as an addition to a storm spinnaker in case all regular-sized chutes were blown out.
4. **SAILBOARD** – medium- or heavy-weather sail combo.

These bonneted sails could be especially interesting to owners of small racers, on which both space and weight are serious considerations. To meet the racing rules, they have to carry a selection of sails that add a couple of hundred pounds of extra weight. On the other hand, bonnets are not practical or worth the expense for small sail-area reductions like we have on our working staysail. We use two rows of reef points and find it easy to tie in the three or four points that hold about 40 square feet of sail for each reef.

Like many of the best ideas in sailing, the bonneted jib is not a new system, but rather an update of an old method using modern materials. Bonnets could come back into vogue just like slab reefing (jiffy or pennant reefing) has. And, like slab reefing, it could give performance-oriented sailors and cost-conscious cruisers durable, efficient sail shape, lower costs, and quicker sail changes.

Note: In 1996, Des MacWilliams of Crosshaven, Cork, Ireland, made our third zippered jib. Although we had found that all of the details of the first bonneted sail worked well, he added a few of his own ideas. Now, after using that sail for a summer of wooden-boat festivals and regattas in the south of England and north of France, plus a six-month voyage to Scotland and Norway, we are completely satisfied. Des cut the sail relatively flat so it would work well for the occasional races we join. Then, to save weight (and a bit of cost), he cut the bonnet from lighter fabric (5 ounces), the upper section from heavier (7 ounces) fabric. Rather than use metal hooks for the securing flaps, he created loops that link together just like the stitches of crochetwork. Lighter and easier to build, they're what we'd use on the next bonneted jib - if and when we wear out this one.

(MacWilliams Sails, Ireland, Tel: 353-21-831505, Fax: 353-21-831700)

CHAPTER

7

A COST-CONSCIOUS SAIL WARDROBE

One of the most obvious places to control the cost of outfitting a boat for local and offshore cruising is in your choice of sails. With a new, 100 percent jib for a 9-ton cruising cutter costing between $1,400 and $2,500 (1998 prices), it is vital to consider a minimalist approach to a sail wardrobe. Space is definitely another consideration on boats used for offshore voyaging. Even on a larger boat, a seldom-used extra sail could mean a cramped cabin or a limited supply of provisions. The following would be our recommendations for sailors who wish to consider their engines as auxiliary - for use in and around marinas rather than for shortening time on offshore passages. In each case, we've made the assumption that the boat carries approximately 83 square feet (7.71 sq. m.) of working canvas per 2,000 pounds (907kg) of loaded displacement (chapter 11).

CUTTER UNDER 6 TONS DISPLACEMENT

1. Triple-stitched mainsail with with 3 sets of reef points
2. Triple-stitched staysail with one set of reef points
3. 100% jib with one set of reef points to reef to working-jib size
4. Nylon drifter, 135 to 150% of foretriangle

SLOOP UNDER 6 TONS DISPLACEMENT

1. Triple-stitched mainsail 2 sets of reef points
2. Storm trysail * (25% of mainsail area)
3. 100 to 110% jib with one set of reef points
4. Storm jib * *
5. Nylon drifter, 150% of foretriangle

First additional luxury sail: 135% 4-ounce genoa with one set of reef points.

* *The area of a triple-reefed mainsail is quite often too far forward on a*

sloop to work well either going to windward or while lying hove-to. Therefore, a long-footed trysail is needed.

** *Since there is no staysail to serve in strong winds, a storm jib is necessary as a backup sail on a sloop.*

CUTTER OVER 6 TONS DISPLACEMENT	SLOOP OVER 6 TONS DISPLACEMENT
1. Triple-stitched main with 2 sets of reef points	Same as for under 6 tons, except the storm jib should be slightly larger than normal, with one set of reef points
2. Storm trysail (1/3 of mainsail area)	
3. Triple-stitched staysail with 2 sets of reef points	
4. 100 to 110% jib with reef points or zipper ***	
5. Drifter	

First luxury sail: number 1 Dacron genoa
    Second luxury sail: spinnaker
*** *A zippered jib or bonneted jib can work exceptionally well here (see chapter 6).*

If you carry a roller-furling headsail, your sail inventory should include the same mainsails and trysails as recommended above, a drifter plus a staysail with reefs either set on a permanent staysail stay or a running staysail stay designed to set in place with a Highfield lever. This way, you have a separate, strong, flat-cut jib to use for high wind conditions. This heavy-weather staysail not only will save wear and tear on your larger roller-furling jib, but it also will give you the flat sail that works best to windward in storm conditions. Should your furling sail or its gear present problems, you'll have a stay with a sail designed to help you claw off a lee shore. This stay will also give support to your mast should the furler stay ever fail. Here's what Dick Deaver, Congressional Cup winner and former sailmaker, said to us when he retired early to set off cruising: "Roller furling lets me sail this 55-footer (16.8m) with less crew, but it has got a lot of moving parts that could break down. So I'd never consider going cruising without at least one stay for a hanked-on headsail that I can guarantee will always go up and always come down no matter what the conditions may be."

CHAPTER

8

THE TWO-FOR-ONE OPTION: A SELF-SUFFICIENT LIFEBOAT/TENDER

All bluewater cruising sailors need a practical shoreboat on board. Most (ourselves included) also would like a lifeboat of some kind, "just in case." For the limited-budget cruiser, the cost of buying and maintaining the normal option – a tender and a separate life raft – can be exhausting. For the sailor on a small cruiser, the space limitations make this quite difficult. Even among those people with both space and funds, there is a growing distrust of CO_2, automatic inflation life rafts. "Will it blow up when I pull the cord? Will the painter yank out? Can I right it after it capsizes? Did the person who packed it have a hangover? How long will I have to wait for rescue?" Questions like these lurk in the backs of our minds and are enhanced as we read accounts of people such as the Baileys, Robertsons, Butlers, and Steve Callahan. Steve (author of *Adrift*), drifted for 76 days in his life raft after losing his small racing boat, and he highlights two other major concerns we have about this soft option when he writes, "It can be nerve-racking to know your life depends on a single, inflated boat with a $1/16$ inch thick skin as you float off in an ocean full of curious, toothy rough-skinned creatures and work with pointy hooks, spears and knives." In his book on survival, Steve analyzes three famous survival voyages and comments, "If the victims had been able to enhance their mobility, they would have dramatically reduced their drifts" (i.e., the time they spent adrift). He stressed that being in a conventional life raft means depending on other people coming to your rescue.

This is in direct contrast to the historical attitude toward lifeboats. Since time immemorial, the ship's whaleboat, gig, or tender was relied upon as a second chance should the mothership sink. Since the crew used this boat to ferry themselves and their supplies to shore and back, they cared and knew how the boat was maintained. If it leaked, they fixed it. If the oars or rig were faulty, the crew could inspect and repair it. They knew how well this boat rowed or sailed and how much load it could carry. Lifting it on board and off regularly, they were, in effect, having regular lifeboat drills. It was generally assumed that there was little hope of outside assistance, so the *primary* thought of the whole crew was to keep the ship herself seaworthy so that they would not have to climb into their shoreboat, a tiny, crowded lifeboat.

Over the past 10, or 15 years, a growing number of people have begun reassessing this old attitude against the problems of the current substitute, instant-inflation life rafts. This has led to the challenge of finding ways to combine new materials with old ideas to create what we call the two-for-one option. By using fiberglass or cold-molded wooden hulls and adding inflatable collars several offshore cruisers now carry tenders that will row well, can be outboard-powered, can sail well to windward, and are stowable with chafe- and puncture-resistant bottoms. They are also light enough for a woman to pull up onto a beach. Combine these virtues with the ability to serve as a sailing lifeboat in the unlikely event of a sinking and you could save outfitting costs, gain storage space, avoid the time, hassle and expense of a yearly life-raft inspection, plus six-yearly replacement and eliminate some of the nagging doubts that life rafts engender. Until recently, there was only one way to do this – what we call the do-it-yourself option. Now there is a newly developed, wave-of-the- future, buy-it option that works for those people who do not have room to stow a hard tender on deck.

The Do-It-Yourself (DIY) Option

Our two-in-one combination came about by an evolutionary process. Since 1969, when we first set sail on *Seraffyn*, we have relied on a fiberglass dinghy. The main reason was cost. By a huge margin the simulated lapstrake (clinker) hull outlasted inflatable boats owned by other long-term cruisers, and it was in excellent shape after 15 years. As we began thinking about building *Taleisin*, we heard about what was then considered a crazy idea, an inflatable collar that could go around a dinghy to make it extremely buoyant and similar to the typical RIB (rigid bottom inflatable) of today. This got us thinking – what about using this as the basis for a combination lifeboat/tender?

From 1980 to 1983, while we built *Taleisin*, Lyle Hess, her designer,

Figure 8-1. *Our tender / lifeboat* Cheeky.

1. *Mast partner.*

2. *Eight-inch (20.3cm)-diameter hatch. This storage locker holds two bailers, a small leadline and a sponge. It can become a secure compartment to hold vital emergency gear once the lifeboat is launched.*

3. *For extra strength, we have made the daggerboard and rudder from solid teak, 7/8 inch thick (2.2cm), which is stronger than plywood. This arrowhead-style foam-filled seat has proven to be very practical and could make a good addition to any do-it-yourself fiberglass tender.*

4. *Watertight bulkhead. The daggerboard case is bonded to the bulkhead for extra strength.*

5. *Dual oarlocks. The canopy bows socket into the forward oarlocks and arch across the tender from port to starboard.*

6. *The aft seat is also filled with foam. There is a 6-inch diameter inspection hatch on the front face of the seat.*

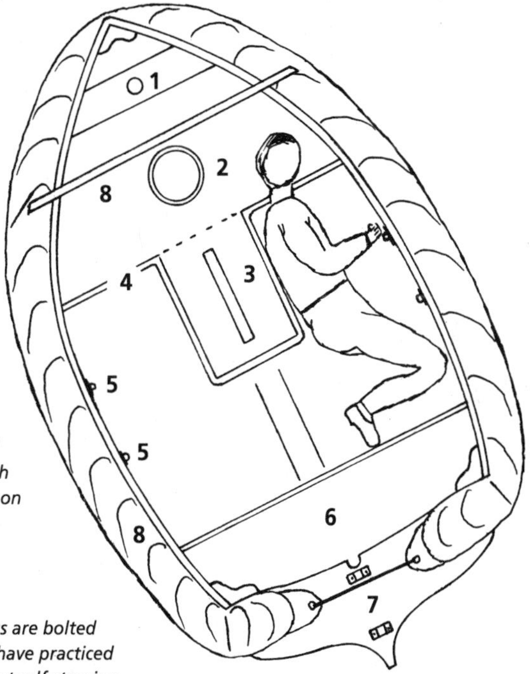

7. *The husky rudder fittings are bolted through the transom. We have practiced using a simple tiller-to-sheet self-steering arrangement on Cheeky, as shown in chapter 9. For the lone sailor, this would be very important, as the crew can retreat to the shade of the canopy and free his hands to fish or navigate while the boat keeps sailing.*

8. *The 10-inch-diameter inflatable collar is held on by a cross strap just aft of the mast. The ends are tied across the transom. It is then blown up and it sticks like a leech. We have used this while skin diving and it has never shifted. Our collar was made by Henshaw Inflatables (makers of the Tinker). Like all equipment on board, it requires inspection on a yearly basis if it is not being used frequently.*

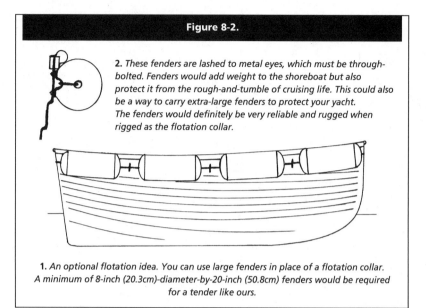

Figure 8-2.

2. *These fenders are lashed to metal eyes, which must be through-bolted. Fenders would add weight to the shoreboat but also protect it from the rough-and-tumble of cruising life. This could also be a way to carry extra-large fenders to protect your yacht. The fenders would definitely be very reliable and rugged when rigged as the flotation collar.*

1. *An optional flotation idea. You can use large fenders in place of a flotation collar. A minimum of 8-inch (20.3cm)-diameter-by-20-inch (50.8cm) fenders would be required for a tender like ours.*

worked on the plans for an 8-foot (2.4m) tender that would fit neatly on the cabintop, under the main boom. We told Lyle about a problem we had with our previous tender. It had thwartship seats, providing only one rowing position, thus making it difficult to row when we carried two people; the stern went down, the bow up. We needed a way to move the rower's weight forward to keep the tender level. The fore-and-aft, movable rowing seat evolved as you see it in (Figure 8-1.) By getting rid of the thwartship seat, this tender became a candidate for lifeboat conversion, as now there was space for two people to lie down inside the boat.

To keep the tender light yet strong, it was built using simulated lapstrake construction. The "laps" act as fore-and-aft stiffeners, allowing us safely to reduce the amount of glass in the hull. The resulting hull weighs only 82 pounds, light enough so Lin can pull it up a beach. She can also winch it right on deck, using the 4-inch-diameter halyard winch. Lyle gave the tender sufficient freeboard so it could carry four or five adults easily. This extra load-carrying ability gave us even more confidence in our sailing lifeboat. When we added an inflatable collar, *Cheeky* became so stable that either of us could stand right on her rail without fear of capsize. Now we had a stable, rugged, almost perfect tender/dive boat combination.

Once we became comfortable with this combination, we began

considering the problems we might face if we needed to use *Cheeky* in a lifeboat situation. We started by working to improve her heavy-weather sailing ability. *Cheeky* sails as well as most 8-footers in light to moderate winds, but in 25 knots of wind, she needed reef points added to her sail. With two sets of reefs, we have successfully sailed this little boat to windward (with both of us on board) in rough sea conditions with whitecaps two and three feet high in winds up to Force 7 (30 knots). Even without her inflation collar attached, this beamy, high-sided boat took on very little water. The next step was to improve and strengthen the rowing and sailing gear until it was as tough as that usually found on a 12-foot (3.7m) boat, sturdy enough to row and to sail to windward in strong winds in spite of being heavily loaded. This ability could be very important if the safety of an island lay just a few miles to windward.

Each time we set sail across a sea or ocean, we store all of the lifeboat-conversion equipment inside the inverted dinghy. The daggerboard and rudder bolt together to create a shelf that wedges inside and onto *Cheeky's* gunwales. The bag of emergency gear, inflatable collar, and sail are lashed onto this shelf. The one- piece mast is kept in a quick-release sleeve and boot on the lower shroud of *Taleisin*. This way, if time allowed we could turn the boat upright and rig it with collar and canopy – otherwise, it could be launched and rigged once it was afloat.

There are several other members of this Build Your Own Sailing Lifeboat Society. Some of their ideas have appeared in *Practical Boat Owner* UK. March, 1998 – the Bluewater (sailing) lifeboat for *Wanderer III* by Theis Matzen, two-time circumnavigator, and in *Cruising World*, 1995, "The Pro-active Emergency Craft," by Steve Callahan.

The Easy Stow, Buy-It Option

For those who have limited deck storage space – either because of boat size, or because of restrictions imposed by mainsheet travelers and dodgers – there is a readymade tender/lifeboat, the first of the foldable RIBs. For almost 15 years, the people at Henshaw Inflatables have produced two soft-bottomed sailing tender/lifeboats called the Tinker Tramp and the Tinker Traveler. There are now more than 6,000 of these afloat, and many regatta authorities have deemed the Tramp and the Traveler as capable of meeting their requirements for a life raft. Recently Henshaw sensed the need for a newer option, because the Tinkers – along with all soft-bottomed inflatables – had drawbacks as the basis for a tender/lifeboat combination. They did not have a puncture-

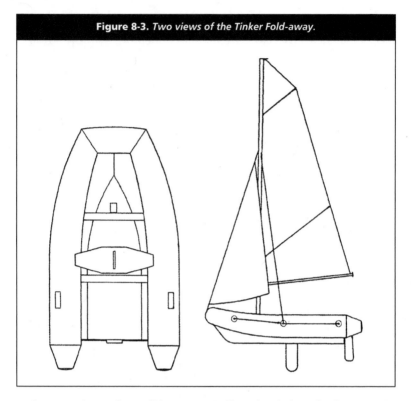

Figure 8-3. *Two views of the Tinker Fold-away.*

and wear-resistant floor, did not row well, and only lasted a few years in the rough-and-tumble of a life as a full-time cruising tender. So now, they have introduced the Fold-away, a true RIB, but it folds to occupy only one-third the longitudinal space of a similar rigid dinghy, and it weighs only 55.5 pounds (26 kg). It can be fitted with instant inflation bottles for both the hull tubes and the canopy.

How do the do-it-yourself and buy-it choices compare? Both have the advantage of simple, easy-to-patch, wear-resistant fiberglass bottoms. Both have enough buoyancy to support two people in a flooded condition without inflated buoyancy tanks. The Tinker has a glass/foam-sandwich bottom capable of supporting about 300 pounds on its own. Its side tanks are divided into three separate sections; any two of the sections will provide support in a life-raft configuration.

Both choices have been fitted with a canopy, sea anchor, survival gear, and sailing rig, but they take different approaches to the canopy, with positive and negative aspects to each. The Tinker Fold-away canopy,

Photo 8-1, left. *The Tinker Fold-away can be sailed under double reefed mainsail in strong winds with a well balanced helm.* **Photo 8-2, right.** *Once folded, it measures 3 feet 3 inches by 2 feet 9 inches by 1 foot 5 inches (1m by 83.9cm by 43.8cm) and weighs 56 pounds (26 kg).*

because of its inflatable tubes, provides extra buoyancy, which helps right the lifeboat in the event of capsize. This canopy covers the whole boat and keeps the crew completely out of the weather. Velcro flaps in the canopy let the crew use the oars to maneuver for short distances. But the canopy must be deflated to sail onward. In contrast, *Cheeky* is set up with a canopy made from a single layer of Dacron that covers only the forward half of the boat to provide spray and sun protection. The mast can be stepped right through the canopy, with a water-resistant boot to protect the crew. *Cheeky* can be either rowed or sailed in this configuration.

Both boats make useful shoreboats that can be sailed or used with an outboard motor. *Cheeky*, a displacement hull, does about 4$^{1}/_{2}$ knots with a 2-hp motor. The Fold-away, with one person on board, is designed to

Photo 8-3. Hard-bottomed boats can be sponged out completely so the crew is less likely to suffer from salt-water sores. This is in direct contrast to survivors in soft-bottom life rafts who have all complained of being continually wet.

Photo 8-4. This inflatable canopy should be a comfort in heavy weather, but it must be removed to use the sail rig, so it would not provide shelter underway.

Photo 8-5. *The minimal canopy on* Cheeky *would be of little use in a storm, but it affords shelter to the crew while rowing or sailing in normal weather conditions. The sail is orange and yellow, so it can be seen easily from a distance.*

plane at about 12 knots with 3^1/$_2$- to 4-hp motor. We have seen it in action, and it appears to handle smoothly.

We have not, as of press time, had a chance to compare the sailing abilities of the two boats, but we have sailed on one of the original Tinkers. It can go to windward, though it is not quite as efficient as a hard-bottomed dinghy of similar length. We can safely assume the Fold-away will do as well or better.

Is it important to be able to sail toward assistance? Again, Steve Callahan states clearly, "In reality, as case histories prove, passagemakers are on their own. No one, *repeat NO ONE*, ever conducted an active search for the Robertsons, Baileys, Butlers, myself, and any number of offshore cruising people who have gotten into trouble. The reason? Search and Rescue (SAR) craft have limited ranges and many countries have limited or no SAR facilities. Unless SAR personnel have a specific target such as a mayday position or EPIRB [emergency position-indicating radio beacon] signal, no one is likely to look for you because it is a bloody big ocean. And you must make a call and be heard (and keep being heard) before SAR personnel will respond. EPIRBs are great, but every year we hear of at least one case in which the EPIRB has allegedly malfunctioned, sometimes while indicating it is working, leading to a survival drift of indeterminate length. Diverted ships may take longer than your EPIRB's (battery) life to reach you." Remember, if you are not rescued within the 48-to-96-hour battery life of your 406 MHz EPIRB, you will be dependent on passing ships seeing you. Thus, to stand a chance of being located and picked up, you must be within range of shore-based air-rescue facilities or near major shipping lanes while your EPIRB is still functioning. For this reason, we have never been comfortable with what we can only call the passive option, the life raft. We want to be able to take an active part in this drama by having a sailing lifeboat, and an EPIRB as a backup.

But back to our comparison of the two active options. To compare the rowing ability of both boats, we took them out in 15 knots of wind with a slight chop and took turns rowing each one over the same distances. We also invited James Lang-Brown (photo 8-3), who has used inflatable boats a lot more than we have, to join in our decidedly unscientific trials. We all agreed that the Fold-away RIB rowed far better than any soft-bottomed inflatable, and in light winds, almost as well as *Cheeky*. But in a fresh breeze, *Cheeky* would be more successful in rowing out a kedge anchor in an emergency situation. James agreed that the Tinker might not be capable of performing that task under oar power alone in the Force-8 conditions that *Cheeky* can handle.

Our afternoon of comparing the two boats led us all to agree that they outshone the more normal option of a separate life raft packed by someone else. We can have do-it-yourself lifeboat practice. Just like man-overboard drill, we can go out in open water in Force-4 or Force-5 winds, heave-to, and practice preparing and launching the lifeboat/tender. This would give us a chance to upgrade any shortcomings we see, and it could save valuable time if and when a true emergency occurred. This is in direct contrast to the canistered-lifeboat option. To practice with that gear, you must either join a special course where you will be given one chance to jump in a swimming pool and climb into a raft, or you have to arrange to practice with your own equipment before you take it in to have its yearly inspection.

It just isn't practical to take your own life raft out into the open sea, practice with it, have it repacked, and try again. The repacking cost is

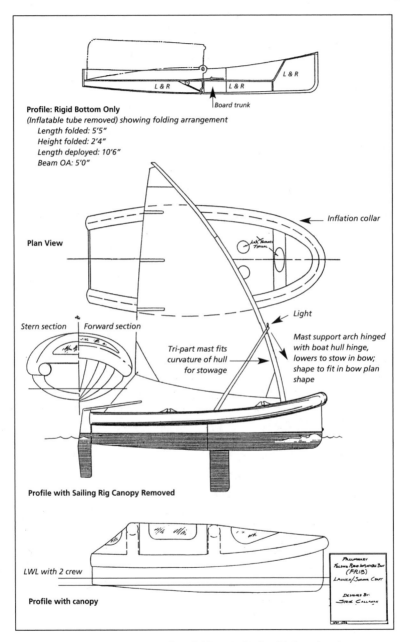

Profile: Rigid Bottom Only
(Inflatable tube removed) showing folding arrangement
    Length folded: 5'5"
    Height folded: 2'4"
    Length deployed: 10'6"
    Beam OA: 5'0"

Board trunk

Inflation collar

Plan View

L & R
L & R
L & R

Light

Stern section | Forward section

Tri-part mast fits
curvature of hull
for stowage

Mast support arch hinged
with boat hull hinge,
lowers to stow in bow;
shape to fit in bow plan
shape

Profile with Sailing Rig Canopy Removed

LWL with 2 crew

Profile with canopy

PRELIMINARY
FOLDING RIGID INFLATABLE BOAT
(FRIB)
LAUNCH/SURVIVAL CRAFT

DESIGNED BY:
STEVE CALLAHAN

Figure 8-4. *Steve Callahan's ideas for a folding rigid inflatable boat (FRIB).*

high. Which leads to what we feel is the greatest gain of these two options (the self-created, solid tender/lifeboat or the folding RIB): taking responsibility for yourself and your own safety equipment. If you are using, on a daily basis, the lifeboat that your life may depend on, you will be well aware if it is becoming worn or developing leaks; you can fix it before you repack it to go to sea. It won't be a case of out of sight, out of mind. Nor is it a case of having to be dependent on a complete stranger repacking your raft. You can deal with the repairs and know they have been done correctly. In other words, you are packing your own parachute.

As we were preparing this chapter, we spoke with Steve Callahan and asked for his personal recommendations based on his own very real experience. Steve said he would "carry both a sailing lifeboat and a CO_2-inflated life raft." Then we asked him what would be his first choice if he were a cost-conscious cruiser who could only justify the money and space for a single boat. He quickly answered, "A well-equipped hard-bottomed sailing lifeboat."

DISCLAIMER

Although we do not feel the need to put a disclaimer on other information we have written in this book, it's important to note that we have never had to abandon ship – and we hope we never do. Like Steve Callahan, if money and space were no barrier, we might be interested in carrying both styles of EPIRBs and both our tender/lifeboat and the folding RIB fitted with CO_2 instant inflation and canopy. At some point, every cost-conscious cruiser has to draw a personal line on expenditure.

We have applied the same criteria to our choice of EPIRB, resulting in choosing the BEEPA MRB4, which broadcasts on 121.5 MHz and 243 MHz and costs $189. Here's why:

1. It has owner-replaceable batteries (C-cell alkaline).
2. The batteries are cheap and available everywhere.
3. Spare batteries can be carried and even replaced in the lifeboat.

4. Each set of eight batteries lasts for seven days once you turn on the EPIRB. This is an enormous advantage, as with a spare pack, this gives 14 days of transmission.
5. There are more than 600,000 of these 121.5 and 243 MHz EPIRBs in use, and they are the only ones that can be produced and used as personal locator beacons.

We are willing to forgo the possible advantages of the 406 MHz

EPIRB when we consider not only its initial costs ($850+) but also the cost of a replacement battery pack ($300 or more), its seriously limited broadcasting time (two days to a possible four days) and the requirement that the unit be returned to a registered repair depot for inspection and repowering every fifth year. The manufacturers we spoke with both said that they would be leery of suggesting that an owner replace his own 406 MHz EPIRB battery, as the connections require special preparation and soldering, and the unit must be properly resealed to make sure it's reliable.

ADDRESSES

Cheeky IS A FATTY KNEES DINGHY, MADE BY EDEY & DUFF LTD., 128 Aucoot Road, Mattapoisett, MA 02739 USA, Tel: 508-758-2591.

THE TINKER IS MADE BY HENSHAW INFLATABLES LTD., South Gate Road, Wincanton, Somerset, BA9 9RZ, United Kingdom, Tel: 44-1963-33237, Fax: 44-1963-34578. Tinker Marine USA, Building 11, 1919, Clement Avenue, Alameda, CA 94501, Tel: 1-510-814-0471, Fax: 1-510-814-8030

BEEPA EPIRB IS MADE BY SEA AIR AND LAND COMMUNICATIONS LTD., P. O. Box 22621, Christchurch, New Zealand, Tel: 64-33792298.

CHAPTER

9

RETURN OF THE TILLER

Improve performance! Save weight! Save money! Cut down on steering failure and cockpit clutter!

Sound like an advertisement? It should be, but it isn't. Since the tiller has little commercial value, no one pushes the clear advantages of this tough little item. Yet slowly and surely, the innovative side of our sport is turning the pages of an old book to discover a new idea. Just as long bowsprits (rig extensions) are now de rigueur on many modern race boats, tillers are making a comeback. A careful look at the advantages makes the opening statements completely justified for cruising boats and race boats up to and even over 40 feet (12.2m) in length. If you then look at some of the subtleties of designing and building the deceptively simple tiller, you might find it the most logical choice for your next boat. If you already have a tiller, some simple ideas and accessories could make it even more user-friendly than ever.

Advantages of a Wheel

Originally, all ships were steered with a tiller. If they were hard to steer, blocks and tackles were added to assist the helmsman. Then along came the wheel – to give easier, faster steering than a tiller with its awkward tackles. Though yachts were far smaller, and thus easier to steer than big ships, many suffered from weather helm. This tendency for the boat to want to head up into the wind if firm pressure is not held on the tiller can have some advantages, but if it is excessive, it exhausts the helmsman. Curing weather helm can mean doing anything from raking the mast forward to moving the whole mast forward, from recutting the sails to adding a bowsprit. But the simplest and most common solution used by many builders was to add extra leverage in the form of a wheel. It wasn't a cure; it only disguised the problem, but it definitely reduced the tendency to stretch the arms of the helmsman. (See Figure 9-1 for some tips on curing weather helm.)

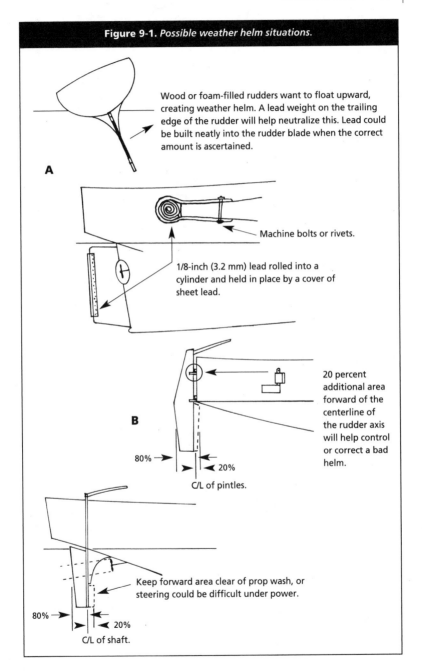

Figure 9-1. *Possible weather helm situations.*

Wood or foam-filled rudders want to float upward, creating weather helm. A lead weight on the trailing edge of the rudder will help neutralize this. Lead could be built neatly into the rudder blade when the correct amount is ascertained.

A

Machine bolts or rivets.

1/8-inch (3.2 mm) lead rolled into a cylinder and held in place by a cover of sheet lead.

B

20 percent additional area forward of the centerline of the rudder axis will help control or correct a bad helm.

80% → ←

► ◄ 20%

C/L of pintles.

Keep forward area clear of prop wash, or steering could be difficult under power.

80% →

► ◄ 20%

C/L of shaft.

Figure 9-2. *Advantages of two types of steering.*

WHEEL

Makes steering less tiring by controlling weather helm

Increases mechanical advantage

Feels familiar – steers like a car

People feel good standing behind a wheel

Pedestal makes a good center-of-cockpit grabrail, compass mount, and table mount

Does not sweep across cockpit so is less worrisome to visitors

Makes installation of a below-decks electronic autopilot easier (definitely better for salt-sensitive electronic gear)

Keeps crew clear of helmsman for racing

Clears cockpit for thwartship crew traffic

Makes installation of a second steering station easier, i.e., for inside and outside stations

TILLER

Ultimately reliable

Ultimately inspectable

Low maintenance (few moving parts)

Simple installation

Low weight

Low purchase price

Clears cockpit for fore-and-aft traffic

Lets helmsman reach winches easily for sheet adjustments (Important for short-handed sailing)

Easy to remove to clear cockpit area

Easier to rig vane or autopilot steering

Faster steering, i.e., you can make radical course changes more quickly

Lets you sense small changes in sail trim or balance of rig

Serves as an obvious rudder-angle indicator for the whole crew (also for photographers)

Enables you to use rudder to scull the boat in light winds

Lets you put tiller between your legs to steer temporarily and free up your hands to handle jib sheet or toss a mooring line

Lets you steer the boat from various positions inside and outside the cockpit – especially with a hiking stick

Less liable to injure crew

Provides a base for tiller-to-sheet self-steering

Keeps weight of crew and gear out of end of the boat

No need for separate emergency-tiller arrangement

Lets helmsman get out on side deck with hiking stick (two wheels needed to do this on racing boats)

Once wheels began appearing on yachts under 40 feet (12m) other advantages became apparent. Now you could invite your favorite uncle out for a daysail and he could take over steering immediately. No more having to explain, "Just pull the tiller this way to make the boat go that way!" You could simply say, "Steer it just like your car."

People feel good about themselves when they are standing behind a large, leather-clad wheel. This appearance can be just as important as the benefit of having a neat position for a compass and cockpit table mount on the wheel pedestal. Yet the most important reasons for having a wheel remains firmly in the realm of big boat racing. Only with a wheel can the helmsman be kept truly clear of the flying elbows of the winch crew.

As Figure 9-2 shows, there are other advantages of a wheel. Yet, when you compare these to the advantages of a tiller, you may begin to wonder if fashion has been the main influence in making wheels so prevalent among boats under 40 feet.

Advantages of a Tiller

Although tillers have always had firm adherents among determinedly practical cruising sailors – ranging from Eric Hiscock to Hal Roth, from Don Street to Bernard Moitessier – it is among the high-speed racing fraternity on their new sport boats like the J class, Melges 24 and 30, and the Mumm 30 that tillers have begun their swift reemergence. The reason is simple. The full-on racer on a sporty boat wants to keep all the weight off the ends of the boat. No quadrant, no cables, no 200-pound helmsman at the back end of the cockpit equals less hobby-horsing (pitching).

The tiller is more sensitive to boat responses than a wheel. Not only does it give faster, more positive rudder adjustments, it telegraphs information back to the helmsman to let him know if the boat is balanced properly. This is important, as even a five- or six-degree rudder angle can cause drag that can slow the boat.

Cruisers might not feel the extra bit of speed is important, but most will agree that a tiller makes installing some form of self-steering far easier, and self-steering is the most important aspect of enjoyable offshore voyaging. Whether wind-vane or electrically operated, it is easy to disconnect self-steering quickly from a tiller. Simply lift the control link free of the tiller lock pin. If for some reason your wind-vane self-steering or autopilot dies completely, the tiller provides a hidden option unavailable to those with wheel steering. With about $50 worth of simple gear, you can rig up a sheet-to-tiller steering system (see Figure 9-7).

Another plus for tillers in combination with an autopilot or self-steering gear is that the best control point for the connecting lines or push rod are usually about 2 feet forward of the rudderhead. This makes the controls far less intrusive and much less of a hurdle for the crew than the port and starboard control lines of wind-vane steering led to a wheel. Combine this with the absence of the wheel itself, and fore-and-aft traffic in the cockpit becomes far easier.

Sculling, using a tiller, is a tactic so useful among small-boat racers that there are special rules governing it. Even on cruising boats up to 44 feet (13.4m), you can use the side-to-side swinging of the rudder to move your boat toward a new breeze, or the few yards forward you need to come up to a mooring or dock for an almost-perfect landing. This tiller sculling is like a secret weapon for racing sailors and those who cruise without engines – onshore or offshore. In very light breezes, it is easy to lose steerage. With a tiller, you can use what we call "the half scull" to swing the bow of the boat so it lies at a close-hauled position to what breeze there may be. This new angle to the wind will get the boat moving faster than it would on a downwind course, because as the boat gains forward momentum, its speed is added to the actual wind speed to give a stronger apparent wind. Once you get moving, you can ease off onto a beam reach and keep sailing, despite the light wind.

To us, one of the most worrisome aspects of wheel steering – and a very important reason to choose a tiller – is the growing number of serious, wheel-inflicted injuries caused by breaking waves washing crew against wheels. Dana Dinius of 44-foot (13.4m) *Destiny* had his femur shattered when a wave smashed him against the wheel during a storm north of New Zealand. Michelle Perot, on board *Maiden*, broke several ribs and bent the wheel so badly it jammed the steering for several minutes until the crew used tools to rebend it clear of the pedestal. Chay Blyth built special guardrails to keep crew on his latest Round the Southern Capes (west-about) Race from hitting the wheel when waves swept along the deck and into the cockpit. He told us, "Last race, wheels caused the only serious injuries, including a shattered wrist when a crew member was swept against the turning wheel."

And finally, even if you have a wheel, you still need an emergency tiller. No matter how carefully your system is installed, the mechanical complexities leave it more susceptible to steering failure. The most common problem (other than seasickness) listed for the 1979 Fastnet

Race storm and the 1994 Queen's Birthday storm (near New Zealand) was wheel-steering breakdown. So some of the following ideas could help even if you only use a simple tiller as a backup for your wheel.

Building a Stout, Reliable Tiller

Your tiller should be strong enough so that when a 200-pound (90 kg) crew falls heavily down onto it, it won't break. How strong is that? Larry: "I like to test a tiller by putting it in a big vise then jumping on it and heaving my whole weight on its forward end (I weigh about 180 pounds). If I can't break it, then it should withstand the test of sailing."

A tapered tiller will have a tendency to bend a little under severe loads and thus is less likely to shatter than a stiff, parallel-sided one. The curve you see on most tillers is for appearance's sake or to assist in clearing obstacles or knees in the cockpit; it is not a necessity. So to make

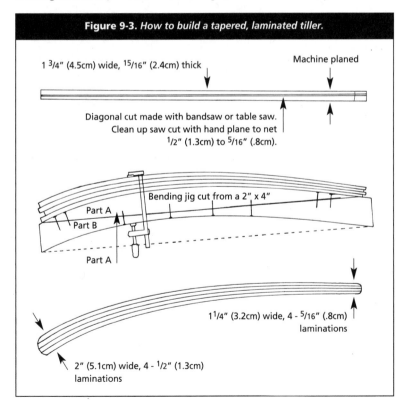

Figure 9-3. *How to build a tapered, laminated tiller.*

1 3/4" (4.5cm) wide, 15/16" (2.4cm) thick

Machine planed

Diagonal cut made with bandsaw or table saw. Clean up saw cut with hand plane to net 1/2" (1.3cm) to 5/16" (.8cm).

Bending jig cut from a 2" x 4"

Part A

Part B

Part A

1 1/4" (3.2cm) wide, 4 - 5/16" (.8cm) laminations

2" (5.1cm) wide, 4 - 1/2" (1.3cm) laminations

tiller-building easier, you can choose a simple tapered, straight shape. Build it out of a rot-resistant wood such as pitch pine, black locust, or teak to ensure longevity.

A one-piece tiller is preferable as the ones we have seen fail are most often curved, laminated ones. If you do decide to laminate a tiller, use heatproof, waterproof adhesives such as resorcinol, Aerodux 185, Aerodux 500, or Cascophen. These adhesives are completely reliable and can even be used to laminate up a teak tiller that will be left unvarnished

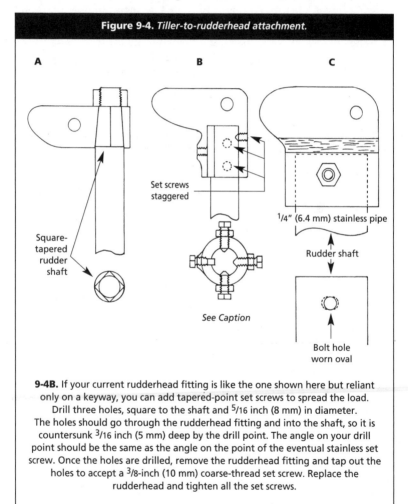

Figure 9-4. *Tiller-to-rudderhead attachment.*

9-4B. If your current rudderhead fitting is like the one shown here but reliant only on a keyway, you can add tapered-point set screws to spread the load. Drill three holes, square to the shaft and 5/16 inch (8 mm) in diameter. The holes should go through the rudderhead fitting and into the shaft, so it is countersunk 3/16 inch (5 mm) deep by the drill point. The angle on your drill point should be the same as the angle on the point of the eventual stainless set screw. Once the holes are drilled, remove the rudderhead fitting and tap out the holes to accept a 3/8-inch (10 mm) coarse-thread set screw. Replace the rudderhead and tighten all the set screws.

in the tropics. The strongest, most cleverly designed laminated tiller we have seen was made from tapered pieces of wood. This meant that the outside laminations did not taper off to leave unattractive feather ends (Fig. 9-3.)

Tiller-to-Rudder Connections

The most reliable, easiest to build tiller-to-rudderhead connection is the mortise-and-tenon type such as shown in Photo 9-1. In most cases this will only work with an outboard rudder. For inboard rudders, a metal tillerhead-to-shaft fitting is necessary. Figure 9-4 shows three different tiller-to-shaft connections with which we have sailed. A is the most reliable, but unfortunately it is least common, because the machining time needed to get a close fit on the square taper makes it the most costly. The square-taper connection works similarly to your propeller-to-shaft connection; it is essentially a squeeze play between the two parts. But it is even better than the prop connection, as the large surface area of the square acts like a huge keyway to resist wear and loosening. B, on the other hand, is prone to loosening. The constant, often forceful, corrections from wind-vane steering gear can distort the keyway during a long tradewind passage. One way to help alleviate this keyway wear is to add tapered-point set screws, as shown in Figure 9-4B. These set screws can be tightened, even at sea.

Version C (Fig. 9-4) shows the worst kind of rudderhead-to-tiller connection with which we have sailed. It is extremely susceptible to wear. During the delivery of one new 35-footer (10.7m), we had 1/4-inch (6.4 mm) of wear in 1,100 miles on a 1/4-inch-thick, 4-inch (10 mm)-diameter stainless-pipe rudder shaft. A larger-diameter bolt can help in this situation, but the best fix would be to weld a tight-fitting compression plug, then use multiple set screws to locate the tiller more firmly, as shown in 4B.

Making the Tiller Work Better for You

It is particularly helpful to be able to remove the tiller completely when it is not in use (Photo 9-1). When we are in port, this clears the cockpit for socializing or sleeping. It also makes the boat theft-proof, as you can remove the tiller and lock it away below. At sea, it is nice to be able to shorten the tiller to make the cockpit feel more commodious. Bernard Moitessier had a telescopic tiller on his last boat, 31-foot (9.5m) *Tamata*

Above, Photo 9-1. Below, Photo 9-2.

(see Fig. 9-5). To achieve a similar reduction in length, you could also make a folding tiller.

But with wind-vane self-steering or autopilot during a passage, it pays to have a good, long tiller. As photo 9-3 shows, this long tiller is accessible from the companionway, so you can luff up in a gust of wind or steer clear of floating logs or weed. We find this long tiller handy during especially wet weather, as the person on deck can go forward to drop a sail and the person down below does not have to don foulweather

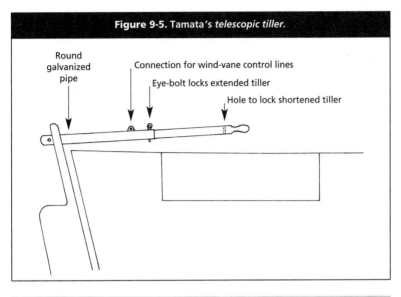

Figure 9-5. Tamata's *telescopic tiller.*

Round galvanized pipe

Connection for wind-vane control lines

Eye-bolt locks extended tiller

Hole to lock shortened tiller

Photo 9-3.

gear to assist in steering. He/she can just reach out and push the helm without releasing the self-steering. The boat luffs up for a bit, the sail comes down, and the wind-vane takes over again.

Simple Tiller Accessories

By adding a thwartships belaying pin to the inboard end of your tiller, you can use adjustable port and starboard shock cords to help your boat

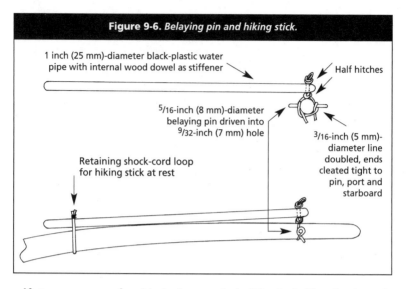

Figure 9-6. *Belaying pin and hiking stick.*

1 inch (25 mm)-diameter black-plastic water pipe with internal wood dowel as stiffener

Half hitches

⁵/16-inch (8 mm)-diameter belaying pin driven into ⁹/32-inch (7 mm) hole

³/16-inch (5 mm)-diameter line doubled, ends cleated tight to pin, port and starboard

Retaining shock-cord loop for hiking stick at rest

self-steer more comfortably in heavy winds (Fig. 9-6). The shock cords can be adjusted to dampen the wind vane's correcting movements and, in effect, act as a shock absorber to cut down on overcorrection. The shock cords can also be adjusted to put in a bit of lee helm or weather helm so the vane helps you track more accurately. This is especially helpful on a broad reach in fresh winds and long, rolling seas.

Even without a wind vane, the tiller belaying pin would be useful for securing sheet-to-tiller steering. Although it is usually offshore cruising sailors who need various options for self-steering, this clever system can be of interest to a wide range of sailors – whether a lone day sailor hoping to enjoy lunch with both hands free or a race-boat delivery crew heading home short-handed. We have included a couple of the basic diagrams from John Letcher's book on *'Self-Steering for Sailing Craft'* to help you begin experimenting (Fig. 9-7). After using his methods on several boats we have to agree when he says, "Sheet-to-tiller gear can do your steering, simply and reliably, on all points of sailing."

The final use for the tiller belaying pin is, to us, one of the most important. It can be the basis of a cheap, easy-to-make hiking stick. A hiking stick on an 8-ton cruising boat? Yes, we find it really useful when we are approaching a dock or mooring ball, as it lets the helmsman stand on either the port or the starboard side deck to get a perfect view of the objective. Since you are now out of the cockpit, it is easy to hand someone the aft mooring line, or to step off and secure the line to the

Figure 9-7. *Sheet-to-tiller steering.*

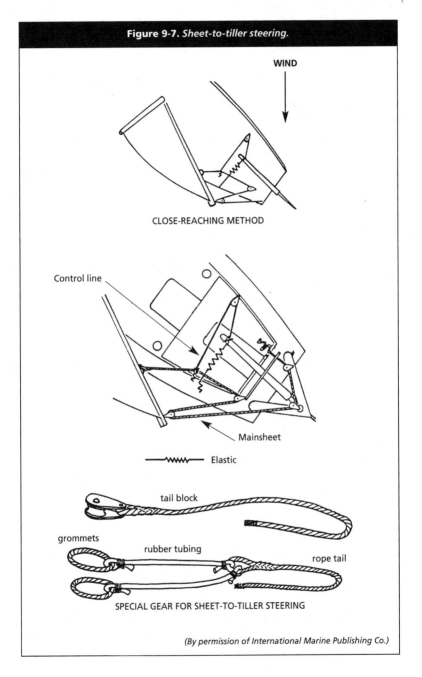

WIND

CLOSE-REACHING METHOD

Control line

Mainsheet

—WWW— Elastic

tail block

grommets

rubber tubing

rope tail

SPECIAL GEAR FOR SHEET-TO-TILLER STEERING

(By permission of International Marine Publishing Co.)

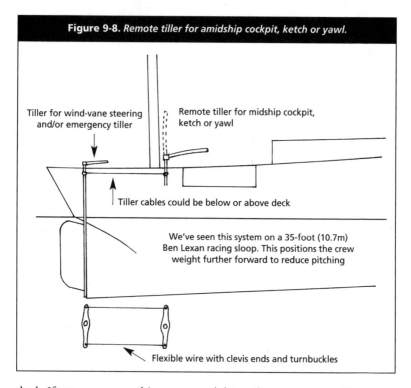

Figure 9-8. *Remote tiller for amidship cockpit, ketch or yawl.*

Tiller for wind-vane steering and/or emergency tiller

Remote tiller for midship cockpit, ketch or yawl

Tiller cables could be below or above deck

We've seen this system on a 35-foot (10.7m) Ben Lexan racing sloop. This positions the crew weight further forward to reduce pitching

Flexible wire with clevis ends and turnbuckles

dock. If you are approaching someone's boat, they are reassured by seeing you standing on the side deck holding a mooring line for them to use to stop your boat as it glides alongside under power or sail. The simple system shown in Fig. 9-6 includes a shock-cord loop to keep the hiking stick out of the way when you don't need it. Complete removal of the hiking stick is easy for offshore sailing.

For the prudent sailor, a potential backup tiller is probably on board right now. Before you set off cruising, adjust one of your dinghy oars so it will fit your rudderhead fitting.

The new wave of sport boats is encouraging designers to recycle the tiller. As they do, they are working to make new boat designs more balanced, so that tiller steering is a breeze. The good news for owners of all types of boats – ketches, yawls, sloops, or cutters: with inboard rudders or outboard rudders – can be read in the balance sheet (Figure 9-9). You could use the money you save to get out cruising sooner.

Figure 9-9. *The Balance Sheet.*

FITTING A WHEEL TO A MODERN 30- TO 33-FOOTER
(based on an average of prices provided by West Marine Products using Edson International components, for boats such as the Pearson 30, Columbia 32.)

Materials only — including pedestal, stainless-steel destroyer-type wheel, chain and rope assembly, and all gear to connect this system to the rudderhead, below cockpit floor level — average **$1,232.00**

Normal accessories

Pedestal guard	109.00
Steering brake	92.95
Labor at $35 per hour, average 16 hours	560.00
Estimated cost	**$1,993.95**

TILLER STEERING

Materials – tiller	54.92
Rudderhead fitting	119.00
Estimated cost	**$173.92**

(Tiller and rudderhead fitting would still be required with wheel for emergency steering.)

GETTING GOOD VALUE FOR YOUR CRUISING FUNDS

WE'VE ALL HEARD THE AXIOM – every job will expand to fill the available time. Now add another truism – cruising will cost as much as you have. Together these statements sum up one of the biggest challenges facing you when you get out cruising: It will be completely up to you to regulate both your time and your expenditures, with few of the dictates of normal shore life to guide you.

The apparent freedom to spend your time any way you want is a wonderful part of cruising. But even though you may not have a job that determines your schedule, you still have the cyclone or hurricane season to consider. Then there is the need to maintain your boat – from regular haulouts to equipment repairs. Crossing oceans, reprovisioning, working to top up funds – the requirements of your new life all consume irreplaceable, nonrefundable time. Some of these time-consuming factors can be controlled, others can't. If you do not find a way to balance and schedule them, to budget your time, you may find yourself wondering when you will be able to savor the adventures you dreamed of – mooring in the middle of Seville while you study flamenco dancing or classical guitar, hiding in a solitary atoll anchorage while you dive to photograph sunken treasures and watch glorious tropical sunsets, or moving into the life of some exotic location to learn how other peoples are facing the challenges of the ever-changing world.

Time is precious, but your cruising funds are too, because they buy you time. Most of your money is going out, little is coming in. You'll find it more difficult to budget while afloat than on shore, as there will be some weeks or months when you are living mainly from your provisions, entertained by the slow rhythm of the sea and shoreline around you, times when you'll spend nothing at all. But then you'll arrive at a major port where you plan to haul out or reprovision, and you'll feel as if your wallet is hemorrhaging.

The following chapters show some of the ways we have found to control these basic costs and maximize cruising pleasures. Each person has to choose his or her own methods of handling this juggling act. Find the proper balance and the time and money you squirrel away can be used to add emotional confidence along with exotic experience as you explore under sail.

CHAPTER
10
COST CONTROL WHILE YOU CRUISE

New Year's is the one time each year when our wide-flung fleet of cruising friends – even those who hate writing letters – puts pen to paper to let us know how they fared. Because this bulging pack of newsletters and notes comes from people all around the world who have broken free to explore under sail, we gain considerable insight into how cruising styles, cruising locations, and personal choices affect cruising costs. And year after year, the same patterns seem to emerge. Although boat size will always affect cruising costs, comparing the experiences of two of our most budget-minded friends over the past year highlights other major factors that keep some people cruising within their financial means while others "break the bank."

The crew on *Siandra*, a 40-year-old, 35-foot (10.7m) Lion-class sloop, stuck to their $500-a-month budget, even though they were exploring in Norway, possibly the most expensive country in the world (one glass of beer, $5). The other couple, on a brand-new, classic-design 22-footer (6.7m) built of GRP, were cruising in Mexico, a country known for its relatively low cost of living (one beer, 50 cents). The latter couple is returning home a year earlier than planned, having overrun their $500-a-month budget by almost double. What are the major differences? The crew on *Siandra*, along with most of our friends who stay on target year-in, year out:

1. made their boats unstoppable;
2. kept sailing in light breezes;
3. were willing to postpone repairs of nonessential gear until a more appropriate time;
4. were comfortable being at anchor instead of in marinas;
5. did not enter races/rallies and limited the time they spent sailing in company;
6. slowed down and spent a lot of their time with local people.

As we discuss in detail these and some of the other less obvious ways you can cut your cash expenditures, you will notice that many offer other benefits. These range from saving time during the ideal sailing season to adding emotional pleasure to your cruise.

MAKE YOUR BOAT UNSTOPPABLE

Achieving this requires that you accept that your boat is first and foremost a sailing machine with an auxiliary engine for convenience. If you outfit it from this premise, then practice sailing to gain confidence in your skills before you set off, you will be en route to unstoppability. The next step is to make sure that all of the essentials – from sailhandling to steering to food storage and preparation to navigation – can be done with gear that can be repaired by you and/or is not dependent on the engine or electrical system. In many instances, this can be achieved by carrying self-contained backup gear powered by solar cells, dry-cell batteries, butane, or kerosene. Back-up sextant, kerosene cabin lights, hand pumps for water systems, a backup single-burner Primus stove such as we carry– all these mean you can sail onward even if the electrical system or the engine fails or you run out of fuel.

When we were at anchor at St. Helena Island, one of the most isolated communities in the world, the owner and crew on a 40-foot (12.2m) ketch arrived, frightened and disillusioned because their engine had thrown a rod and nothing on board worked – no lights, refrigeration, navigation gear, or anchor winch. Because all of their pumps were electrical, they had no way to get fresh water out of their bilge tanks. Now they had a real dilemma – the next scheduled supply ship wasn't due for eight or 10 weeks. Because of the rugged terrain, no airplanes can land here, and the nearest airport was 800 miles away on Ascension Island, a military base where visitors are definitely discouraged. The owner used the island telephone to contact the Royal Cape Yacht Club and arrange for another yacht to bring parts and a delivery team. Six weeks of lying in the swell-tossed roadstead gave him time to realize that he wasn't comfortable having his life controlled by machinery; he wasn't ready to, and did not know how to make his boat unstoppable. So he reconsidered his dream. When parts arrived and repairs were finished, he and his crew returned to South Africa, where the boat was sold. An extreme case? No. We've seen variations on this story all over the world. The cost of trying to get sophisticated gear fixed "right now" in Tonga could be twice the cost of waiting until you sail to New Zealand, where parts and repairs are not only available but also dependable.

Even with non-interdependent gear, some people cannot bear the idea of knowing that something on board is not working correctly. They want it fixed, and fixed "right now." We were in laid-back Bora Bora, French Polynesia, when a fellow named Dave decided he was going to solve the problem of batteries that didn't seem to stay topped up. The boat was a fine sailing machine and Dave and his wife were both good sailors. In fact, we were all at dinner together when his wife suggested they live with the problem and sail on to American Samoa, where they knew good repair people were available and it would be relatively inexpensive to buy new batteries if required. But Dave grew more and more determined, and the repair turned into a three-week saga of ever-increasing phone bills from the local hotel to Papeete, of living with a disassembled boat and a frustrated family. Over cocktails one evening, his wife said, "It's not the money that hurts, it's that we are here in the middle of paradise spending day after day being too upset to enjoy it all. And now we've used up the time we wanted to spend at Suvarov before we have to move on to a safe place for the cyclone season." Dave finally had to fly to Papeete and carry back new batteries. When he installed the batteries, he was heartbroken to find the whole problem had been the fault of a bad connection between the ground strap and the engine block.

On the other hand, Laura and Randy Hacker-Durbin assumed an unstoppable attitude. They were cruising the Pacific for two years on their self-built 40-foot (12.2m) cat-ketch *Pollenpath*. Laura wrote about their concerns when the approaching cyclone season made it important that they set sail from Lautoka, Fiji, to the safe haven of New Zealand, even though their engine had packed up. After 10 days of sometimes fine, sometimes difficult sailing, they reached the entrance to New Zealand's Bay of Islands, where a new adventure began. The breeze died down to a whisper and as Laura wrote in *Sail* magazine (February 1998), "Randy began digging the dinghy and outboard out of the forepeak to lash it alongside and motor us in. But for me it became a challenge to see if we could sail the whole way from Fiji. We began ghosting up the channel on the incoming tide. The satisfaction was immense when we dropped the anchor. The passage became a real accomplishment for both of us – we had sailed the whole way."

LEARN HOW TO KEEP YOUR BOAT SAILING IN LIGHT WINDS

This is discussed in even more detail in the next chapter. Not only will you save money on fuel and reduce wear and tear on the engine, but life on board will be more pleasant without the machine noise. If you can use this light-air sailing time to do some routine maintenance jobs, you could arrive in port with a lot shorter work list. Then you can use your valuable shore time to join in the local harvest festival or beach barbecue.

LEAVE REPAIRS OF ALL NONESSENTIAL GEAR UNTIL HAULOUT TIME

Because you need to schedule your haulout stop well in advance, you can save shipping costs by ordering specialized parts ahead of time. Allow a few weeks to do this yearly pit stop, so that you will not be frustrated should there be a holdup due to customs or shipping delays. But you may find that, as is often the case in the most popular cruising haulout ports, boatyards already stock the parts you need. Furthermore, skilled repair people seem to gravitate toward these areas, and careful discussions with other sailors and local craftsmen might help you find "the right one" to save you the emotional and financial costs of having to redo makeshift developing-world repairs. A final bonus is that you only have to put up with the boat being disarranged and invaded by the mess of dockside repairs once during the year.

MAKE LIFE AT ANCHOR PLEASURABLE

This is essential; if you don't feel comfortable and secure at anchor, you and your crew will need to spend more time in costly marinas, or tied

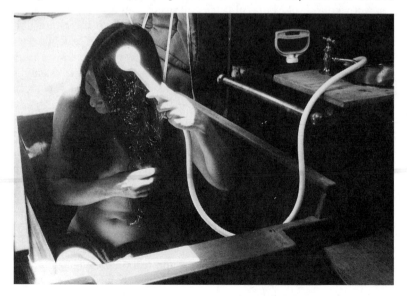

alongside quays, which in turn generates other costs. Life alongside is noisier, affords less privacy, and attracts shore dirt and pests – from cockroaches and rats to unwanted salesmen who can make their pitch more easily. It takes time to get your boat securely tied alongside or in a berth, so once you are there, you are less likely to set sail serendipitously. (If you're at anchor, you can easily take newfound local friends out for an afternoon's sail or fishing or move to a more pleasant anchorage on the other side of the island for a few days, then return to the "big smoke" and join the crowd for some city delights.) A final drawback is that your boat is more prone to scuffs and paint damage as you maneuver in the close confines of a quay or marina, and as other yachts come alongside. So work toward making your ground tackle convenient to use. To gain peace of mind, rig up your stern anchor and a second bow anchor so it is easy to put out extra ground tackle. Have a good rowing boat and a long set of oars and experience "the joy of rowing." Then, if your outboard engine becomes balky, it is only a nuisance, not a serious problem. Work at making your on-board bathing facilities easy and convenient so your crew does not feel the need to be in a marina just to have a shower. (See *The Care and Feeding of Sailing Crew*: Keeping Clean.)

AVOID RALLIES AND RATION THE TIME YOU SPEND CRUISING IN COMPANY

Although rallies provide enjoyable camaraderie, along with the spur-to-action of an absolute departure date, this is definitely not a cost-conscious way to cruise. First there are the entry fees, then the cost of rushing to buy, install, or repair various types of rally gear to meet the organizer's liability-insurance requirements. If this final outfitting is done at a rally starting port, local service and supply people will charge more because they have a captive audience. Since you will be urged to keep pace with the rest of the group, you will be rushed into fixing gear "right now," no matter what the cost, rather than sail to another port with more competitive prices. From outfitting and provisioning to the clothes you wear, to entertaining on board and restaurants on shore, "keeping up" is a hard part of rally life that could drain your cruising kitty as well as your feeling of self-esteem. An editor of *Yachting Monthly* highlighted this when he wrote of interviews with participants in the 1997 ARC Rally (*Yachting Monthly*, March 1998). The owner of one of the budget-minded boats told him, "I went on board the Oyster 55 *Kanaloa* (also in the ARC) and left with nothing but envy for his yacht and shame and embarrassment at mine."

Then there are the other costs. *Rally* implies lots of boats moving at the same time, which usually translates into boats racing. This leads to wear and tear on sails and gear far in excess of what you may have experienced during day racing, far in excess of that of normal laid-back cruising. This rush mentality may add unexpected tensions among crew who pictured cruising as an antidote to shore life. And of course as part of a rally, you'll gain a lot of sailing friends in the fleet, but you'll lose the time to involve yourself in the local culture. Because you arrive as part of a readymade floating community, you often will be cut off timewise and socially from local people, the very people who could show you the most fascinating sights in their area and advise you where to shop inexpensively for everything from services to entertainment. (This is discussed in detail in *Seraffyn's Mediterranean Adventure*, pages 127-29.)

RATION THE USE OF YOUR RADIO TRANSMITTER

Not only do radio transmitting systems themselves add costs to outfitting, but offshore they seem to be among the most frequent items on the "repair or upgrade" list. Once again, radios cut you off from local people simply because it is tempting and enjoyable to accept dates with other international cruising friends long before you reach port. "Let's meet for dinner as soon as you get in; let's rent a car together." The more time you reserve to get to know local people, the more likely you are to exchange homemade meals, homemade entertainment. These onshore acquaintances can lead you to special, lesser-known anchorages and destinations.

BALANCE YOUR CRUISING TIME

If you make occasional two- or three-day passages instead of trying to harbor-hop around the world, you'll save money because you'll have more time in each port you visit to explore and find what you need at reduced prices. Balancing your time between major ports and visits to isolated anchorages or tiny villages means you'll also save money and broaden your chances for memorable experiences. During the three fun-filled weeks we anchored right at the waterfront in Papeete, we spent seven times more just on entertainment than we did when we sailed onward for two months in the outer islands. Away from the bright lights, we still went ashore for occasional meals, but we stopped being tempted by sexy French lace knickers, mouthwatering French patés and cheeses, and twice-a-day gatherings with fellow sailors at the ice cream shops and cafés. At the more traditional outer islands, our time was filled to the brim with skin diving, bicycle forays along the palm-fringed paths, and evenings with local dancers as they undulated and drummed in preparation for the annual Bastille Day competition in Papeete.

STOCK UP

Use your boat as a miniature warehouse and buy extras whenever you see low prices on your favorite nonperishable goods. In most island areas, items you see one day may be gone the next. In others, prices may be double. The corollary to this is, find local substitutes for provisions that must be imported, and therefore could be costly. (U.S. peanut butter in Rio de Janeiro is $5, local crushed peanut creme is $1.)

TRADE CHARTS AND BOOKS

It is not necessary to carry the latest charts of any area. Not only do rocks rarely move, but even the latest charts will be at least a year or two old by the time you use them – and they may have been based on surveys from 60 or 70 years ago. Instead, carry the latest Light List, and practice heaving-to until morning to enter new places in daylight. Although we would not sail without a very detailed set of coastal charts (secondhand, if possible), we have spent less than $200 a year on charts since we set sail on *Taleisin*. We have traded for those we needed either by posting an ad in cruising ports along our route or by placing a request in the OCC bulletin or the SSCA newsletter six months before we plan on sailing to a new area. (Ocean Cruising Club, c/o Averil Johnson, 93 Desborough Road, Eastleigh, Southampton, SO50 5NT, United Kingdom. Seven Seas Cruising Association, 1525 South Andrews Avenue, Fort Lauderdale, FL 33316, USA.)

At other times, we have helped form what we call a "Chart Club." If eight or 10 cruisers are headed in the same direction, we all pool the charts we have acquired and one person catalogs them. We then chip in to buy the few extras we need to have a complete set and arrange for full-size copies at one fourth the cost of the originals. (U.S. government charts are not copyrighted, but British ones are, so be careful here.)

Trading for secondhand cruising guides saves money. Even the information in the newest guidebook could be at least two years out of date by the time you get to your destination. What you need are details of interesting, out-of-the-way anchorages, historical notes, and information on local attractions and mores. These will not change drastically from one year to the next.

AVOID "GETTING ON-LINE"

This seems to be the newest way to overload a cruising budget and consume time that could possibly be put to better uses. It is definitely a sales-driven, emotion-laden subject. For who wants to be "computer illiterate" or to use "snailmail" or to miss out on the chance to keep in touch with "everyone" immediately? Unfortunately, computers (yes, even the newest ones) and their attendant parts, from printers to modems, are sensitive to salt air, just like other electronic gear. But, even more frustratingly, these usually have to be returned to the country of purchase to be repaired. So far, not one cruising friend has shown us a breakdown of savings that equals the capital investment, maintenance, and upgrading costs of having a computer system. Two interesting facts emerge from our New Year's mailbag: about 30 percent of our friends' letters come from those who have some type of computer on board, and only a third of those were able to use their computers to generate their letters. Each of the others made apologies from "printer out of order" to "can't figure out how to get this to ....."

Interestingly, not one of our cruising friends who write articles has found that an editor turned down a piece because it was submitted as a typed manuscript. Good writing and photos are still the key.

LEAVE YOUR CASH AND CREDIT CARD ON THE BOAT

Impulse buying will destroy your cruising finances. We find it hard to resist spending money like....well, like a drunken sailor, on our first few days in port. This is especially true after a long ocean passage or after being in areas with no major shops or ice cream for three or four months. So we carry only enough cash to buy us a nice restaurant meal and if we see something we think we really need, we are forced to wait until we can go back to the boat for money or our credit card. By that time, we often have talked ourselves out of the item or thought of a more affordable way to solve the problem.

WHAT ARE THE WISE AND REWARDING WAYS TO SPEND YOUR MONEY?

Spend money on upgrading your sails before they blow out. Have the seams restitched as soon as you notice any sun deterioration. Add new chafe or sun-protection patches early. Consider adding a full-length 4-inch folded leech tape when your mainsail or headsails become two or three years old. Remember that your sails are *the* component that keeps your boat unstoppable (see *The Capable Cruiser*: Cruising Canvas Care).

Use the telephone to solve problems, as this gives you person-to-person contact and can combat feelings of homesickness. Several-call back companies offer either prepaid or charge-card options that make international calling amazingly inexpensive. In 1998, we paid only 12 cents (U.S.) per minute to call from the United Kingdom to the United States. We keep an account with AT&T called the True Choice Military Option, which costs nothing unless we use it and gives us immediate, quick credit-card calls at about half of normal prices. We use this to connect ourselves to our New World System to use the cheapest rates we know of. (United States to Trinidad, 18 cents per minute, Puerto Rico to the United States, 12 cents). Contact one of the companies listed below or look for others in the classified pages of international magazines such as *TIME* or *Newsweek*.

AT&T True Choice Calling Card Customer Service, 1-800-225-5288.
    From outside the United States call collect: 816- 654-6000.
Swift Call UK, 0800-769-0022, has the best prices from the United
    Kingdom to other countries.
New World USA, 1-201-287-8400, has the best prices anywhere outside
    the United Kingdom to anywhere else. There is a minimum usage
    requirement of $10 per month.

Kallback USA, 1-206-599-1933, has prices to some countries better than *New World*, with no minimum charge.

Avoid flying home because you are homesick. Your trip home will cost far more than just the airfares. You must also consider gifts, car rental, living and hotel costs while there, storage fees for your boat, and the temptations of your local chandlery and book-store. The only times we travel back home are when we sail our boat there, when there is a death in the family, and when we deliver someone's boat for them. This last option, though, is one to consider. A delivery job or crewing position could give you the money to cover these costs. Or, if you aren't too far from home, you could use some of the money saved by not flying home to rent a lovely hotel room for some family and friends. Invite them for three days of festival in La Paz, Mexico, or Seville, Spain – you'll cut their costs and add an interesting element to your cruising style.

Do not try to save money by avoiding all shoreside treats – whether meals or horseback riding or occasional car rentals. If you eliminate treats like these, you and your partner may feel you have given up everything to live on a boat with little reward to balance it. A definite highlight of our Brazilian sojourn cost us about $400 and was worth every bit of that and more. We secured *Taleisin* in a safe marina right next to the center of Rio de Janeiro, got out our bikes, packed a travel bag, and bicycled 4 miles (6 km) to a well-recommended family-style hotel overlooking the Copacabana Beach. For three nights and four days, we joined life along 14 miles of the world's most beautiful, most joyously used beaches. (Larry almost fell off his bicycle by keeping a lingering eye on the nearly invisible Brazilian bikinis.)

Do include expensive-sounding countries in your itinerary. Avoiding places such as Norway and Italy just because of their higher costs of living can be a mistake. If you reprovision in lower-priced areas (we loaded 120 bottles of wine at $1.50 and 24 of whiskey at $12 in France and Scotland), then arrive laden with stores, you can live reasonably in places like Norway (wine starting at $12 a bottle, whiskey at $45). Put off by the high prices in the shops, we spent far less cruising there than we had in lower-cost countries, yet we made friends we'll have for life. If you are earning as you cruise, you'll often find that the wages offered in these first-world countries more than offset the costs. And, in many of the more expensive countries, it is easier to get around the work restrictions than it is in less-developed areas.

Finally, three places we don't feel it is wise to try to save money all relate to tiring and boring cruise-related jobs. It definitely pays to have your laundry done on shore. Is it logical or fair to ask a woman who is successful in her own right to spend hours hand-scrubbing clothes? If at all possible, wouldn't it be more encouraging and less aggravating to spend even $40 or $50 to have someone do up those three huge bags of soiled clothes after a long passage? There will occasionally be times when you have no other choice, and if you both pitch in to scrub, wring, and hang clothes once a week, it can be a chatty, even charming experience. But whenever possible, definitely pay for laundry service.

The same advice goes for taxis to carry your once-a-week load of groceries back to the boat and also to deliver the piles of food you'll need at reprovisioning time. By walking or busing one way, then using a taxi to return to the boat, you may well get better prices, since you then expand your choices to include out-of-town shops and discount warehouses.

As the ultimate sign that you've found a good balance among your cruising funds, your time, and your ability to earn as you go, consider hiring help for the dirty part of the year, haulout time – someone to scrub, prepare and paint the bottom of your wind-powered magic carpet. This choice might even save you money, as it could reduce the cost of additional days in the yard.

There is no simple formula that will ensure you get the best value from your cruising funds, the most pleasure from your adventure. As a review of the foregoing suggestions will show, the two major challenges facing you are learning to control maintenance costs by keeping your boat unstoppable and balancing the very sociable life you will be entering. Most of us find that the bonus of cruising is the people you meet along the way, other cruisers as well as locals. Because cruising leaves you free of the strictures of shore life, it is tempting to spend every afternoon and evening socializing. Full-time socializing at home ashore would be expensive and impractical, and it is no different when out cruising. Find the right balance and you can truly feel you are enjoying a champagne cruise on a beer budget.

CHAPTER
11
KEEPING HER MOVING: LIGHT AIR SAILING

W e can't remember a more welcome landfall than Sri Lanka. Our Pilot Charts had forecast a 14 percent chance of gale winds for at least part of the 2,200-mile passage from Aden, Yemen, but we'd had breezes so fitful that *Seraffyn* sat motionless for hours at a time. Instead of averaging 100 miles a day, as we usually did, we had averaged only 63 on this passage. When we told Don Windsor, the port captain at Galle, Sri Lanka, about our frustrating 35-day passage, he said, "You did very well. The seven boats that have come this way since the Suez Canal reopened took 50 to 64 days to make the same trip. There's never much wind out there." He also told us that these sailors had motored, hoping for more breeze, often ignoring the 5- or 6-knot winds along their way until they ran out of fuel. Unfortunately, their boats hadn't been prepared to sail in the light winds they had had to rely on for the remainder of their passage.

In most cruising discussions, light-air performance is given a much lower priority than gale tactics. Yet light airs predominate in the islands strung along the equator in the South Pacific, and in much of Indonesia. If you can keep your boat moving under sail there, you'll be able to reach remote goals that could make your voyage unique instead of having to determine your route by refueling ports.

Some of the principles of light-air performance that apply to race boats can be useful for cruisers, but there are three major problems rarely considered on boats designed for performance under specialized rules. The majority of cruising boats will be, to put it bluntly, overweight; they will be short of crew power; and they'll usually have a limited inventory of "luxury" nylon sails on board. But the cruising sailor determined to overcome these handicaps can achieve rewarding, cost-effective results with a combination of new sailing tactics, good sail choices, and design improvements.

We've heard dozens of people announce that they'd shortened their mast to go offshore, as if a shorter mast would somehow be safer. There is little logic to this unless your boat is underballasted (tender). A shorter mast means you'll either have to resort to large overlapping sails to get light-weather sail area or, as often happens, have to install larger fuel tanks to overcome the distances in light-air cruising zones. A boat's potential speed in light air is most accurately calculated by computing the frictional drag of the underwater areas of the hull (a function of the amount and distribution of wetted surface) and comparing it to sail area. But through years of watching cruising-boat performance – both by crossing oceans under sail and by joining handicap races in dozens of different ports – we've come up with a simple rule of thumb to determine a boat's likelihood of good light-air performance. Our formula may leave room for errors of ± 5 percent, but it lets you compare half a dozen boats quickly. Divide by 2,000 the boat's displacement in pounds, that is, designed weight plus 1,500 pounds per crew member. [1] Now compute the working sail area in square feet (the total of the mainsail and 100-percent jib) and divide the sail area by the previous figure. If the result is much less than 83 (square feet per 2,000 pounds), you'll find it difficult to set the light canvas required to keep your boat moving in light airs (this is equivalent to .85 square meter per metric ton of displacement). Light-air flyers such as the Schock 55 carry 110 square feet of working sail area per ton; with the 150 percent genoa, the Schock 55 carries 132 square feet per ton. *Seraffyn* carried 88 square feet of working sail area per ton, 127 square feet with her big genoa; the figures for *Taleisin* are similar. At the other end of the scale, Tahiti ketches and Wm. Atkin 32-footers (9.8m) carry 55 to 60 square feet per ton, 70 square feet when luxury sails are added; in effect they are running on three cylinders. There is *no way* an undercanvased boat can perform in light air, because this performance is directly related to the sail-power needed to propel the boat in actual cruising form – not when it is being calculated perfectly loaded to a designer's preferred waterline, but rather when it has reached its true cruising weight, including wine, bicycles (maybe even a motorcycle), sailboards, and the 150 or so books many of us carry on board.

The soft, wineglass curves of classic long-keeled hulls, plus their inherent heavier displacement, often are a positive contribution to light-wind performance. The fuller-bodied hulls present less wetted surface for

---

1. The displacement usually listed by designers is total sailing weight of the boat, with half the provisions required to feed its crew for a two-week voyage. By adding 1,500 pounds per crew-person, this number will come closer to the true displacement of most 28- to 40-foot offshore boats. We have chosen to use short tons (2,000 pounds) to simplify this equation. Marine architects more often use long tons (metric tons, equal to 2,240 pounds) in their calculations.

their displacement than do flat-bottomed, fin-keeled racer/cruisers. The additional weight, if combined with a good spread of canvas, helps keep the boat moving between puffs of wind. So, contrary to popular belief, older designs such as 1950s CCA boats, RORC-inspired hulls, and classics like Cape Dorys and Pacific Seacraft often perform better than more contemporary ones in light airs. One famous century-old Falmouth Quay punt, *Curlew*, has been cruising the world for 25 years, turning modern racing fleets on their ears in light-to-moderate airs. This well-sailed, long-keeled 28-footer (8.5m) wins a high percentage of races in which it sails, boat for boat against modern 28- to 35-footers, because it spreads a substantial amount of canvas in relation to its total displacement and wetted surface area, plus its weight keeps it moving through the wakes of fishing boats and ferries that toss lighter boats and shake the wind from their sails.

Curlew has another light-air performance-enhancing design feature – no propeller, no aperture. Scott Jutson, a yacht designer who is making his mark by paying constant attention to underwater drag factors, has created the accompanying chart (Fig. 11-1), which shows the speed loss caused by using a fixed propeller instead of a folding one. As it shows, the drag of a propeller is most detrimental to your boat's performance at very low speeds. Your day's run can be increased by 8 to 12 percent in winds

Figure 11-1.

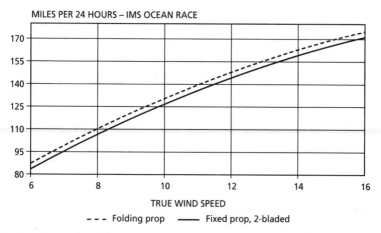

5.6 TON DSPL./ 9.3 M. WL
FOLDING PROP vs. FIXED BLADE

MILES PER 24 HOURS – IMS OCEAN RACE

TRUE WIND SPEED

- - - Folding prop ——— Fixed prop, 2-bladed

Scott Jutson Yacht Design 1991

below Force 3 by choosing a folding propeller over a fixed, three-bladed one. Even with a two-bladed fixed propeller, the difference is close to 10 percent. As the wind freshens, the percentage of loss does drop, but the propeller drag still hurts and can cut 5 percent from each day's progress. So even though three-bladed fixed propellers are more fuel-efficient and possibly smoother-running, choices that enhance efficiency under nylon power can pay dividends for economical voyaging.

We've noticed an interesting correlation between a boat's efficiency under engine power and the hours spent motoring rather than sailing. Yachts with auxiliary motors fitted to the older cruising standard of 1 hp per ton of boat usually power at about two-thirds of hull speed and tend to make fewer fuel-dependent long-distance passages than those with the current recommendation of 1 hp per foot of length to gain equal speed under sail or power. Smaller propeller, lighter engine, less fuel tankage, more space for light-wind sails – all add up to better light-air performance. But it may be the emotional acceptance that this is a sailing vessel first and foremost that keeps you looking toward your sails when the wind whispers.

Certain other factors also contribute to successful light-air performance. For instance, a clean bottom is essential. Knowing this, racers choose hard bottom paints so they can be scrubbed down before each race. For offshore voyagers, an acceptable compromise is a leaching bottom paint designed to be wiped off by a snorkeler three or four times between haulouts.

A clear deck also helps in light airs. Bicycles, water jugs, spray shields, and dodgers – all cluttered on deck cause the breezes blowing near deck level to curl and become less efficient. [2] Besides, to handle light- air sails, you will need to move around on the side decks and foredeck. The clearer these areas are, the easier and safer sail-handling will be.

Choosing the right light-air sails is difficult, as sailmakers will pressure you to try ideas culled from the racing world or invented purely to coax more money from your pocket rather than speed from your boat. We've found that the most economical light-air sail is one that is easy to set, easy to control, and capable of being used all the way around the wind rose. If light-air sails are difficult to handle, many of us will take the cockeyed-optimist approach, thinking, "If I wait a bit, the wind will freshen." Meanwhile, we curse the slatting jib and, instead of moving along at a possible 3 or 4 knots, fumble along with our sails banging and

2. Tests have shown that in 6-knot breezes, air-flow patterns will be distorted for up to four times the height of any obstacle.

chafing, barely having steerageway. Or we start the engine and tolerate its noise.

After trying a variety of light-wind sails, we've found the most versatile and simple one to be a nylon drifter. Ours for *Taleisin* is cut from 1.5-ounce nylon and has 600 square feet (56 sq. m.) of area, just like our number 1 genoa, but it is cut with a higher clew. It can be set free-standing on its own low-stretch, Kevlar-core luff rope. But it does have four jib hanks spaced equally along its luff. Unlike the multipurpose spinnaker (MPS), this sail can be used for going to windward in 4 or 5 knots of apparent wind. When closehauled, we use the hanks to help hold the luff tight. Twenty degrees off the wind, we forget about the hanks and set the sail free-standing. We carry it downwind in up to 15 knots of breeze, or until its 1/4-inch (6mm) sheets start to get skinny. Our drifter weighs only 15 pounds (6.8kg) and can easily be stuffed into a space the size of a five-gallon (22.7 liters) pail.

There is no reason to fold a nylon sail, as the most diligent crushing seems to have little effect on it. *Taleisin's* drifter was never folded, and despite frequent use, was in fine shape after 10 years of voyaging.

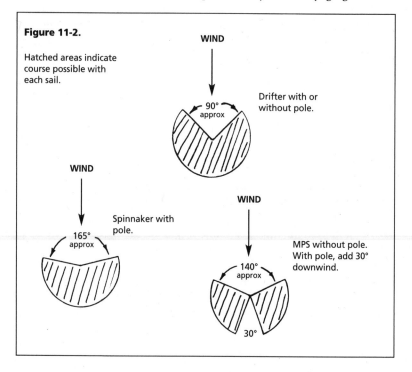

Figure 11-2.

Hatched areas indicate course possible with each sail.

WIND

90° approx

Drifter with or without pole.

WIND

165° approx

Spinnaker with pole.

WIND

140° approx

30°

MPS without pole. With pole, add 30° downwind.

A drifter does not chafe against the headstay as much as an MPS or spinnaker would in sloppy conditions, nor does it have the same tendency to wrap around the forestay in fluky winds.

In winds above 10 knots, we usually run wing-and-wing, with the mainsail and 100 percent lapper set on a whisker pole. As the wind drops, we get out our drifter and set it flying (i.e., no hanks) to leeward. Its sheet is led to a fairlead block, which is seized to the outhaul fitting of the mainsail boom. From there, the sheet leads forward to the jiffy-reefing winch, which is under the boom next to the reefing-pendant cleats. Since the drifter's sheet and halyards are right at the mast area, setting and lowering the sail can be a one-person job. To steady the drifter, we push the main boom forward and use a preventer vang to hold it in place. The main boom thus works as a drifter strut and lead. Once the drifter is set, we drop the mainsail into the lazyjacks. The two headsails – jib on its pole, drifter on the main boom strut – give us almost as much sail area as we'd carry in a cruising spinnaker, more than we'd have with an MPS (Fig. 11-3), yet we have more versatility and little risk of chafe or wraps. If the wind drops or the sea gets lumpy and the

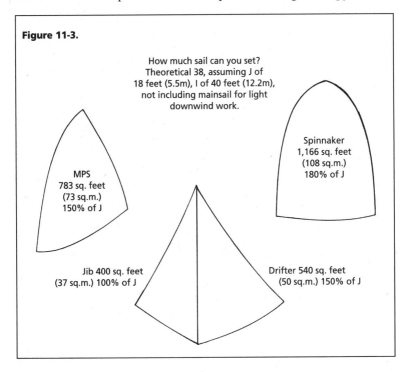

Figure 11-3.

How much sail can you set? Theoretical 38, assuming J of 18 feet (5.5m), I of 40 feet (12.2m), not including mainsail for light downwind work.

MPS
783 sq. feet
(73 sq.m.)
150% of J

Spinnaker
1,166 sq. feet
(108 sq.m.)
180% of J

Jib 400 sq. feet
(37 sq.m.) 100% of J

Drifter 540 sq. feet
(50 sq.m.) 150% of J

Photo 11-1. *The working jib on our whisker/spinnaker pole, the drifter sheeted to the end of the boom. The best of light wind sailing, smooth sea, sunny skies and only 8 knots of wind.*

Photo 11-2. *Detail of the tack arrangement with two headsails. The drifter is set flying, the hanks you can see are used for closehauled sailing.*

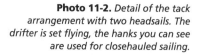

Dacron jib starts to slat or bang, we drop it and use only nylon power. This is quiet and less disturbing to any crew who may be trying to catch some sleep. If the wind freshens as we're running wing-and-wing, it's easy to douse the largest sail, the drifter. Just hoist the mainsail (ours has no headboard or battens so can easily be raised on any point of wind), ease the spinnaker halyard, and stand in the lee of the main to gather in the softly billowing expanse of nylon. If the drifter does get into the water as it's dropped, there's little concern, as it can be stored wet temporarily and brought back on deck to be dried later. If the wind shifts forward and remains light, we can drop the jib and its whisker pole, sheet

Photo 11-3. *The drifter sheet is led through a small block at the clew fitting of the mainsail, then forward along the boom to a reefing-pendant winch on the bottom of the boom.*

in the main boom and drifter, set the mainsail, and be properly canvased for beam reaching or later going to windward.

When cost determines your sail choices, the combination of a drifter opposite your 100 percent jib represents the thrifty way of gaining sail area downwind. Sailmakers often recommend snuffers to encourage their customers to use either a spinnaker or an MPS to improve downwind performance. Unfortunately, snuffers are expensive and bulky and they sometimes fail to work properly in the rougher conditions found offshore. Worse, they can cause chafe at the head of your sail. By dividing your downwind rig into two headsails, you end up with a drifter that can be handled easily without special containment gear.

Of necessity, furling jibs are built to cover a wide range of winds, so sailmakers usually choose heavier fabric than normal. Then they add a layer of sun-protection cloth along the foot and leech of the sail, thus aggravating the weight problem. So most roller-furling sails will droop and slat in winds that could keep normal headsails flying. The cost of carrying a light-weather furling genoa, plus the difficulty of changing from one furling headsail to another, could mean you'll just roll up the jib and switch on the engine. A nylon drifter, cut flat so it can be used close to the wind, or designed to be set flying, could keep you enjoying your sailing machine in light airs and will definitely prolong the life of your roller headsail.

Mainsails are usually cut from fabrics that are too heavy to work well in light breezes, especially in choppy seas. The slatting of even the most tightly vanged and prevented mainsail can wake a sound sleeper. So when we are trying to cross seas left over from a 20-knot beam wind, using only a light following zephyr, we find it best to drop the mainsail and rely completely on our nylon headsail. It's quiet, with little chance of chafe, but because the area is all forward, it's only effective off the wind. We have tried steadying the mainsail by tying a shock cord to one of the reef-point lines and securing this to the shrouds. Beware, though: This helps stop the sail from slatting, but it could be a ripping experience if someone forgets to untie the cord before tacking. As our mainsail grows closer to the end of its life, we've erased this method from our inventory of light-air tricks and instead begin getting out the light-air sails out sooner or easing off our course so we can sail under drifter alone.

Fully battened mainsails have been suggested as a solution to this problem. But, as discussed in chapter 5, the cost of universal-joint batt-cars to make sure the sail goes up and down properly, the common problem of batten-pocket chafe on the shrouds, and the difficulty of raising and lowering the sail at any time other than when you are directly head-to-wind, make us feel this type of mainsail is too expensive for the trade-off of larger roach area, less chance of luffing, and simplicity of stowing.

Dean Wixom, who cruises on a Norsea 27, took a different approach to this light-air mainsail problem. He has a loose-footed, loose-luffed, flat-cut nylon mainsail in addition to his normal one. He uses it in conjunction with his nylon drifter and says it provides wonderful, quiet sailing in the leftover chop often found along the coast of Central America.

A definite laziness affects all of us when the wind falls light and the air temperature rises. Yet time and again, we've felt the magic when a dragging night watch – marred by slatting sails, rolling boat, and stagnant DR position advances – turns into a gliding swish across a much smoother sea with the use of some light air sailing tactics. It's worth getting off one's duff to dig out the nylon sails and get the boat moving through the water with a far steadier, quieter, and infinitely more satisfying motion. You'll find that the time spent working to gain advantage over the light breeze creates a happier state of mind, and the hands on the clock no longer seem to crawl. Even though we know it happens, it still surprises us when we get the boat moving closehauled and find that the apparent wind speed increases until the boat comes alive and reaches speeds of 3 or 4 knots under the nylon drifter. To keep the boat moving in these light zephyrs, it is important to try anything that will keep the sails still and shaped to catch the wind. Inducing a slight heel – either by getting the crew to lounge or sleep on the leeward side or by moving a few water jugs to leeward – will help. Both on the wind and freed off, it's important to use a vang to hold the mainsail out and down so it doesn't pump out the wind on each swell. Downwind in very light breezes, it pays to wing out the jib and, if necessary, put a downhaul on the whisker pole to steady it. A smaller 100 percent headsail, which can be held out tight and steady on the pole, will work better in these conditions than a longer-footed genoa that undulates and curls.

One racing tactic that pays dividends for light-wind cruising is to avoid running dead downwind unless the breeze is fresh and steady. By reaching up about 20 degrees, even if it is off your rhumb line, you'll keep the boat moving better and, in the overall passage, cover little superfluous ground. The boat will stay steadier and the speed gain will be substantial, with less risk of an accidental jibe.

In a laden cruising boat in light airs, you'll find it pays to keep off the true wind after you tack – to "let her breathe," as the old-timers would say. Instead of pinching right up, let the boat off five degrees more than you would in fresher winds. Get the boat moving and trimmed on this easy-breathing course, then slowly work closer to the wind, sheeting in the sails, inch by inch. As the boat gets moving, the apparent wind will increase and move forward, so you'll soon be able to reach a fast, closehauled course.

Most other axioms for light-air racing apply to light-air cruising. Ease the halyards and clew-outhaul tensions on all sails so there are slight wrinkles but no puckers along the luff or foot. This gives your sails a fuller, more powerful shape. Ease the mainsail a bit to relieve any weather helm so the rudder can be kept aligned with the keel to reduce drag. If your boat develops lee helm – as many do under large headsails in light winds – sheet in the mainsail a bit more to trim her. Steer to traverse the seas instead of heading directly into leftover swells or chop, and ease the sheets to keep her moving. Over the long distances of a passage, you'll soon make up for any course deviations.

Of course, most of us cruisers soon tire of sitting at the helm and turn to our wind vanes to take charge. If your vane is designed to operate well in light breezes, you'll probably work to keep moving under sail instead of resorting to the noise pollution of your engine. A well-designed vane gear can steer in amazingly light winds, especially to windward. We've found our vane will keep control as long as there is enough wind to keep the boat moving. The following chapter discusses ways to improve light-air wind-vane performance.

Skimming across almost mirrorlike seas in light zephyrs is a magical treat – comfort sailing at its best, warm and utterly carefree-feeling. In these days when everyone is more aware of the environment, using your sails to propel your boat with a renewable, low-cost resource (the breeze) gives you an extra sense of satisfaction. Light-air cruising may be an acquired taste for those who cruise close to home. But for those who eventually visit far-off shores, 60 to 70 miles a day for free can look pretty cost-effective. Carrying the right equipment and learning the basic tactics early will make these light-air days a rewarding part of your voyage.

CHAPTER

12

LIGHT-AIR WIND-VANE PERFORMANCE

"NO ONE EXPECTS TO SAIL IN WINDS UNDER 8 KNOTS, so I've concentrated on making this gear work well in real breezes," the builder of a well-known vane told us when we rendezvoused in a Polynesian port. He was on his first wind-vane-guided cruise. By the time he reached his destination, he had learned, as Eric Hiscock often wrote, that the majority of voyaging is done in winds of 12 knots or less. Now the vanes built by this voyager have been re-engineered to work in light breezes.

Vanes can be amazingly sensitive. We've watched ours control *Taleisin* in breezes so light the wool telltales barely lifted. Among commercial gear with which we've sailed, we've seen the Aries vane take charge in any breeze strong enough to give the boat steerage.

Some steering gears come with two vanes of differing area and weight. One is for use in light airs, the other for moderate-to-heavy winds. We have approximated this by having a sail-fabric light-air vane that furls to reveal a smaller (40 percent of the area), heavy air-vane of $1/8$-inch (3-mm) plywood. Once the winds are over 25 knots, there is lots of wind power, so we can furl the Dacron; if the winds become gusty or very strong, the smaller vane stays stable and does not vibrate or shake the gear and backstay. Our gear uses a vertical-axis vane, but the same is true with horizontal-axis vanes such as the Aries or Fleming or Monitor; the smaller heavy-air vane lies more quietly at anchor in strong winds. The light-air vane is vital when the breezes become fitful.

We've seen some interesting ways people have chosen to increase their vane area in light airs. One friend had two holes in the after edge of his vertical-axis plywood vane. During zephyrs, he attached a light nylon flag and found it improved vane performance. Other sailors using horizontal-axis vanes simply attach a corrugated-cardboard addition using clothespins. If your gear is limited in light breezes, try either of these ideas to get an idea of the potential improvement.

Friction is the enemy of light-air vane performance. Check over your whole steering system, from the main rudder to each part of the vane, and free it up to get fingertip movement. Your main rudder should swing easily on its pintles. Instead of using metal-to-metal bearings, you can achieve smoother turning by adding replaceable Delrin bushings to your gudgeons and pintles or rudder-shaft bearings. These bearings should be at least $1/16$-inch (1.5mm) loose so the rudder will not bind. Properly fitted and with appropriate bearings, your rudder should be free enough to swing to the breezes when it is dried out in a shipyard.

Commercially built or home built, every moving part of your steering-vane gear should be smooth-running and working on needle, ball bearings, or bushings. Turning blocks for control lines should use low-friction, self-contained ball-bearing sheaves such as those engineered by Harken Brothers.

Many wheel-steering systems have enough friction to prevent a vane from working well in light winds. Therefore, a vane gear that steers independently of the ship's main rudder would be the ideal choice for use with hydraulic wheel steering or any other system on which friction cannot be reduced. Some cruisers have designed ways to unclutch their wheel-steering gear, then hooked their vane control lines directly to the emergency tiller to reduce friction.

Once friction is worked out of your steering and vane system, it is important to avoid reintroducing it by improper control-line adjustments. In light airs, leave the control lines from tiller to gear quite loose. Our lines actually sag about $1/2$-inch (13mm) along their 18-inch (457mm) length to get optimum light-air control. When we did sea trials on a 47-foot (14.3m) tiller-steered cutter, sailing out to sea for 10 days, we left with the owner saying his off-the-shelf gear was useless. Then we noticed he'd tensioned the chain linking his gear to his tiller so the control line was firm to the touch. By easing the tension until the control lines hung in an easy scallop, the Fleming self-steering gear immediately took charge and brought the boat on course and a contented smile to the owner's face.

In light air, it is helpful to have a telltale close to and just above the wind vane. Though your masthead telltale may say the wind is on the beam, this may not be so at vane level. To get the vane adjusted properly, it needs to be aligned with the wind direction at its own level. We have tied a 10-inch (250mm) piece of knitting wool to the backstay, a foot above our backstay-hung vane. Not only does this help in setting the gear in light winds, it also tells us if we've changed course due to a local wind shift, because if the vane is aligned with the telltale, the gear is doing its job. If, on the other hand, you find you need to adjust your vane so that it does not align with the telltale to get it to steer a proper course, this is an indication that something is wrong with the vane or your boat's trim. It might need different counterbalancing; you might have weather helm because of improperly set sails; your control-line tension might be too tight. Work toward getting the telltale aligned parallel with the vane in very light winds and your gear should be doing its best.

Getting your cruising boat to steer without human power or electricity is well worth the patience. Attention to details will make your vane do its job. The rewards go beyond being freed from the tyranny of the tiller, for an efficient self-steering gear can improve your light-air passagemaking to windward. Unlike autopilots (which stick to magnetic compass courses), or human helmsmen (who have short attention spans), your wind vane will automatically catch each change of wind direction to steer your boat closer to the optimum course. It is in light breezes that this aspect of vane steering seems most like magic. Once you get your vane working well in zephyrs, you'll feel free to wander forward and find a perfectly shaded, sail-padded lounging place from which you can watch your quiet, wind-powered gear control your course across a smooth and glistening sea.

13

IMPROVING LIFE
AT ANCHOR

Roll, pitch, corkscrew, doze off. I brace myself in the bunk, then I roll over again to try to get comfortable. The motion is relentless. Here Lin and I are at anchor and I know I'd sleep better if we were beam reaching in a Force 5 wind and sea. You, too, will have times like this, times when you have to seek shelter in anchorages that are relatively safe for the ship but uncomfortable for the crew. In fact, we found anchorages like this are common in the South Pacific, the Marquesas islands, and inside Australia's Great Barrier Reef, where many of the roadsteads and even harbors are subject to deflected swell and considerable wind chop. Conditions in some of these anchorages made *Taleisin* pitch and roll so badly that at times the cook wouldn't cook and sleep was next to impossible. As there was lots of interesting skin diving and exploring on shore along these coasts, and few better anchorages, I gradually worked out some motion-dampening tactics that helped us live more comfortably in spite of the motion.

My first move was the easiest. I set a riding sail. Any flat-cut sail, set well aft of the rig's center of effort, will help reduce rolling. In moderate winds, those of Force 6 or less, I set the double-reefed mainsail and outhauled it, then tied down the reef points down tightly to make it as flat as possible. I secured both the mainsheet and the preventer-vang tackle to locate the boom slightly to one side of amidships. With the boom secured, not only doesn't the boom bang around when gusts swing the bow of the boat through the eye of the wind, but the sail is amazingly well-mannered and quiet. When the boat does tack, the sail simply flaps once or twice, then lies on the other board with little fuss. You'll probably find that yawls and ketches lie more comfortably at anchor with their mizzens sheeted the same way to act as riding sails. Schooners should lie best with the mainsail sheeted flat and reefed to reduce the area.

In winds over Force 6, I use our triple-reefed mainsail as the riding sail. This leaves an area of approximately 80 square feet (7.5sq. m.). *Taleisin's* total displacement in cruising trim is 18,000 pounds (8 tons), so a riding sail of about 9 square feet (0.9 sq. m.) per ton of displacement should give you similar results without too much heeling motion in heavy gusts of wind. Most sailmakers design mainsails so they become flatter as they are reefed. This is so with ours – which, as you can see in the photo – is quite flat when it is working as a riding sail. Our storm trysail is also cut flat, and we have confidently lain at anchor with this rig in winds of up to Force 10 with occasional heavier gusts during the williwaws that come off the hills of Australia's offshore islands (photo 13-1).

The next step I use to increase our comfort in marginal anchorages requires a bowsprit. Pitching, sheering, and chain overriding can be reduced by rigging a nylon bridle through a single block at the end of the bowsprit, as shown in Figure 13-1. On *Taleisin*, this 1/2-inch (1.3cm) diameter three-strand nylon line is rove through a block that lives at the end of the bowsprit. Both ends of the bridle line are tied inboard at the lifeline stanchion closest to the windlass. Any time I wish to use the bridle, I tie one end of the line to the chain using a rolling hitch, then winch the hitch out until it is near the block. I then let out extra chain to hang in a loop, which goes below the water. This stops the slack chain

Photo 13-1.

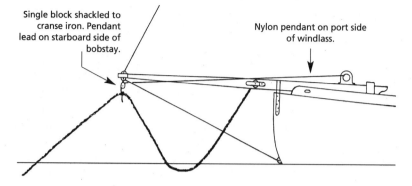

Figure 13-1. *Bowsprit-led anchor pendant.*

from banging against the bobstay. By leading the pendant right to the end of the bowsprit, the boat is held down by the long lever and has less tendency to pitch. I have found that *Taleisin* will lie quite sedately in a wind chop of up to $2^1/2$ feet (76.2cm) with this bowsprit-end fairlead and bridle. Without it, her pitching motion is quick and disquieting. I have also found that chain used this way will dampen the pitching motion much better than a lightweight nylon anchor rode. The extra weight of the chain seems more determined to hold down the bowsprit, and the friction created as the chain drags over the bottom also slows the sheering momentum.

Many yachts, especially those with a cutaway forefoot or fin keel, tend to try to sail at anchor, sheering port and starboard, then fetching up with a jerk at the end of their anchor rode. These yachts take up more space in a given anchorage, and sometimes their sheering anchor cable will foul, then drag their anchor backward. This wild sheering, and the fear of being to leeward of a dragging yacht, makes nearby sailors nervous, especially during a midnight blow. The longer lever offered by the bowsprit-end fairlead and bridle is especially helpful here, as it minimizes the sheering and helps the boat lie more quietly in gusty winds. [1]

Some people with whom we have spoken worry about using this bowsprit-end pendant, feeling it could cause damage to their rig, as the strains from it are directed not onto the windlass or bow rollers, but

---

[1] If you do not have a bowsprit and your boat is subject to charging around at anchor, you could use a solution suggested by Dean Wixom who cruises on a Nor Sea 27. Attach a nylon pendant to the main anchor rode using a chain hook or rolling hitch, two feet in front of the bow roller. Lead the pendant aft, outside and clear of all the lifeline stanchions and secure it on the sheet winch. Ease out the main anchor rode until the bow of the boat lays off approximately 20 degrees from the wind. This should keep the boat from tacking at anchor.

rather onto the headstay and whisker stays. This should not be a concern, as any one of these stays is usually three times stronger than the anchor chain on the same boat. Furthermore, three-strand nylon is stretchy, so it absorbs shocks that otherwise would be directed right onto the fittings of the boat. After using this system for some 30 years, I feel quite good about using a pendant as a snubber in waves of up to 3 or 4 feet if I can't find a better anchorage. I do watch the mast, though, and if ever I noticed it starting to bend forward more than a slight bit with each surge, I would become reluctant to continue using the pendant. If I sailed in a boat with a fractional rig or a gaff rig, I would set up both running backstays before attaching the pendant to the anchor cable, to prevent what could be an embarrassing situation, a self-induced dismasting at anchor.

Two final reasons to use this bowsprit-end bridle: It serves to keep the anchor chain away from the hull so that it doesn't scar up the topside finish in wind-against-tide situations when the boat tries to override its own cable. And the nylon pendant line is softer and stretchy, so it is far quieter than chain left on its own on a metal bow roller.

Though most modern boats are designed without bowsprits, we have seen owners of cruising boats such as the Norsea 27 and Cape Dory add short bowsprits just for anchoring purposes. These bowsprits or platforms can be used to rig anchor bridles and also serve as a convenient place to store anchors clear of the foredeck thus reducing the incidence of stubbed toes.

Figure 13-2. *Bow protection ideas.*

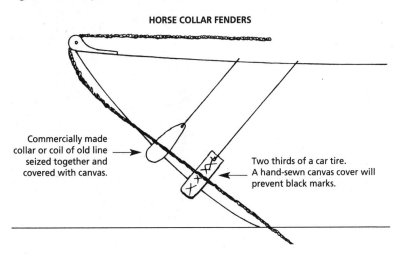

HORSE COLLAR FENDERS

Commercially made collar or coil of old line seized together and covered with canvas.

Two thirds of a car tire. A hand-sewn canvas cover will prevent black marks.

Those without bowsprits can reduce the noise and chafe caused when the boat overrides its chain by using a bow collar. Figure 13-2 shows examples of some of the bow collars we've seen as we cruised.

A final line of defense against restless nights at anchor in less-than-perfect anchorages is the homemade, low-cost flopper-stopper we have used successfully over the years. The main part of the flopper-stopper is simply a strong, heavy-duty plastic carry box (just like the stacking storage boxes sold in many children's furniture stores). I chose one with solid sides and a sturdy mesh bottom. I then sewed two 8-ounce folded and doubled Dacron flaps to the bottom to produce a simple, one-way valve, as shown in Figure 13-3. A bridle line of $7/16$-inch-diameter line is led through the handles on the box, then up to a bowline. By trial and error, I learned that a swivel needs to be fitted to this line. Without the swivel, the line tends to twist and could eventually become hockled. The upper end of this line is tied into a bowline, and the loop of the bowline is snapped onto the spinnaker-pole end. I found I needed weights on the bottom of the box to make it sink quickly; the ones I used consisted of a spare length of chain

Figure 13-3. The flopper-stopper

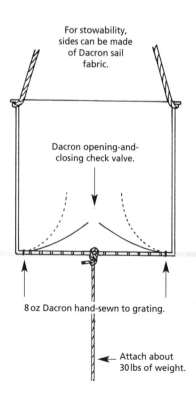

For stowability, sides can be made of Dacron sail fabric.

Dacron opening-and-closing check valve.

8 oz Dacron hand-sewn to grating.

← Attach about 30 lbs of weight.

Photo 13-2.

Photo 13-3.

and a dinghy anchor, which I lashed in place with a short piece of line to hang below the bottom of the box. I then set the spinnaker pole about square to the centerline of the boat, using the staysail halyard on a topping lift, and held it in place with fore-and-aft guy lines. I adjusted the length of the bridle line so that the flopper-stopper box always remained below the surface of the water, but with its weights kept clear of the bottom. This flopper-stopper works amazingly well, because as the rolling boat tries to lift the box clear of the water, the Dacron flaps close and the weight of the water in the box counters the motion. On the rollback, the anchor and chain pull the box back down and the flaps open upward and fill the box with water again. If the swell is approaching from port, we set the pole on that side, and vice versa – this helps keep the boat more synchronized with the motion of the sea (photographs 13-2, 13-3, 13-4). We have now made this flopper-stopper more stowable by replacing the plastic sides with Dacron.

Our spinnaker pole is 19 feet 8 inches (6m) long. With this long lever, we find that an 18-inch-by-18-inch box, plus 30 pounds of weight, is all we need to cut the snappiness out of the rolling motion and steady the boat. If you have a proportionately shorter pole, or a larger boat, then a larger-volume box or heavier weights would be needed to produce a similar roll-dampening effect. For larger boats, another option would be to set up flopper-stopper boxes in series, choosing boxes that could store inside one another when not in use.

If a flopper-stopper such as this is used in a busy harbor at night, it would be prudent and correct to attach a light to the end of the pole to prevent collisions. In out-of-the-way anchorages and roadsteads, we relied on the anchor light, which we secured 8 feet (2.4m) up the staysail stay to show our position and illuminate the pole. We felt this was sufficient, as few yachts should be maneuvering within 15 feet of our anchored boat.

Few anchorages in the South Pacific have perfect, 360-degree swell protection. So if you choose to cruise this area, it is a sure bet

Photo 13-4.

you also will be forced to anchor at places such as High Island, inside the Great Barrier reef, where we lay to wait out a three-day southeasterly gale on our way south and east to New Zealand. We felt this was far preferable to giving up a hundred hard-earned miles of weathering by running back to a better anchorage. During those three days, we used all three of the methods described – a riding sail, bowsprit-end bridle, and flopper-stopper. By doing so, we turned a miserable cross-swell-induced roll into a slow-motion dance that let us get lots of rest, read some good books, and, most important, kept the cook interested in cooking.

CHAPTER
14
SHIPYARD SAFETY AND SECURITY

"I'LL BET YOU'VE HAD SOME SCARY EXPERIENCES AT SEA!"
"Ever worry about losing *Taleisin* when you were in a storm?" We hear these questions frequently, yet, though it sounds ironical, it is in shipyards that we are most concerned about our boat. The number of prudent voyagers we've known who had serious difficulties at sea, difficulties that caused injuries, heavy expenses, or long delays to their cruising plans, is low compared to the number of those who have had cruise-delaying shipyard accidents. Although the majority of haulout problems we have seen could be traced to faulty shipyard equipment or procedures, in almost every case the yacht owner could have taken preventive actions that would have averted the problem. He or she could have insisted on safety lines, looked over the equipment with a more critical eye, or added extra supports once the boat was out of the water. But to do this, boat owners need to know some of the guidelines for handling their graceful, waterbound creature when it becomes an ungainly, landlocked object.

Even though careening may not be the ideal way to put a fresh coat of paint on your boat, you may some day save it from sinking by knowing this technique. To make emergency repairs after a collision, to check for hull damage, or to put on bottom paint where there are no tidal grids or haulout facilities, you should look for a well-protected harbor or enclosed bay with a gently sloping sand beach, then careen your boat on a falling tide.

First inspect the beach at low tide to be sure it is clear of sharp objects before you bring in your boat. On the next tide, a half hour before high water, position the boat beam-on to the shore with the keel just touching. Heel the boat toward the shore either with a line led from the masthead or with weights or chain on the side deck. By settling the boat before the high tide, you are assured it will lift off on the next tide. Be sure to close any hull ports. Then protect any paint work that will touch the sand by sliding soft pads under the turn of the bilge as the boat settles. A gentle surge – say, less than five or six inches of rise and fall – will cause little problem when you careen. If the boat is laid with its mast up the slope of the beach, the occasional wake of boats passing at under 5 knots (the in-port speed limit) should have little bouncing effect. But we would avoid careening where heavy workboats, such as tugs, are likely to pass. Except for doing emergency repairs, careening might not be a good option for very deep-draft fin-keelers with lots of flare to their topsides above the waterline. These boats will tend to lie with much of their topsides against the sand, which could scuff the paint. But few cruising boats fall into this category, and most will lie with only their bottom paint touching the sand.

If your boat has a keel profile that lets it sit evenly on the bottom with little tendency to lie bow-down and no tendency to lie stern-down, a safe and inexpensive way to dry out for a scrub-off is on a tidal grid or on legs. [1]

In many parts of the world, tidal grids are provided by sailing clubs and marinas. In some places, you can set up your own grid with a few minutes of work. If you are in an area with a tidal range that is about two feet more than the draft of your boat, a crew of two can scrub and paint the bottom of a 35-footer (10.7m) in one tide. We regularly dry *Taleisin* on a grid in New Zealand and England. We bring her in just before high tide and settle her as the tide drops. We go have breakfast and do a few on-deck jobs until the water is knee deep, then we dip a scrub brush in a bucket of sand and use it to remove the growth from the bottom. This sandy brush acts just like wet-and-dry sandpaper. Since the sanding is done while the tide is falling, the job is less of a health risk, as we do not inhale bottom-paint dust as we work. If we plan to apply new paint, we hose or bucket the bottom down with fresh water. (Our pump-up shower unit is perfect for this job; a siphon hose led from jugs of fresh water set on deck would also work for the final rinse-off.) When the bottom is dry, we paint from the keel up. One of us uses a long-handled paint roller, the other follows closely behind, smoothing the paint with a 4-inch-wide brush.

The boat has not been moved by machine, never had to run up an

---

1. In New Zealand, even the owners of fin-and-skeg boats, which lie stern or bow down, dry out their boats on tidal grids without damaging rudders or bows. They hold up the bow with lines led from the anchor winch to the dock or pilings, or they lead a line under the stern cleats and leave them secured until the tide recedes. They then use props or steel drums to support the boat while they work.

Photo 14-1. *To induce a little heel (2°) toward the dock, you can pull her over with a halyard or put your anchor and chain on the side deck.*

incline. She is as close to her natural element as possible, and best of all, we can do only six hours of hard labor before the tide returns to give us a break until the next day. [2]

For this job, it is important to choose a spot with no surge. A slight swell and even some chop will cause little problem other than a few thumps on the wood bearers as the boat settles. But a surge could keep the boat from settling where you wish it to (surge is more of a problem while drying out alongside, than while careening.) Look for substantial uprights to support the boat – either the pilings of a wharf or a sea-wall – but the uprights do not have to be strong enough to support the total weight of the boat. If your boat floats perfectly level side-to-side, she would want to sit upright on her own when she dried, and if there was no wind, you could probably hold even a 40-footer (12.2m) in that position with only a few pounds of support.

Once you have found a place to dry out – preferably a spot with a firm bottom rather than a muddy one – you can stake down two timbers at low tide to make your own grid so that you can scrub and paint the bottom of your ballast keel. Be sure to add the height of any timbers to

2. In areas where tidal grids are common, bottom paints are formulated to work in quick scrub-and-paint situations.

your depth calculations to avoid being neaped. If the tidal range is within a foot of the draft of your hull, try to go onto a grid during a period of rising tides.

Position your boat over the grid, using well-spread springlines, and induce about a three-degree heel toward the dock pilings or seawall. We usually do this by leading a halyard to a line that is secured to the far side of the wharf, or by setting an anchor abeam and leading its warp to a halyard. Watch your boat as it settles to be sure it keeps this heel. If you plan to stay on the grid through another tide cycle, it could be necessary to ease off the halyard tension as the boat rises, unless your masthead line is led to a point well away from the boat.

If you cannot find a structure against which to lean the boat, or if you are not sure the one you have found is strong enough, and your boat has a fairly long keel, you can use beam anchors led from masthead halyards to hold the boat upright. A properly stayed mast will spread the strain through the rig easily. We once surveyed a worm-infested 35-footer (10.7m) in Porto Bello, Panama, by using anchors led from the masthead to each side, a line ashore, and a third anchor astern to keep her aligned facing square between the beam anchors. The tidal range was only 3 feet,

Figure 14-1. *Legs for taking the ground.*

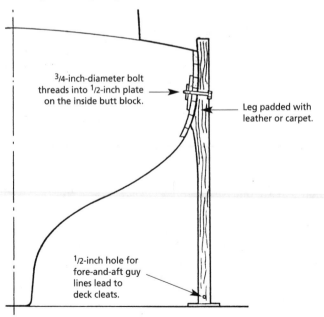

3/4-inch-diameter bolt threads into 1/2-inch plate on the inside butt block.

Leg padded with leather or carpet.

1/2-inch hole for fore-and-aft guy lines lead to deck cleats.

Photo 14-2. *(above left) The legs for this boat are cleverly splayed out to give a wider support base.*
Photo 14-3. *(above right) A steel boat naturally has to have galvanized pipe legs.*

but we were able to leave her positioned this way for three days so that temporary repairs could be done. This tidal work let the owner sail clear of the Caribbean before the hurricane season arrived.

A variation on this dry-out theme is legs. Yachts and working boats dry out on specially fitted legs all along the rivers of southern England. Most use legs positioned with bolts that thread into strong fittings in or near the chainplates, backed up with fore-and-aft preventer lines led to the bottom of the legs (Fig. 14-1). But you could use two 4 by 4 timbers lashed to the shrouds instead. Before using legs, it's essential to check that the seabed is firm and flat – not only where the keel will rest, but also where the legs will touch. For security, it pays to have an 8-inch-by-8-inch-by-1-inch plywood foot pad on each leg.

Even if you are able to use the tide for routine maintenance, there will be times when you need shipyard facilities. To practice preventive haulout procedures, you have to consider both the device that will lift your boat from the water and the cradle or supports she'll sit in once she's dry. From discussions with shipyard owners in more than three dozen countries, a conference with the local surveyor for Lloyd's of London, and our own experience, the consensus is that for safety a dry dock would be first choice, a floating dry dock second, then a vertical hoist, a marine railway, a Travelift, and last, a crane and lifting straps.

Since dry docks and floating dry docks are relatively difficult to find, our usual choice is a vertical hoist. On a vertical hoist, the boat can be settled into its cradle and lifted gently until it is about one-third dry. The supports and wedges can be checked at this time, before the boat is moved or the cradle is subjected to the vibrations of rolling along a track. Since the hoist lifts the boat to the level of the surrounding yard, there is no need to contend with a long haul up a slope.

It is this slope that can be the biggest concern on a marine railway. Without proper precautions, a boat can slide off the cradle while she is being hauled or relaunched. Because of the boat's concentrated weight, once the ways car starts moving along the slope, the boat will want to keep moving, even if the ways car jams or stops quickly. The most potentially catastrophic accident of our 11-year cruise on *Seraffyn* happened as she was being prepared for relaunch in Jamaica on a relatively steep marine railway. We had not been notified it was time to move her, so only one of our usual safety lines was in position. The yard men only planned to move her 30 or 40 feet aft to rest until the crew cleaned sand off the tracks farther down the slope. But the cradle didn't stop when they stopped pushing it. Instead, it picked up speed. The yard man didn't think to just let it run out into the water; instead, he panicked and locked the brake on his cable drum. The cradle stopped with a crash and *Seraffyn* slid back, bending the metal after-supports of the cradle. Only the single safety line kept her from falling completely off the cradle. Getting her back into an upright position, then repairing the damage (which fortunately was not structural) took four days. Without that single safety line, the whole boat could have tumbled off the cradle and been holed. After that shock, we began keeping safety lines in position whenever the wheels of any cradle were unchocked. This paid off royally 13 years later, when we were relaunching *Taleisin* after a haulout. Larry had secured two mooring lines, one each side of the boat from the forward cross member of the ways car aft through the stern hawsepipes onto the sheet winches. We tensioned them firmly. Since the shipyard owner encouraged what he called "both belt and braces," we also tied the upper part of the cradle arms together. Just as *Taleisin* was rumbling down the tracks, some youngsters ran onto the launching area. The ways car was stopped abruptly and *Taleisin* began to slide aft along the cradle. But her safety lines stopped her after she'd moved less than 6 inches aft. The only sign of the potential mishap was a scratch from a wedge that wiggled loose. Some shipyard owners might discourage your extra safety precautions, saying, "Don't you trust us?" But we've learned to persist in adding safety lines and being involved – if only for our own peace of mind and the feeling that we've done the best we can to protect our home and lifestyle.

If you are hauling out either with a vertical hoist or a marine railway, be sure the rails for the car carrying the cradle are at least 60 percent of your boat's beam apart. This wide base will make the whole arrangement more stable. Be sure the boat is firmly settled in the cradle before it is moved. When you move from side to side on deck, the boat will shake a bit, but it should not have any sideways movement. Any wedges or chocks should be secured with retaining pins, nails, or clamps before the rumbling move begins. Otherwise, the vibration could shake them loose. If the uprights supporting the boat look too light, tie the top ends together across the boat, using a block-and-tackle or a lanyard to tension the line. Once the boat is in its layup spot, check any wedges again and be sure the car wheels are chocked before you get a ladder and climb aboard.

Marine railways are the most common way of hauling yachts outside the continental United States. But Travelifts and cranes are becoming more common in other areas in the world. They are an efficient way of moving boats quickly and placing them anywhere in a storage area, free of the constraints of rail tracks. They make lifting fin-and-skeg boats easier, as the cradle supports for the bow and stern can be built when the boat is out of the water, so there is no guesswork about exactly what height they should be. Unfortunately, in our experience Travelifts have frequently been the cause of scuffed paint, cracked bulwarks, and broken impellers. Because they are relatively easy to operate, the operators tend to be less experienced than those working at marine railways in well-established shipyards. So we generally make Travelifts our second-to-last choice at haulout times. When we attended a launching at a Travelift yard run by Kevin Lidgard, a well-experienced, third-generation New Zealand shipwright, he told us, "Remember that the rated lifting weight painted on the Travelift machine is for a new machine with new cables and new lifting straps. It takes into account the safety factor necessary to compensate for jerky motions. But as the machine gets older and the cables wear, the safety factors decrease. It would be unwise to use a Travelift rated within 30 percent of your boat's total displacement (including the extra cruising gear that has it 5 or 6 inches down on its lines) unless the machine was relatively new or recently inspected and recertified." Preventer lines on the lifting straps should be arranged in a way that will keep the forward strap from sliding up the stem of the boat. Kevin had $5/8$-inch-diameter lines spliced onto his lifting straps. Once the straps were snugged up under the floating boat, these lines were led aft through chocks or fairleads at deck level and secured around cockpit winches. We also saw them secured before any boat was lifted from its cradle to begin its journey through the yard for relaunching. For a straight-keeled boat such as a centerboarder, these safety lines are tied between the lifting straps to keep them from spreading and slipping along the hull if the Travelift comes to a sudden stop.

Ideally, on a long-keeled hull, the lifting straps should be on the ends of the ballast keel, well clear of the rudder. We had to haul *Seraffyn* with a Travelift in Canada. I was on my own, without Larry, when the lifting took place, and the after strap had been placed only 8 inches from the end of the keel. The lift operator refused to lower the boat back into the water about 3 feet in order to move the strap forward. He gave me the "men know best" routine until I threatened to start shouting, 'Rape.' Two days later, he came by to apologize and said, "I never realized the back end of the keel would be so thin." It may feel embarrassing at the time, but insist that the straps be positioned where they belong before the boat is hanging over hard concrete. Remember that there is a conflict of interest in many commercial shipyards. The yard man is interested in getting his job done as quickly and easily as possible; you are interested in protecting your boat and its paint job. But it is your dreams and cruise that will be affected if things go wrong, not the lift operator's.

For a fin-and-skeg hull, be sure the straps are clear of the skeg and at the gently rounded section of the hull. Make a mark at deck level to indicate the forward and aft ends of your propeller assembly and any impellers or depth-sounder fittings, so the straps can be positioned clear of them.

To avoid the minor cosmetic damage often caused by the stretching of the lifting straps at relaunch time, we have had good-to-fair results with two layers of corrugated cardboard (18 inches by 30 inches) placed at the high-load points under the lifting straps. We wet the inner layer and hull so it sticks and stays put. Any strap slippage should then occur between the two dry layers of cardboard. For a chine boat, you should add cardboard and build shaped plywood protectors to keep the lifting straps from crushing into the edges of the chines.

The least safe way of hauling would be with a crane, where all of the lifting straps lead into a single cable. If this is your only choice, be sure the crane operator adds spreaders well above deck level so the straps are held out from your toerails or bulwarks. Without the spreaders, the rails could be crushed inward. The spreaders also reduce the amount of strap that will lie against the hull. The more length of lifting strap against the hull, the more chance of skidded-off paint.

WHERE THEY PUT YOUR BOAT

If you are hauled on a marine railway, you'll have little choice regarding the location of the boat unless the yard has a shuttle transfer system. But given a choice, ask to be well clear of other boats and near some shade. By making your wishes as clear as possible, your boat will be safer and you'll be less likely to have your paint ruined by overspray from painting operations on the boat next to you.

If the yard has a Travelift, ask that your boat be placed away from any intersections and away from the area near the lift. We watched a forklift operator hit the end of the bowsprit on a boat that was stored at a yard intersection in England. The collision caused the boat to twang like a bass fiddle. The damage was slight, but the nerves of the two people working inside their boat were badly shaken. For long stays, especially during stormy seasons, try to get your boat situated away from other sailboats. Request a position next to power craft, which have a lower center of gravity when on shore so are less likely to fall over in extreme winds. Avoid long rows of deep-draft sailboats, especially if their rigs are in place. The owner of an Australian cruising boat named *Domino* lost not only a year of cruising but also a lot of money when an 85-knot gust of wind from a mini-tornado hit his boat beam-on. She toppled against the boat next to her and started a catastrophe that ended with six boats crushed and lying on their bilges amid the shattered remains of their cradles. The owner did say he had commented to the yard people that his cradle, with its single-chain arm retainers, looked a bit light for his ferrocement boat. Had it been reinforced or backed up with extra supports, it might have avoided what came to be known around the waterfront as the "*Domino* effect."

SUPPORTING YOUR BOAT ON SHORE

To help judge whether the cradle your boat will be using is designed to take the stresses and strains of shipyard life, look at the drawings and photographs accompanying this chapter. In each case, the best cradles have the uprights triangulated in two directions, with the unsupported length of the upright never more than the supported length (Figs. 14-2

Figures 14-2 through 14-5.

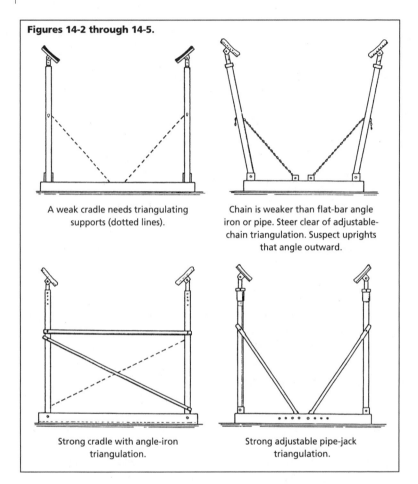

A weak cradle needs triangulating supports (dotted lines).

Chain is weaker than flat-bar angle iron or pipe. Steer clear of adjustable-chain triangulation. Suspect uprights that angle outward.

Strong cradle with angle-iron triangulation.

Strong adjustable pipe-jack triangulation.

through 14-5). If the cradle uprights are held in position and triangulated by chains instead of solid pipe, or if the arms angle even slightly outward, add supports (often called poppets) as soon as possible. In no case should the width across the base of any cradle be less than 70 percent of the beam of your boat.

The keel of any hull should be supported so that it is taking the majority of the weight of the boat. For a long-keeled boat, this would mean at least two heavy cross members under or very close to the ballast keel. For a fin-keel hull, a steel channel or trough the length of the keel is ideal.

A steel cradle should be well bolted or fully welded at all joints. A

Photo 14-4. *This cradle is definitely too narrow for the boat; extra side supports should be added. The longish keel will support the boat fore-and-aft.*

Photo 14-5. *A well-triangulated long cradle with adjustable legs and big carpeted pads against the hull. Proper job!*

wooden cradle should be secured with bolts and well triangulated, with as broad a base as possible. The adjustable pads or wedges that touch the hull of the boat should never be narrower than 6 inches by 6 inches; if

they don't conform to the shape of the hull, they could mar the boat.

If, instead of a cradle, uprights are used, be sure they are firmly wedged or screw-tightened so they cannot sink into the ground or skid out from under the boat. Use at least three per side on boats between 28 and 40 feet (8.5m-12.2m) plus a support for the bow and stern overhangs. Before you climb on board your cradled or poppeted boat, step back and look at the whole arrangement. If there is a strong wind, will the vibration loosen or start any poppet wiggling?

Photo 14-6. *The legs for this deep-draft hull are extended to their maximum. Extra supports should be added.*

Photo 14-7. *With a short fin keel like this, lots of supports are needed to hold up the ends of the boat.*

If it does, are the poppets set in such a way that they will not fall out from under the hull? They should have a tendency instead to fall or wiggle inward. Consider the squared area of the pads lying against the hull and make sure none of them look like they are going to apply too much point pressure. This is important; we saw a fiberglass boat with an obvious flat spot along one bilge after it was left for a winter with the aft starboard poppet carrying too much of the weight.

A final safety precaution rests completely on your shoulders. Before you move any support arms or poppets to paint or sand, contact the yard manager. Either have him assign yard personnel to do the moving or have him approve your proposed method. That way, he is accepting legal responsibility for the change, and any consequent problems.

HOW FREQUENT IS YARD DAMAGE?

Shipyard accidents, like automobile collisions, theoretically shouldn't happen, but because human beings are involved, accidents occur. Although the operators of better haulout yards will insist this chapter portrays a bleak situation, that their crews rarely damage even toerails or paintwork, they can all cite examples of major damage occurring in other yards. Probably because we voyage and talk with a lot of sailors who have had to do their haulouts away from home, we have heard of and seen far more accidents than those we have mentioned here, and some have

Photo 14-8. *Taking responsibility for our floating home.*

occurred in yards of very high repute. One common thread ran through most of the serious accidents. The people in charge at the time were usually "new marina" boat handlers or financially uninterested parties – i.e., not the boatyard owner or the boat owner. To change the odds so they are highly in your favor at haulout time, it pays to know how your boat should be handled. You can use this knowledge to choose the best facilities. We've been most comfortable at well-established shipyards with long-term reputations to protect, or in locations where the owner of the yard takes a personal interest in the haulout and relaunch. Once you leave home waters, it is harder to learn about the reputation of local haulout yards, and your choice of yards might be quite limited, so the chances of damage could increase. If you aren't comfortable with the yard facilities and there is sufficient tidal range, it might be better in the long run to take full personal responsibility for the situation and set your boat on a tidal grid.

If you use a shipyard and there is a language barrier, find a translator to be with you at haulout time. Have a drawing of the underbody of your hull to show the shipyard operator before he starts to lift your boat. If you do not feel mechanically qualified to make definite decisions about the safety of yard equipment or procedures, ask lots of questions. If the personnel say, "Don't worry," or "We're insured," it is time to worry. If you are told that cradle setup is billed by the hour, as it is in Tahiti, allow an extra half hour in your estimate of costs so you aren't inclined to rush personnel. If you hear of a particular yard that is out of the way but highly recommended, make the detour. A hundred-mile detour, even a 500-mile one, could lead to a pleasant shipyard experience instead of one that creates the kind of hassles you went cruising to avoid.

PREVENTION IS EASIER THAN CURE

The planned two-year voyage was nearing its midpoint. WB and his wife had enjoyed their reach through the South Pacific. As the cyclone season neared, they headed south toward the safe haven of New Zealand, where their plan was to haul the boat for two weeks of maintenance work, tour New Zealand by car, then sail westward four months later, when the cyclone danger was past. A misplaced moment of politeness changed all that. And even though W was not responsible for the near-tragic accident that almost cost one man his life and definitely shortened the Swan 55's voyage, he said, "I did it before and I did it now. Just because I was going into a professionally run shipyard, I relaxed my grip, stepped back, and left the responsibility for my boat in their hands."

The Swan 55 had been hoisted from the water and settled in a cradle that looked a bit small for her. The yard men said the cradle had been built to hold a local 60-foot racing boat. When Mrs. B complained that the boat seemed to rock a bit too much, she was told, "Don't worry, little lady; if we drop it, we'll buy you a new one." Even when she and W complained that they saw what looked like cracks in the cradle arms, the yard people assured them, "Don't worry, we know what we are doing."

Ten days later, a New Zealand woman who owned a boat farther along in the yard instigated a rather noisy screaming match when gales were forecast. She demanded extra supports, saying she'd steal them if necessary. She got them. But the owner of the Swan 55, like many socially aware visitors, wanted to be polite and not cause a scene, so they dropped the matter.

The gales arrived, 35 knots with occasional gusts over 40. The highest winds recorded by the meteorological office two miles away were gusts of 50 knots. At lunchtime, the Swan 55 slowly began to topple. With a horrendous crash it went over, throwing her owners and four lunch guests right across the cabin. Her rig hit the rig of *Sappho*, a 40-footer (12.2m) in the next cradle. *Sappho*, too, went over, and only luck saved her owner. The crash sent *Sappho's* rudder flying, and it knocked him unconscious so that he, fortunately, fell between the keel and the turn of the bilge. But for a few inches, his head would have been crushed.

Immediate inspection showed that the cracked arms of the cradle

Photo 14-9. *This can spoil your whole year!*

holding the Swan 55 had not failed, but the opposite ones had. The yard owner lost no time in getting the boat craned upright, her rig removed, and the battered hull shipped off to another yard, where repairs to her interior and side could begin immediately. The repairs took four months, cost $50,000, and were satisfactory. That was the only easy part of the solution. Though the original yard immediately said, "Our insurance will cover everything," the insurance company did not agree, pointing out a clause in the contract that said they were not responsible if, "there is a design failure in any yard equipment." The cradle holding the Swan with her 8-foot-plus draft had been designed for a centerboarder drawing only 6 feet; the shipyard crew had welded the cradle-arm extension. Problems also surfaced with a second clause, which stipulated that there had to be a contract between the yacht owner and the shipyard for the yard and its insurer to be held responsible.

So, instead of being a carefree cruiser, for six months WB and his wife were stuck in the city fighting legal battles in a foreign country where, even though the language was familiar, the laws and customs were not. The insurance company finally did pay – outside the doors to the courtroom, literally minutes before the case was to be heard. Fortunately for W, he had money to live on while he fought, the patience to fight, and the funds to finance immediate repairs to his boat. Without those extra funds, W might not have been able to hire a lawyer and would have had to wait until he received the insurance settlement before he could start repairs. So the six-month delay experienced by W could have become closer to a year.

In looking at other shipyard problems, we've learned that this is one area where insurance coverage is ridden with loopholes. Many cruising policies do not cover storage on shore, assuming the shipyard will have coverage. Even non-offshore policies can have what we call " no-mans'-land traps." While *Taleisin* was under construction, we had builder's and sea-trial insurance. Specific clauses said that while being shifted or transported by anyone other than the builder, she would not be covered. The trucking firm warned us their coverage started only when her cradle actually was resting on their truck or rollers, and it ended whenever shipyard employees began using shipyard equipment to offload her: "If something happens while her cradle is resting half on our trailer, half on their ways car, you'd have a possible fight on your hands with three insurance companies trying to get out of paying." For insured sailors – but especially for uninsured voyagers, as we are now – here are some pointers that could make any battle more equitable:

1. Protect yourself. Check the reputation of any shipyard or boat mover before using their facilities. Ask if they carry insurance. Inspect their equipment and watch their boat-handling methods.

2. Get a signed note agreeing to the terms of the haulout; be sure the note includes your name, your boat's name, and the signature of a yard representative. This doesn't require a formal form; it can even be the quotation of costs with your proposed haulout date and time. This will serve as proof that the shipyard has accepted responsibility for the job.

3. If the shipyard is not insured, remember that you may have to prove "gross negligence" on the part of the shipyard to make a claim in court. (This is very hard to prove.)

4. If you intend to leave your boat stored on land, provide your own insurance. No shipyard policies can cover theft, the most common storage-yard problem.

5. If you carry insurance, try to have it written so that damages to your boat are covered by your own insurer and repairs can start immediately.

6. If an accident does occur, take detailed photographs immediately. Show your boat in relation to others in the yard to indicate that the accident was specific to your boat and that others were not damaged by the same winds or forces. This proves the accident could not be called an act of God.

7. Learn how your boat should be handled and stick to your guns, even if you are made to feel like a nuisance. Even if there are no insurance hassles, even if the shipyard does the repairs caused by faulty haulout procedures or equipment, as WB found, no one will pay for the cruising time he lost, the seasons he missed, or the guilt he felt as his boat, which had served him so well, crashed to the ground.

EMOTIONAL COST CONTROL AS YOU VOYAGE

IN OFFSHORE VOYAGING, AS IN LIFE, you need to learn to walk before you try to run, to practice your sailing and cruising skills before you set off across oceans. If you skin your knees where you can easily find a Band-Aid, then try again; you will be able to consider those small bruises as part of the growing process. If you gain experiences and skills close to home, and learn to overcome each problem before you set off on the Big Voyage, you will watch your confidence – and your crew's confidence in you – grow. Then, once you have made that first foray across an ocean, you can begin planning the next, bolder journey.

The wonderful thing about cruising is that it is a constant learning experience. There are always new goals, new challenges and destinations. The chapters in this section show that getting away is only the first step. You'll be headed toward a broad horizon of new friendships and new adventures.

C H A P T E R
15
VOYAGING WITH CONFIDENCE ALONG THE TRADEWINDS

I remember when my dad, the only sailing enthusiast in our family at that time, used to drive the whole family a hundred miles once a year to rent an 18-foot daysailer for two hours of sailing at Newport Beach, California. "Come on Lin, let's go out into the ocean," my brother would shout as we ran down the dock. We were only 8 and 6 years old then and we'd point to the sea, a direction I later learned was dead downwind. "No," Dad would say with a longing glance toward that open expanse of adventure, "we'll beat to windward first, then reach around the upper bay. If we run downwind, we might not get back in my $20 time limit, and if we don't, we won't have enough money left for hamburgers on the way home." We'd groan and settle in, hiding under the shelter of the tiny foredeck as Dad tacked contentedly up the bay, spray wetting the place we'd have preferred to be.

His words kept coming back years later as *Taleisin* grew to reality and voyage planning began to occupy Larry and me. We wanted to go to the South Pacific. We'd voyaged east around the world on our little cutter *Seraffyn* and during more than 11 years of sailing had never once been below the equator. We'd delivered a dozen boats across oceans yet never seen the South Pacific. Besides, we had an invitation to visit two friends in New Zealand. They were convinced we'd enjoy seeing that distant, slow-paced country where sailing was a national sport. Then there was the lure of Papeete. Dozens of voyaging friends had described their lazy days moored along the quay while pareau-clad beauties flashed by on motorscooters only 50 feet away. It intrigued me to think that Papeete was the main city of an oceanic nation that covered almost a quarter of the globe, yet it had less land than the state of Vermont.

"If we head for Europe again, we might never get to the South

Pacific," Larry agreed as our sea trials came to a close. My answer summed up the lure that had ensnared many new sailors who choose this route: "just for once, let's do something the easy way. Let's sail downwind. Let's take the Milk Run."

We're not sure where the term *Milk Run* came from, or who first used it to describe the route from Southern California to Mexico then to the Marquesas and on through the Tuamotus to Tahiti. Voyagers from Europe and the east coast of the United States pick up the route (also called the "Hiscock Highway," after legendary voyagers Eric and Susan Hiscock) at the Galapagos, then jump on the equatorial countercurrent and easterly tradewinds for what promises to be a sleigh ride to paradise.

We headed out, and we did have what amounted to a sleigh ride through the tropics. The winds were rarely forward of the beam and the weather was warm – sometimes too warm. We found wonderful skin diving and added the nights at Lou Pescadou's café to our list of favorite times and places. But after sailing on the Milk Run and beyond, after seeing a large percentage of new voyagers' illusions dismantled piece by piece, we've tried to come up with a balanced assessment of this popular route.

Like most voyagers, I was eager to taste the pleasures of tradewind sailing.

Sixteen years earlier, in 1969, when we first set off wandering on *Seraffyn*, we avoided the South Pacific route just because it led dead downwind across vast areas of oceans. I was absolutely new to voyaging. Larry had a few hard windward journeys under his belt – up the coast of Baja California into the 20-to-25 knot "Mexican trades," plus a voyage to Hawaii and the return trip along the blustery northern edge of the Pacific High. "Until you are completely sure you enjoy this life, I don't think we should get too far from home, too far downwind," he told me. "Let's stick to Mexico, where we can avoid long passages." Looking back now, I can chuckle at his slightly devious plan. By avoiding long passages for the first two years of our voyage, by letting me feel I could always return home easily – by land or by sea – he seduced me into loving the cruising life so much that by the time I did have to face a hard beat to windward, the 450-mile passage from Colombia, South America, to Jamaica – I managed it and still wanted to cruise afterward.

In the spring of 1985, when we set sail from Mexico for the Marquesas on *Taleisin*, more than 70 other yachts did the same; for the overwhelming majority of those sailors, this was the first voyage of more than 100 miles from land, the first time they had to keep watches for more than two or three nights in a row. Most of these sailors planned the downwind phase of the voyage, never considering that to get home from a downwind sail, you must sometime, somehow, go to windward – unless you circumnavigate the whole Pacific basin. Even a round-the-world voyage along this route still leaves you closehauled from Panama to California for the homeward leg. After 2,800 miles of running to reach the Marquesas, then 800 miles more to the Tuamotus and on to Tahiti, a return trip to any point on the West Coast of the United States means first laying close on the wind for 2,200 miles to Hawaii. Then it's on to California, another slog northward hard on the wind in search of the northwesterlies for a second voyage of 2,200 to 2,500 miles.

One disillusioned sailor bought us a drink at a café across the street from his boat in Papeete and sighed, "I hated the passages, tired me out and left me scared." He was not alone. We met or heard about at least 10 first-time voyagers from the West Coast who were looking for delivery crews or trying to sell their boats in Papeete. Fortunately, this particular sailor reconsidered after a month of rest and recreation. He compared delivery costs, and sale prices for boats in Tahiti. Then he screwed up his courage and set off northbound for Hawaii, where he sold his boat and returned to work. His next goal was to buy a coastal cruising boat for exploring shoal and river areas. He later wrote us: "I'm glad I finished

The pleasures of life along the tradewinds have changed little through the years. The anchorages may be more crowded, but the Polynesian dancers have not lost one bit of their charm.

what I started but I'm just not an offshore voyager. I got bored out there, then I got worried and it became no fun, so why do it?" He agreed that a trial voyage from San Diego, offshore to San Francisco, would have helped him plan less ambitious, more enjoyable cruising.

The more successful voyagers we met along this route had already made other passages or had the time and/or the money to contemplate the alternatives open to them. For those with only a year or two of cruising time, Tahiti was the gateway to thousands of islands and dozens of cultures. They then planned to sail south to New Zealand, where it is relatively inexpensive to arrange to ship a boat home on the deck of a ship. (The costs for a delivery team would be far higher than those for shipping if a boat is under 40 feet on deck.) In 1997, the cost for freighting a boat from Auckland to any port on the U.S. West Coast was $5,000 to $7,000, including mast removal, cradle, and insurance. Auckland has two shipyards next to the main marina. They are accustomed to building the necessary supports and cradles and ships go directly to the United States bi-monthly. Costs are about 25 percent lower in Auckland than they are in any port in Australia. Among the 18 voyagers who shipped boats home from New Zealand in 1987, 12 had come along the Milk Run when we did. A few were using this alternative as the planned end to a wonderful downwind voyage and a few had to quit because of unexpected family or business emergencies, but most chose this option because they couldn't face the beat back home.

Our voyage along the first long leg of the Milk Run was amazing: wing-and-wing day and night averaging 140 to 175 miles a day. It took 16 1/2 days to cover the 2,550 miles from Mexico's offshore island of Socorro to Taiohae Bay in the Marquesas; the weather was sunny and warm, but we rarely had the steady, dream-like trade-wind sailing we'd read about. We hit a year of strong winds – technically called reinforced trades. Instead of the average 12 to 16 knots of normal years, our winds for nine months of sailing through Polynesia averaged 20 to 25 knots. Our passages were quite fast, but when we finally dropped south of the tropics, we were glad to have some comfortable, light-air sailing. Other South Pacific veterans told us of years when the opposite was true. When El Niño currents caused the trades to die altogether, some had to beat 35 or 45 days to reach the Marquesas, instead of running quickly from Mexico as we did.

Our first landfall on the Milk Run still ranks as the most spectacular view we've ever seen: the jutting black peaks of Nuku Hiva, the steep, green-covered, black-stone cliffs and leaping waterfalls, the complete

The warm waters of Polynesia offer up the delight of our favorite eating fish, the mahi-mahi. But, store-bought provisions are not as easy to find in many of the outer islands.

absence of traces of human habitation, the two 50-foot dozing whales we passed as we swept down the eastern side of the island. Then a 10-pound tuna took our lure and leapt like silver fire above the white-tipped rollers. To the south, the almost-phallic peaks of Ua Pou came into view. This is a sight that all ocean voyagers should see once in their lives.

We arrived off Taiohae Bay just after sunset. The abrupt tropical change from day to night found us making the first long tack between the pair of volcanic caps standing sentinel just outside this port of entry. The

5-mile-visibility sectored red-and-white light guided our ever-shortening tacks up the long bay, and as we came to anchor, our thoughts turned to all the fresh food I'd buy the next day – tomatoes, ice cream, a good steak, crunchy fruit.

But our gastronomic dreams were not satisfied, and, in fact, we were very glad we'd bought all of the stores *Taleisin* could hold before we left Southern California. The provisions available in the smaller island groups throughout the South Pacific not only were extremely limited in variety but also very expensive. In Nuku Hiva, all we found were bananas, shallots and over-the-hill potatoes. Buying tomatoes or cabbage meant getting up before dawn and walking a mile, hoping to be the first person there when the local farmer checked his one-acre field looking for ripe vegetables.

Algerian table wines were plentiful and cheap, especially in the one-liter plastic bottles commonly called Château Plastique by the cruising fleet. Some frozen foods could be found, also. This is not to imply that sailors arriving in these islands without stores would starve; they wouldn't, but corned beef and canned fruits are the only reasonably priced provisions available in the shops.

Within a month we were anxious to press on toward the variety of foods we'd heard awaited us in Papeete, but we stopped in the Tuamotus and enjoyed the unique hospitality of the French-run hotels. Yachtsmen were made welcome there, since their anchored boats livened the view and their custom at the hotel bar kept the place interesting. Some hotels in these islands even offered free laundry service to lure visiting yachtsmen away from their competitors. Within a short time, we felt like we'd become "local color." The chef at the Kia Ora Hotel on Rangiroa in the Tuamotus told us that the captain of the inter-island freighter sometimes had a private stock of fresh fruit he sold to earn extra money. We chased the semi-monthly freighter but were only able to buy one kilo each of crisp apples and pears. We gave one pear to the hotel bartender as a gift. Later that evening, he presented us with a bottle of good French wine in exchange.

Although there is a bakery on almost every inhabited island in Polynesia, the bakers often make only enough for local customers. If half a dozen cruising sailors arrive at the same time, there will be a shortage, and regular customers come first. So here was a trade-off: You could wait in line, fingers crossed, or bake your own bread in the heat of the tropics. Fortunately, the flour and yeast sold throughout the islands was inexpensive and good quality.

Ice is available in some of the islands, but where it wasn't, shopkeepers were willing to freeze 20-pound blocks in each of three plastic wash basins that we keep stacked in the bilge for this purpose. Their average charge was 50 cents a block if we bought provisions at their shop. On the other hand, refrigeration mechanics are almost unheard-of outside of Papeete and Fiji, and even those have few spare parts on hand. So be sure your freezer unit is in good working order if you sail along this hot route; carry spare freon and parts or be prepared to switch to ice (i.e., have a well-insulated box equipped with a water drain).

Then came Papeete. We have never tasted finer French pâté, more wonderful freshly made ice cream and cheeses. Fresh food prices ran about 50 percent higher than in California or Florida; canned provisions cost 100 to 200 percent more. Much more reasonably priced provisions were later available in American Samoa, Fiji, New Zealand, and Australia. Fresh provisions, in fact, were cheaper in most of the islands west of French Polynesia.

A provisioning rule we learned through many years of cruising held true on the Milk Run. When you see it, buy it. If you spot your favorite variety of Greek olives when you stroll past a shelf, buy enough to stock your locker right then and there. You may not see any more for months.

Our biggest regret as we voyaged through French Polynesia was that neither of us spoke French, thus severely limiting our encounters with local people. Even though in other parts of the world, English is the second language, here it's French and only a few islanders speak a bit of English as their third language. The people in small villages tried to make us welcome, but the language barrier prevented close encounters. The French-speaking crew of the Canadian yacht *Skye II* lived with a family on a Tuamotus atoll for three months, learning to spear sharks, weave fine baskets, build woven homes. They rendezvoused with us in Bora Bora full of stories of their adventures ashore that made us regret our lack of linguistic skills.

There are two distinct types of voyagers along the Milk Run – the convoy enthusiasts and the independents. Both can have a good time, but both will have very different experiences. Those in convoy often set sail from each port together, keep in close radio contact, choose the same arrival port, and plan their entertainments together. Some of these people become lifelong friends, and some continue around the world together, but since someone in any group will always need or want to do some shopping, these convoys quite often end up anchored near the lure and expense of hotels and shoreside restaurants. The independent loners can stay away from provisioning centers for a month or more, so they often can explore the more secluded anchorages and get to know the local people on a more personal basis. Some even learned to speak a bit of Tahitian or French.

It seemed a common complaint that there are no beautiful deserted island anchorages left along the Milk Run, yet loners told of wonderful dream-like settings only 20 to 30 miles from the fleshpots of the cities. The skin diving was far better at these special places, since the locals have decimated the fish populations along the reefs within rowing distance of their homes. The loners did miss some of the raft-ups and excursions planned regularly by the convoyers during their morning radio schedules, but since each customs port in the islands was essentially a funnel for foreign cruisers, the loners did meet up for the fun, partying, and gossip to be found whenever a group of voyagers gets together.

We had been lent a set of U.S. hydrographic charts for this voyage and when we reached Tahiti, we purchased excellent French charts. These detailed French charts enabled us to sail inside the barrier reefs of places like Raiatea, where we wandered for 25 miles to find the highlight hidey-hole of our cruise – a spot where two favorite cruising friends joined us in quiet seclusion to anchor in 10 feet of water on a sandy bottom absolutely clear of coral heads. We dove on a reef face that dropped off sheer from eight feet to over 100 feet, only 100 yards from where our boats lay perfectly sheltered from the thundering, rolling seas outside the reef.

Many cruisers we met had invested in reduced-size charts sold by printers who capitalized on the fact that nautical charts are not protected by copyright laws. After comparing charts, we decided that the copies reduced to one-third normal size are potentially dangerous. What looked like smudges on the small charts showed as reefs or rocks on our larger ones. Soundings were hard to read, with no color differentiation; identification of potential anchorages was more difficult. Before investing in these reduced charts, be sure to compare them to the originals.

If at all possible, plan your haulouts before you set sail along the Milk Run; the next good places are New Zealand, and Fiji on this route. Haulout facilities in Tahiti are well run but expensive, and their schedules are usually very full. To the west, haulouts are possible in American Samoa and at Neiafu, Tonga. The Samoan yard is a commercial tuna fisherman's yard, and prices are high. The Tongan yard, run by an experienced yachtsman, has only one ways car and one slipway, so again schedules are tight. Fijian yards are good, but the unstable political situation and currency problems mean that many basic yacht-repair supplies are not available.

As with shipyards, safe places to leave your boat while you fly home on business are few and far between, especially if you need a place where your boat will be secure against potential cyclones. Along with this, airfares can be very pricey. So fly-in guests will be far less frequent than they would be if you cruised Mexico or the Caribbean.

Aside from the practical aspects, what were our impressions of this almost-trackless expanse of ocean? We'll never forget the early morning chats with Amelia, the Tahitian woman (born on Pitcairn Island) who rowed over each morning to share a special piece of fruit and a mischievous story or two. Nor the spell of a three-day, honeymoon-style twentieth anniversary spent slowly pedaling our bicycles around the brooding peaks of Moorea during the day and dining and sleeping in luxurious thatch-roofed hotel rooms at night. Nor the sight of Larry wrestling with a six-foot octopus on his diving spear at an isolated anchorage in back of Bora Bora. Nor the magnificent image of beautiful, strong Tahitian women and men skimming across the lagoons during the Bastille Day paddling races. But like many others told us, west of French Polynesia, beyond the Milk Run, beyond the heavily promoted tourist areas, lay the real magic of South Pacific cruising.

Some New Zealand friends preparing for a cruise came to visit us and outlined their plans: "We've decided to pack up and head straight off to windward for five days next month, then turn and come home and fix anything that doesn't work right, fix any deck leaks exposed by being hard on the wind. Then we'll do it again. Then we'll be ready to cruise, because if we aren't afraid to go to windward, we will never have to worry about going home if and when we want to." We couldn't agree more. It's an old cliché that even a cardboard box can sail downwind, even a novice sailor can get to Tahiti along the Milk Run. But experience and preparation, along with windward sailing ability, can make the voyage a true Milk Run, full of the rich cream that is the dream of any sailor.

CHAPTER

16

THE PSYCHOLOGY AND PHILOSOPHY OF LONG-TERM VOYAGERS

"DID YOU HEAR Sandy and Andy got married up in Samoa?" Jan commented as six of us lounged in *Taleisin's* oil-lit cabin. "That's great," Larry said. He adjusted the cabin heater to fight off the winter chill and went on, "I'm pretty sure it will be a good match: they've been sailing together for 10 years that I know of."

"Did you see *Jakaranda's* forward cabin before Andy and Sandy left Tonga that first time?" Russell asked. "They couldn't get in it. It was full of baskets and mats their Tongan friends gave them." The stories went on; tales of accidental rendezvous when a week or two slipped by in company with someone you met only because you chose to visit one island instead of another; stories of a crazy excursion to try whitewater rafting that left nine ocean voyagers white-knuckled and willing to face even a Tasman Sea crossing before setting foot on another river.

This was an unexpected rendezvous with two voyaging couples we'd met in Tonga five years earlier. By chance, we'd all been in Sydney, Australia: Larry and I as we worked to earn funds for our next year's voyaging: Russ and Michelle Minto as they began their fourth offshore voyage with two young daughters on a boat they'd just finished building. Peter and Jan Metherall had just driven up from Melbourne, where they were earning funds to let them set off for "lots longer than a year next time."

As dinner settled and red wine mellowed the mood, the conversation seemed to drift away from tales that made us laugh to those about the basic underlying realities of an offshore voyaging life. "I heard you got caught in an early cyclone off Fraser Island a few years back," someone said. My description of lying to a parachute anchor for 2 $1/2$ days, then beating against 40-knot winds for another two, only to encounter breaking seas across the entrance to the only safe harbor in reach, evoked other stories of hassles with uncomprehending officials, of being trapped in miserable anchorages for days by foul weather, of discomfort and loneliness, of nights when thoughts of dragging anchors kept the weariest sailor from sleeping. As we listened to these stories, I began to wonder why some people are addicted to crossing oceans, to inviting problems into their lives, to living with the only constant being change.

It is easy to understand why people spend years dreaming and preparing for their first long voyage – adventure, a reason to chuck work for a year or two, an excuse to sail as much as they want instead of just for an hour or two on weekends, a goal. Larry's inspiration was John Guzzwell's story of sailing off on a self-built 20-footer (6.1m) with $500 in his pocket, to return five years later with $300 still intact. It showed him the one way he could satisfy his urge to travel on a working man's wages. For me, that first voyage had been a chance to be different from my civil-service-oriented family background. For other friends, it was an opportunity to show their children the outside world, to influence their early years.

But of 10,000 people who dream of setting off cruising, maybe 1,000 get their boat and life together and sample adventures in far-off ports. Of that 1,000, probably only 100 stay away from home for two or three or five years. The vast majority of that successful group of 100 voyagers return to their home base feeling sated and complete, ready to settle into the life they left behind or eager to move on to some new scheme or dream. Though many of those who completed a successful cruise look back with fond memories of days spent blissfully snorkeling along a pristine coral reef, or evenings listening to the chants of Polynesian revelers and say, "Someday I'll be off again," not many do it. From our observations, that number could safely be set at 5 or 10 percent – people who, like Eric and Susan Hiscock, set off on voyage after voyage, seeming more at home anchored in a foreign port than seated next to a warm fire in their own hometown.

So, as we absorb the fact that our eight-year old rigging wire has to be replaced – which means another month's work before we can safely face the unpredictable winds of the Bass Straits – I ask Larry why people like us go a second or third time. It would probably be easier – physically and mentally – to do just about anything else. "Short memories," is his simple reply.

Michelle Minto is no more helpful as she tries to herd two unruly, slightly tired youngsters into a dinghy full of groceries without destroying the eggs that threaten to slide off a seat. "Suburban life just doesn't hold any real interest for us," she says.

For someone like myself, born with gypsy blood prickling through my veins, it is difficult to be objective about "repeat offenders." Many we know are not always ones the sea has treated kindly. In fact, an overwhelming number have cruised beyond the moderate weather of the tradewind belt and have chosen to test themselves against the Roaring Forties or endured passages to windward to reach destinations one- time voyagers usually reach by road or airplane.

The Bushnells, who raised two girls during a seven-year circumnavigation on their 31-footer (9.5m) *Dove*, rolled repeatedly and were dismasted in storms near South Africa's Agulhas Current. Yet five years after completing that voyage, they set off again, along with a young son who had been born in Africa. That time, their goal was a voyage to the north of Japan and then the Aleutian Islands. Mike Kris beat for 35 days to reach the Marquesas when an El Niño year reversed the tradewinds, yet he set off again and again in 55-year-old *Gilpie* to cross the Tasman Sea or traverse the Cook Strait, the last time with his wife Barbara and year-old son on board. No, fair-weather stories are not a common thread among second-timers. In fact, we've heard more stories of wonderful sailing from one-timers than from those who keep on doing it. I wonder if it has anything to do with the feeling of sheer accomplishment that comes from coping with a definable problem. Even the fiercest storm lasts only a day or three, and, like every voyage, has a definite beginning and end. This is in direct contrast to life on shore, where problems with jobs, family, and governmental bureaucracies seem to drag on with little hope of complete resolution. I've become addicted to this aspect of voyaging. Set a goal, begin, act, end. I crave the feeling of losing sight of land and knowing that nothing I have forgotten to do, to buy, or to bring along matters, not until this voyage is over. More than once, I've been tempted to slow the boat as a landfall approaches so we can sustain this feeling of being in a world organized only by ourselves and the weather. But like the person caught up in an exciting novel, I also long to rush to the end to see how it all finishes, to enjoy the sense of completion. Most addicted voyagers (AVs) say the same, commenting on their impatience with the seemingly insolvable problems on shore.

AVs rarely are blessed with much money; wealth actually seems to guarantee limited-duration voyages. Larry, in his succinct way says, "Why

After five years of voyaging, Niki Perryman and Jamie Morrison who have sailed from Sydney, Australia on their Lion Class 35-footer, found the desire to travel off the normal cruising route lead them to choose a winter in Northern Norway. The people and experiences they had there made them even more addicted than before.

should anyone cook and shop and take care of themselves in the confines of a boat when they could just as easily stay in the Hilton and be waited on?" But I wonder if it is the need to work along the way that keeps people involved, gets them off their boats and into local life, where they satisfy a need to feel viable, capable of turning their hands and minds to new trades, new conditions. I look at Andy and Sandy Peterson, who made friends throughout the Pacific by building sails and sailcovers. Their work breaks not only got them in touch with local people but also gave them a change from moving on, a chance to have mail catch up with them, to have friends visit without the problems of coordinating flight schedules and cruising plans. Those with independent incomes often have no excuse to stop for five or six months in one place, so they can complete a circumnavigation in two or three years, sticking pretty close to a predetermined sailing plan. In contrast, the most common news we get from AVs on limited funds is that a completely different plan has emerged because of someone they met as they worked for "freedom chips" in unexpected places.

AVs are not, as a rule, highly organized people. The reality of a cruising life means that plans, both big and small, must often be rearranged. Weather can delay a passage by weeks. A worn piece of gear or the need for a haulout can mean diverting from one destination to another where supplies or communications are better. An invitation to visit a new acquaintance's farm for a few days can coincide with a departure date – turn down that invitation and you might miss the highlight of your cruise. Since I thrive on organizing anything that stands still, this aspect of long-term voyaging has led to internal conflict that is, after 30 years, only partially resolved. "Go with the tide: there's no deadline to meet, no fortune to be lost if you change your tidy little plans," Larry has often repeated. "But if you miss this opportunity to explore, to enjoy, it may never come by again."

This deep-down sense of curiosity is a common thread among AVs. They delight in dropping into people's lives for a week or a month to see the mechanics underlying another society's organization. Pete Sutter, a well-known San Francisco sailmaker who went off wandering the Pacific on 37-foot (11.3m) *Wild Spirit* for seven years, beat (yes, *beat*) back to the same isolated Fijian island three different times to spend three seasons teaching the women sailmaking and helping the local men refine their sailing canoes. "Doesn't it make you feel good, helping those islanders?" I asked Pete. "That's not it," he answered. "I like being part of their village life. It's good to stop being a modern yachtie and see what it's really like using a canoe to gather your food, earn your living."

The opposite side of this coin is that few AVs are easily bored, though they may get restless when outside influences dictate inaction. I once thought it odd that the two of us could sail into a quiet cove and let five days or a week slip by before we launched the dinghy to go ashore and explore. But other AVs tell how much they enjoyed a week or month when they read good books or tended to some hobby, only pausing to throw together a meal. Leslie Swann describes her fondest memories of three different voyages, including one around The Horn, as those quiet times when she could devote hour after hour to the quilting that for her is more addiction than hobby.

Handicrafts, handiness: most AVs are practical people, mechanically inclined, more interested in solving physical problems than in playing mind games. I remember Larry's excitement at the prospect of building a new boat when the plans arrived in Malta seven years into our voyage on *Seraffyn*. "I guess I'm a bit bored with this boat," he'd finally admitted. "I've solved the problems on her, maximized every inch of storage, got the rig working as I want it. Now there's only maintenance to do – no improvements, no new technical challenges."

In contrast, one of the main reasons a single voyage proves to be sufficient for many sailors is the frustration of dealing with the technical hassles inherent in offshore-voyaging equipment. The people who are successful enough to buy a cruising boat could also afford to buy good-quality home appliances, which gave them little concern. Ashore, they bought that refrigerator and forgot about it for 10 years. Afloat, the same type of appliance can prove endlessly unreliable, and no amount of money will guarantee its success. The reason is simple: Refrigerators for houses are built by the millions. Huge companies have large research and service departments to ensure their reliability. But even the most popular equipment for use on cruising boats is produced in limited runs of, at most, 1,000 items. So the relatively untested, unproven mechanical or electrical items on a boat become a source of insecurity if you are dependent on them and unable to fix them yourself, or unable to find parts or service people in foreign ports. One excellent sailor said once was enough because, "I hated being hostage to the only person in Tahiti who could repair a transmission like mine. The more I look at what could break down on this boat and give me problems, the more uncomfortable I get." A boringly similar strand of conversation emerges as you talk with AVs – simplicity. Paul Johnson, on his 40-foot (12.2m) double-ended *Venus*, came to visit us in New Zealand – 19 years after we'd first sighted each other off the entrance to St. George Harbour in Bermuda. Paul was eager to show us how he'd made this boat even simpler than the 28-footer we'd known. "It's got to be simple so it's ready to go any time I am," he said. "That's why I live on a boat, so I can move any time I want to." He has proved this by sailing across the Atlantic four times in one year – just because something happening on the far side sounded intriguing.

A lot of people prefer a life with preset organization, a reason to get up each morning besides thirst or hunger. The steep learning curve of a first long voyage requires a schedule that is almost as rigorous as that in the busiest life on shore. But the second time out, the learning curve flattens to a large degree, and some people find themselves sinking into a sort of lethargy, with no good reason to move on. We've seen them in many easy-living foreign ports. They arrived, planning to sail onward, but a year later they're still there, comfortable but unsatisfied. Eventually, they drift back to a shore-based life, glad of the time out, the adventures to remember, but not interested in going again. In contrast are those who have what could be called a strong work ethic. "Come on, let's get up and do something today," I can almost hear Ardith and Mike on *Sanctuary* saying as they plan another goal for their eighth year of Pacific explorations. While most visiting yachtsmen drifted up to watch the dances and inspect the crafts displays of the 10-day Festival of the South Pacific at Townsville in Queensland, Australia, Ardith and Mike had a schedule of the festival's ethnic films and lectures and were up at the crack of dawn to catch them.

There is a sense of dislocation that discourages a number of successful voyagers from setting off on long-term cruises a second time. By being away for three or five or eight years, you do miss out on the daily activities, you become an outsider in your own hometown or profession. When Larry and I meet old shore-based friends, we realize we missed the excitement and concerns of the 1970s as our U.S. generation saw it: the rise of feminism, the struggle to end the Vietnam war, the beginnings of affirmative action. Our view of those years was of revolutions in Portugal, industrial/union changes in Britain, the effects of the European Union on poorer European countries such as Italy and Spain. Wander too long and you become a foreigner no matter where you are, even to your own family.

We're not surprised – as we discussed in chapter 1 – that the most common excuse given by AVs who settle back into shorelife is grandchildren. There are three time periods when we've seen family people most successfully break away for a long-term voyage: before children arrive, when the children are old enough to adjust easily to life afloat, and when the children leave home. But there is a narrow window of escape in the last because few people can resist being nearby to savor and be involved in the fascinating pleasures of grandparenthood. Some people, such as Spence and Dale Langford, who shared three years of voyaging with their own children, are off sailing again now, but they are voyaging closer to home so they can meander back to share in the early days of each new grandchild's life. Others, such as the Bushnells, have been addicted for so long that their children cater to the abnormalities of their parents by planning rendezvous at distant landfalls to show off new grandchildren.

Abnormality is a word that must be remembered when trying to explain why some people go voyaging time and again. It isn't *normal* to leave the assurances of family and friends, to do without the familiarity of places you know, rules and regulations and languages you understand. It isn't *normal* to accept being an outsider, or to put yourself in situations where you know you'll be cold or tired or concerned. It can't be short memories, as Larry jokingly insists, because many AVs we know are extremely introspective people. Eric Hiscock probably most succinctly summed up the reasons for this strange addiction after sailing almost 170,000 miles on five different boats: "Crossing oceans under sail is rarely comfortable, but it is always very satisfying."

CHAPTER
17

HOW TO REDUCE RISKS WHEN YOU CHOOSE YOUR OWN DIRECTIONS

Christmas Day 1993, Durban, South Africa. A dozen passagemakers from seven different countries relax at the "International's" barbecue. We look out to where our boats lay waiting to carry us west, north, or east, and the conversation turns to favorite way-points along the diverse routes we've all taken. "Port Davey, Albany" – without hesitation, Larry and I recall the surprisingly fine sailing we had as we reached around the southern tip of Tasmania to explore one of the most isolated, hard-to-reach natural parks in the world, then west through the amazingly docile Roaring Forties to Australia's rarely visited southwest coast. Other long-term voyagers speak of special places in Africa, China, and higher latitudes that were far off normal cruising routes. And of course the conversation turns to the passage that lies just ahead, the voyage along the infamous Agulhas Current, past the Cape of Good Hope. "Be patient," says a second-time South African circumnavigator. "*Ocean Passages for The World* shows a lot of northeasterlies for February." Thus, the conversation turns to a fascinating part of voyaging – one in which snowbound winter sailors often indulge – gathering the information to plan successful fair-weather passages. Careful use of the excellent publications available to all seamen, plus use of less orthodox sources, can let you go far beyond the normal tradewind routes and make high-latitude passages enjoyable as you catch the correct side of a high- or low-pressure system, the correct currents to speed you on your way.

After more than 150,000 miles of sailing together, including several voyages against prevailing winds to deliver someone else's yacht and top up our cruising kitty, plus a one-way east-about circumnavigation and three-fourths of another west-about circuit using sail-power only, we've come to have tremendous respect for the old-fashioned manual of route planning, *Ocean Passages for the World*, published by the British Admiralty and available from most major yachting book outlets. The information used to formulate this book (*OP* for short) has been gathered from the records provided by sailing-ship officers for 300 years, plus reports over the past 100 years from motorized shipping. To get the best results from *OP*, we first look at the Sailing Ship Routes section at the back of the book, then study all of the information on weather and currents and warnings described under the powered shipping section for the same areas. The large foldout maps included with the book allow quick visualization of this information.

With the increased demand for sailing books aimed toward cruisers, some yachting writers have tried to compile user-friendly guides to route planning. Unfortunately, it's problematical to use any routing book written by yachtsmen. At best, the information is provided, by a few dozen nonprofessional sailors who make one or two passages across any one area. These cruising sailors tend to choose downwind routes and, like ourselves, avoid traveling during seasons considered less than ideal. Therefore, the yachtsman's information will be sketchy for unusual destinations, unusual routes. Another problem is that any guide written by one person will be biased toward the type of sailing, type of vessel, fuel capacity, and type of passages he or she enjoys. So unless you are using tradewind routes, it would be best to go first to those rarely advertised publications compiled by nonprofit governmental agencies.

Once we've begun thinking of a general destination, our next step is to get out our Pilot Charts for the months recommended by *OP*. Both the U.S. Defense Mapping Agency and the British Admiralty Printing Office compile these amazing charts, which show in intimate detail the average wind directions and speeds, currents, wave heights, and more for each of the world's oceans for each month of the year. (See the list at the end of this chapter.) These charts are amazingly low-priced treasures, and since they, like *OP*, are compiled from centuries of records, one set will last your voyaging lifetime. (They are also far superior to Pilot Charts created and marketed especially for yachtsmen.) Although the British charts (called Routing Charts) and the U.S. Pilot Charts look slightly different, both contain essentially the same information. We prefer the U.S. publications, possibly because we have used them for so long, but also because they show wind roses over coastal areas as well as sea areas, and because they contain storm-frequency charts that are easier to interpret. The British Routing Charts, on the other hand, contain more concise information about wind speeds for each direction shown on each wind rose, plus the actual number of ships' reports on which each wind rose is based. Whichever of these charts you choose to use, remember that this information is based on averages, and weather can be affected by unusual sunspot activity, volcanic eruptions, El Niño occurrences, or even daily temperature fluctuations over large adjacent land masses. So even where Pilot Charts show an 80 percent chance for easterly or northeasterly winds at Force 4, you could, as did many people bound from Mexico to the Marquesas during 1983 (and again in 1989 and 1997), encounter fresh westerly winds for days or even weeks at a time. Furthermore, these publications are compiled by reports submitted by shipping companies, so the more frequently traveled a particular area is, the more accurate the information will be. The Australian Bight and Tasmania, though not on major shipping routes by today's standards, were prime destinations for British sailing ships plying the wheat and wool trade until the late 1920s. So we found excellent information regarding route planning on the Pilot Charts and also in *Ocean Passages for the World*.

Once you have chosen a general route you can find more detailed weather information in the various Sailing Directions volumes published by either the U.S. Hydrographic Office or the British Admiralty. There is a Sailing Directions volume published for each coastal area in the world – 38 volumes of U.S. directions (or Coast Pilots), 71 volumes of British directions. The information in these volumes can be invaluable – not only when you set off to cruise these coastlines but also when planning your coastal approaches. The climatic charts for selected locations in each book give excellent information for sailing within 50 miles of shore. We have no preferences when choosing Sailing Directions. The U.S. ones tend to have slightly more detailed information about small-boat anchorages. The British ones tend to have more profile diagrams showing approaches from offshore. Both give excellent warnings of potential dangers to shipping. Given ease of access to both, We'd look for U.S. directions for U.S. coastal waters, and for Central and South America. We'd use British publications for European and African waters and for the Orient.

Another source for off-standard route-planning information is guides written by local sailors and intended for local cruisers – i.e., South African cruising guides written by South African sailors, guides to Maine written by sailors from Maine. In European waters, we found invaluable information on local weather and currents in the new Macmillan *Almanac* and the Royal Cruising Club guides.

The original spark that led us to choose a southerly route around

Australia to visit Tasmania and easily reach the Indian Ocean in one season without rushing came from Kevin Lane's guide to anchorages he had visited during a circumnavigation of his homeland. Though you might not agree with the assessment of various ports in guides written by home cruisers, their lifetime of experience with changing weather patterns, currents, and tides can be almost as helpful as the more formal publications.

Commercial fishermen have been an excellent source of route-planning information as we voyaged. If you take along a loaf of fresh bread or a few beers when you visit them, they often will share advice on local seamanship. These men cannot choose the best weather for their work and are usually quite pelagic. Fishermen we met in New South Wales could tell us what type of anchors to depend on in the far reaches of Tasmania, what currents and weather they found, "three years back when I fished off the west coast of Australia." We have learned that fishermen working on fisheries such as cray trapping, scallop or prawn dredging (inshore fisheries), will be willing to lie in anchorages that cruising sailors should be terrified to enter. These men depend on large engines, which they maintain constantly, backed up by tremendous experience working in and among rocks and reefs that become as familiar to them as the path to their local pub. So they know how to get out past unlit reefs late at night should a storm fill in to turn their anchorage into a cauldron. Therefore, we've learned to accept their route-planning information and their comments on bottom conditions for anchoring, but to be slightly dubious when they say an unsheltered- looking anchorage is "great, even if the wind does go a bit easterly."

Yacht delivery skippers have also given us good information for offshore routing. When we did our first deliveries up the coast of Baja California, and later from Florida down through the Caribbean, we had to go during times we definitely would not have chosen. (Why else would they pay us to do it?) By talking with sailors who had been delivering yachts and fishing boats for years, we learned about countercurrents and wind shifts, so our deliveries along each of these routes were far easier than would otherwise have been expected.

A more recent addition to our routing information came when we finally purchased the expensive but excellent – *Admiralty List of Radio Signals, Volume 3 – Radio Weather Services*. The American equivalent is Worldwide Marine Weather Broadcasts. We found we could pick up on our Sony 2001D receiver many of the shortwave single-sideband broadcasts for areas we planned to visit. As we listened to the forecasts in

Figure 17-1.

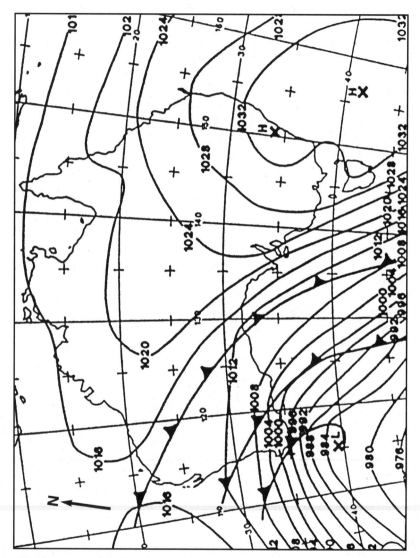

Weather map – July 3rd, 1991. Australia – The winter and spring weather pattern.by listening to radio reports and studying newspaper weather charts we began to understand what to look for.

Figure 17-2.

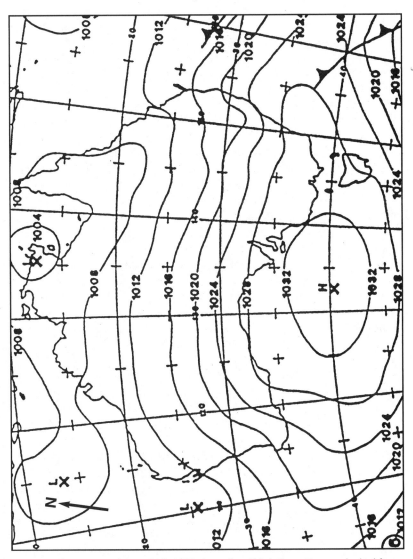

Weather map – *February 26th, 1992. Australia – This is the pattern we looked for, an excellent weather window that tends to occur late each summer.*

the months before we set off, patterns became obvious, so we could see which combination of highs and lows guaranteed fine sailing, which promised gales. Better yet, these reports showed that even during so-called bad seasons, there were often fine patches and favorable winds.

Every bit of research we put into finding less-traveled routes as we voyage or deliver boats seems to be rewarded. This was doubly so during our voyage south of Australia. On a previous visit, we'd spent six months exploring the Great Barrier Reef, and, like many voyagers, we prefer choosing new destinations whenever possible. By going south around, we did this, gaining the time and chance to spend a wild and wonderful week on horseback exploring the isolated Black Bluffs of northern Tasmania, the opportunity to visit remote whaling ports and the almost-deserted inland sea of Port Davey, where dolphin and black swans were often the only other occupants of the many fine and protected anchorages we visited. Best of all, by being in place, ready to use the six-week window that our research showed would provide good sailing westward across the Southern Bight, we cut out 2,400 miles of hot, humid, often windless, current- and ship-infested reefbound sailing through the narrow Torres Strait. Our final reward was a broad reach to the windswept towns of southwest Australia, where wondrous birds fill the beaches and sea life abounds. Foreign arrivals are a once-a-year occurrence – the excuse for a round of parties that prove beyond a doubt that cooler climes provide very warm welcomes.

USING THE AVERAGES: PILOT CHART INTERPRETATION

If there are bargains in the sailing world, they must be the Atlas of Pilot Charts prepared by the Defense Mapping Agency in the United States, the Routing Charts prepared by the British Admiralty. Months before we set off on any passage, we pore over one of the five regional atlases, studying the wind-speed roses, currents, tracks of previous storms. We always reread the explanations of each detail at the sides of the monthly pages, along with the synopsis of general weather information for the particular month. But, since the information is based on averages, we know there is little guarantee that even the most perfect route planning will give us perfect winds, perfect currents. We have, though, learned some tricks that help us hedge our bets toward a preponderance of relatively fair-wind passages.

Instead of looking just at the page for the month during which we hope to make a particular passage, we always look also at the preceding and following months, assuming that weather patterns can change earlier or later than the norm. During 1991-92, this was true for the southern summer, with blustery spring weather continuing late into January in New South Wales and Tasmania. So even though *Ocean Passages for the World* indicates that January and February are the most favorable months for a westbound voyage, we found fair winds and relatively low storm frequencies on the March page of the Pilot Chart Atlas. When we were forced to delay our start until several frontal systems crossed over us in mid-February, we were glad to see "summer" weather patterns fill in late in the month and persist for most of March (fig. 17-3, 17-4). We later learned that the same had been true in South Africa, where calmer, summerlike weather patterns arrived when autumn should have begun.

Although the wind directions indicated by the roses are the first item we examine, what most often influences our planning are the smaller diagrams showing cyclone tracks for each month. If possible, we avoid sailing anywhere near cyclone tracks. But in areas such as the Bay of Bengal or the China Seas, where cyclones have been known to occur at any time of year, we look for the month with the lowest risk and a route outside normal cyclone tracks. When we sailed east from Sri Lanka to Malaysia we noticed that the Pilot Chart showed few tropical disturbances formed below 3° N. Though it added 150 miles to our passage, we sailed south to pass 200 miles below this area and were glad, as a major cyclone passed just 150 miles north of us, sinking a 50-foot (15.3m) cruising yacht (six people lost) and going on to devastate northern Sri Lanka. We hove-to through 12 hours of heavy squalls but escaped the fury that was lying on the rhumb line we might otherwise have chosen.

Some Pilot Charts and Routing Charts show storm tracks right on the main chart instead of on a separate chartlet. This produces a far more daunting-looking picture. But by referring to the index of storm tracks at the side of the Routing Chart, and by eliminating any tracks other than those recorded as cyclone or hurricane strength, you will get a more accurate picture. It is safe to do this, as the majority of well-found cruising boats, given enough sea-room to heave-to can and should be able to withstand storm-force winds (50-55 knots), but cyclonic tropical disturbances can create winds double or even triple this ferocity.

Currents are the next thing we check on the Pilot Charts. A favorable current could make it worthwhile to go along a different route adding miles but also comfort to your voyaging. The Pilot Charts for the North Atlantic showed a countercurrent near Panama that increased in speed during March and April to give us a big assist to the east (against the

Figure 17-3.

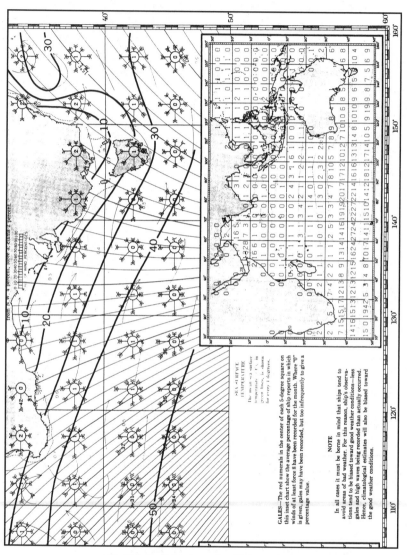

U.S. Pilot Chart for Australian Bight – July.

Figure 17-4.

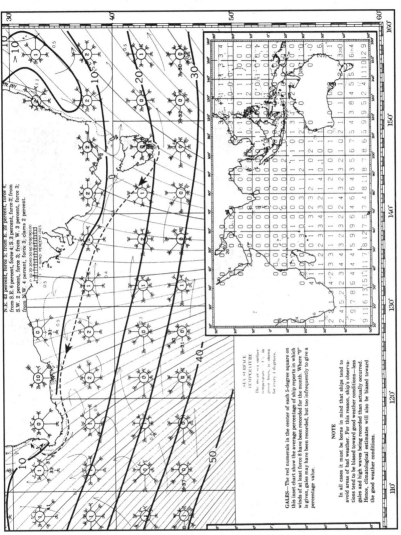

------------ Taleisin's route late February 1992

U.S. Pilot Chart for Australian Bight – February.

easterly tradewinds). By sailing along this current to Colombia, then heading north to Jamaica, we added about 250 miles to our voyage, but we had a relatively easy voyage on *Seraffyn* in spite of the Gulf Stream and the fresh-to-strong tradewinds of the Caribbean. (It is these smaller-counter currents that are missing on many yachtsman's Pilot Charts and routing books.)

Each Pilot Chart contains information on the percentage of ships reporting gale-force winds in each sea area. On the U.S. Pilot Charts, this appears on a separate chartlet. We have found that by adding up all of the gale percentage numbers along the route we'll be taking, then dividing this total by our average projected passage time (we figure 135 miles per day for *Taleisin*), we can get a good idea of the chances of encountering gale-force winds. If the resulting number is less than .6, we usually have gale-free sailing. If the number is over 1.1, we have almost always encountered one or more storms along the way. But, if the number of gales is particularly high in the area nearest our departure, we usually discount this first figure, as we can delay our departure until we have a gale-free weather forecast for two or three days. For example, a voyager leaving for the Canary Islands from the northwest coast of Portugal in November would find a 7 percent chance of gales for the first 200 miles of sailing, but only 2 or 1 percent in each area thereafter. By waiting for a good forecast, you could be clear of the 7 percent area very quickly and into a definite fair-wind voyage percentage. Though waiting can be complicated if you are running to a schedule – as occurs among race and rally participants, charter-boat and delivery skippers – timing is the key to enjoyable cruising and passagemaking.

One of the most heavily colored elements on the charts has relatively less importance for small sailing vessels than for larger ships. The thick red lines running through the main body of each chart indicate the percentage of wave heights 12 feet or more. As you study the Pilot Chart, you'll learn that these waves are often generated hundreds of miles from where you'll be sailing. So unless high-wave frequencies of 20 percent or more occur where gale percentages are 3 or more, the steadying effect of your sails will mean that you can discount this information. When we crossed the Australian Bight, we did encounter southerly swells of more than 3 meters (10 feet) (as indicated on the Pilot Chart) generated 300 to 600 miles south of us by frontal systems that did not affect us. Although these swells were only an annoyance because we reached on fresh northeast breezes, they precluded a visit to the exposed Recherche Archipelago east of Albany, as the surge made all the anchorages uncomfortable.

Figure 17-5.

U.S. PILOT CHART

A comparison of the U.S. Pilot Chart (this page) for November and the British Routing Chart (next page) for the same period.

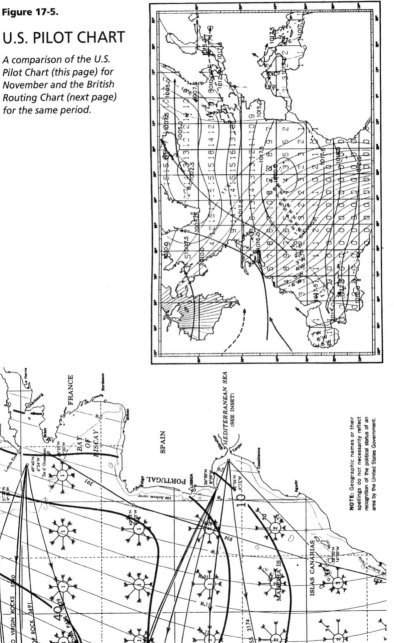

Figure 17-6.

BRITISH ROUTING CHART

A comparison of the U.S. Pilot Chart for November (previous page) and the British Routing Chart (this page) for the same period.

WIND ROSES - The arrows fly with the wind. Their length indicates percentage frequency on the scale

0% 10 20 30 40 50%

Their thickness indicates force thus

1-3   4   5-6   7   8 – 12

The frequency scale is 2 inches to 100%. From the head of the arrow to the circle is 5% and provides a ready means of estimating the percentage frequency. The number of observations is shown by the upper figure, the percentage frequency of variable winds by the middle figure, and calms by the lower figure in each rose.

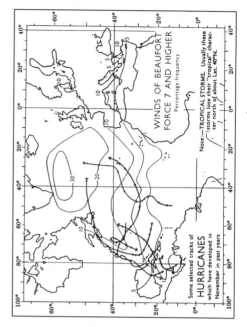

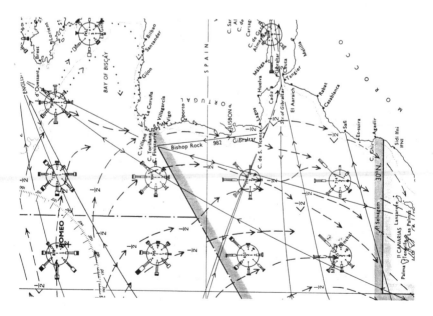

Unlike many other charts and publications, the Pilot Charts do not have to be replaced because of age. The averages change little through the years. The 1979 Indian Ocean Atlas we've used for the past two years is just as accurate as the newer edition. The 1992 Atlantic Ocean Atlas looks little different from the one we used 22 years ago.

As with all informational publications, our favorite reading is often the disclaimer. The Pilot Chart has one well worth considering: "Note – In all cases it must be borne in mind that ships tend to avoid areas of bad weather. For this reason, ships' observations tend to be biased toward good weather conditions – less gales and high winds being reported than actually occurred. Hence climatological estimates will also be biased toward the good weather conditions."

PUBLICATIONS USED FOR ROUTE PLANNING

U.S. PUBLICATIONS

- Pilot Chart Atlases – Northern, North Atlantic, Central American Waters, South Atlantic, South
- Pacific and Indian Ocean
- Worldwide Marine Weather Broadcasts – National Oceanic and Atmospheric Administration.
- U.S. Sailing Directions and Coast Pilots – 38 volumes: purchase en route
- Planning Guides – North Atlantic, North Pacific, Southeast Asia, Indian Ocean, North Sea and Baltic, Arctic Ocean

All of the above are available through the National Oceanic and Atmospheric Administration (NOAA), National Ocean Services, Distribution Branch, Riverdale, MD 20737-1199 USA.

BRITISH PUBLICATIONS

- Ocean Passages for the World – one volume only
- Routing Charts – North Atlantic, South Atlantic, Indian Ocean, North Pacific, South Pacific; sold by the month as individual, chart-size sheets
- Admiralty List of Radio Signals, Volume 3 – Radio Weather Services and Navigational Warnings
- British Pilot Books – 72 volumes

All of these are available from the Hydrographic Department, Ministry of Defence, Taunton, Somerset, TA1 2DN, United Kingdom.

CHAPTER

18

PREPARING YOURSELF AND YOUR BOAT FOR MORE ADVENTURESOME DESTINATIONS

A fiery sunset silhouettes Maatsuyker Island, lying just five miles ahead, marking the southernmost tip of Tasmania. The foamy surge rising against the Mewstone, two miles to leeward, glows pink, and I can just make out the shapes of the seals we hear barking. I chuckle along with the mutton birds that litter our wake and call to Larry, "I'm sure the Sailing Directions gave a mean average wind speed of 37 knots for Maatsuyker Island all summer, but maybe I looked at the wrong column."

"It's a bit ironic," Larry answers as he settles into the pilot berth for his off-watch. "Here we are carrying the drifter through the middle of the Roaring Forties. But I told you this was a logical route. Does Port Davey seem such a formidable destination now?"

The breeze that carries us westward is too fitful to control the vane on our self-steering gear, but the wool telltales on the shroud lift about 30 degrees, so I put on a light sweater and steer to keep *Taleisin* moving at just over a knot. The big nylon drifter undulates to the constant south westerly swell that surges up from Antarctica, 900 miles to the south. I laugh as I remember checking each seam on our storm trysail and watching Larry tighten each screw holding the storm-trysail track to the mast once we'd decided to sail south to visit the most isolated national park in the Southern Hemisphere. My trepidation about once again straying from more traveled cruising routes had been unfounded.

After leaving Sydney to cross the Bass Strait, then sail around Tasmania's southern tip to Port Davey and eventually west across the Australian Bight to wonderful Fremantle, the strongest winds we encountered at sea were less than 30 knots. In fact, the entire voyage was memorable for its lack of adrenalin-producing moments. Memorable were the uncrowded cruising conditions, the enthusiastic welcome given us by local sailors in isolated hamlets along our route, the hospitality of local fishermen, and the amazingly low costs. As we'd learned years before during an east-about circumnavigation on *Seraffyn* – to Finland's Arctic Circle edge, to the very north of the Adriatic, and through all three China Seas – cruising to nontropical, nontradewind route destinations, where ever-changing seasons add constant diversity, can be enormously rewarding.

The joys lying along the tradewind routes have been documented by legions of sailors: beautiful, clear waters, the chance to explore those amazing coral atolls, a preponderance of downwind sailing with steady breezes that Eric Hiscock told us averaged Force 4 (11-16 knots) for all of his three circumnavigations. There is the chance to cruise in company with other families so children can look forward to friends to play with, plus company for adults that will help soften the pangs of isolation that sometimes weigh heavily on people who loosened their ties to family and friends.

The disadvantages of voyaging along what some call the "Milk Run" and others call "The Rally Route" is that the relatively easy sailing attracts the vast majority of potential voyagers. Latest estimates (1996-97) show 450 to 600 cruising yachts of all nationalities moving westward in a circumnavigation along the Pacific equatorial islands. This means that favorite anchorages can be quite crowded and it's rare to find truly isolated places where you can feel like the first adventurer to discover a perfect hideaway. When dozens of cruisers congregate at the same stops, local people become less interested in inviting visitors home to share their lives and more interested in providing professional services. Voyaging along the tradewinds has become more expensive simply because there are more things on which to spend money: full-service shipyards, chandlers catering to offshore sailors, organized native feasts, marinas.

But, it is the hot, humid weather that we do not enjoy for long periods, and the threat of tropical cyclones, that have been the most important factors leading us to do much of our voyaging in temperate latitudes. And in these less-visited places, we've met wanderers who seek the rewards lying off the beaten track. From looking at the boats they use, it is obvious that a purpose-built boat is definitely not a necessity. If you choose your seasons with care, most well-found sailing vessels can successfully take you to the wilds of Alaska or the waterways of southern Tasmania. The only non-Australian cruising boats to reach the amazing isolation and black-swan-dotted reaches of Port Davey in 1992 (to our knowledge), besides *Taleisin*, were *Runaway*, a 30-foot (9.2m) Swedish coaster; *Riyal*, a British Rival 36; and *Northmore*, a 44-foot (13.4m) Hood cutter – and we each had the 20-square-mile maze of inland river estuaries to ourselves for much of our stay.

We have also found that an engine isn't even a prerequisite for offbeat destinations. *Curlew*, a 28-foot (8.5m), 100-year-old engineless gaff-rigged cutter owned by the adventuresome British couple Pauline and Tim Carr, went to South Georgia Island after three seasons of exploring the Patagonian channels and Antarctica.

What we have noticed about voyagers who make repeated forays into higher latitudes is that they tend to look at their boats more as a serious sailing machine than as just a downwind cruising home. They accept that there will be times when they must get their boat to windward efficiently for several days at a time – not only in moderate to heavy winds, but also in light winds. Hanked-on jibs to back up any roller-furling headsails, a storm staysail hanked onto its own stay, a storm trysail ready to hoist on its own track, an extra light, well-cut, large genoa plus nylon headsails, a folding propeller, and a ballast-to-displacement ratio of at least 38 percent – all are necessary. This is because you *will* have to make occasional windward passages if you wander toward the fjordlike Marlborough Sounds of New Zealand. Clear, easy-to-work-on side decks, accessible sail storage, and interior gear designed for changeable conditions are vital, as you will have to work your ship in more variable winds, changing from a beam reach to a run to closehauled all in one day as you explore the rewarding islands of northern Japan.

Simplicity is a common theme among the voyagers we meet who choose nonstandard destinations. Repair facilities and parts will definitely be more difficult to find along these routes, so it becomes more important to choose systems that are isolated from the main engine. You'll also want alternate sources of electricity, such as solar panels or wind generators. Having such systems means no voyage has to be aborted just because of engine failure or diesel shortages. These sailors use gas (butane or propane) or kerosene for cooking. Manual pumps back up any electrical ones throughout their boats; wind-activated self-steering is used for passagemaking and as a backup for any electrical autopilot for coastal work. Ground tackle on these boats tends to be oversize and generous. We see oversize windlasses – manual ones on smaller boats, hydraulic or manually backed-up electrical ones on larger boats. In each case, these cruising people expect to do their own maintenance and repairs, including rigging and sailmaking, and they carry an extensive spares inventory and large tool selection.

We have not met one high-latitude voyager who chose rod rigging for his/her boat. One reason is the ease with which wire can be replaced anywhere in the world. Fishermen in the most isolated villages use galvanized or stainless wire. Even sailors who do not have wire-splicing skills find that they can fit a new end of one type or another (bulldog clips, Talurit, Nicopress, Norseman, or quick splice) to the length of spare wire they can coil easily to fit in a small locker. This gives them on-board self-reliance.

A well-vented heater that works both in port and underway, upright and heeled, becomes vital once you sail beyond the tropics. In fact, one of the major reasons we chose to spend more than three years building our new cruising boat was to add room for a heater. We used an unvented propane heater on *Seraffyn*, and we learned the hard way how dangerous this can be when I was overcome by carbon-monoxide fumes during one stormy night at anchor. The search for a perfect vented heater is not easy. The traditional wood-burning stove is definitely the simplest and cheapest to install, but the fuel it uses produces very little heat relative to its bulk. To ensure we could carry enough hard coal to provide 5,600 Btu of heat or enough to warm the cabin to 65°F (18°C) when outside temperatures were 47°F (8°C) for a 40-day period, we needed 14 cubic feet of storage space. Ten gallons of kerosene or diesel could provide the same number of Btu and required less than two cubic feet of storage space. We chose kerosene as we already carried this on board for our major lighting needs. For those with generous fuel tanks, diesel would be the wise choice. We have found both diesel and kerosene available in most isolated villages, and easier to obtain than butane in many cases.

The heater we use on *Taleisin* is a wick-type (2⁵/₈-inch-diameter round wick) kero burner we modified and set inside a solid-fuel stove body with a 4-inch stovepipe. This gives us adjustable heating with no need for electricity or fans. The vented heat does wonders to dry out the dampest days. We did have to experiment with several smoke heads until we found one that let the heater work even as the boat rushes rail down in gusty winds and at anchor in winds to 50 knots. Most people find that no matter what type of heater they install, smoke-head selection is a matter of trial and error. Surprisingly, this heater has been a bonus even in the margins of the tropics, adding a cheery glow to chilly evenings in Mexico and the Tongan islands.

Easy-to-use bathing arrangements become vital when you spend long periods exploring less-cruised areas. Beyond major yachting centers, there are few formal shower facilities. Furthermore, crispy evenings are wonderful for strolls on shore, but definitely not inviting for on-deck showers. We've designed our bathing arrangements right next to the cabin heater, so even in the freezing conditions we occasionally encountered when we wintered in Sydney, Australia, we were able to bathe in comfort. As a further luxury in cooler climates, it helps if your bathing facilities can be usable underway. This requires a safe seating arrangement. In our case, we shower inside a Japanese-style sitz-tub with a permanent seat. This shower is located well aft, where motion is less of a problem. On other boats, we've seen separate stalls adjacent to the aft head compartment, with water-containment sills and safety seating. Curtained-off areas in a toilet enclosure are difficult to use at sea, as few people enjoy sponging down a toilet once we are clean.

Whatever area you set up for bathing, water monitoring is vital. Pressure showers using main tank supplies can easily drain 10 or 15 gallons of water per use. So, it's important to have an on-demand system that encourages bathers to wet themselves down, turn off the water, soap, then turn on the water just for a rinse. Isolating your shower-water system so it uses a separate supply is also necessary for monitoring purposes. The Hiscocks used a three-gallon plastic, pump-up bug-spray container for their showers. A one-gallon kettle of hot water heated on the stove and added to two gallons of cold water gave them both a satisfying but water-efficient shower. We have adopted their idea and added a push-button demand shower- head on a flexible hose. Even with my thick hair, I find I can get a generous clean-up (two shampoos and a rinse) yet still leave Larry enough for his shower on a three-gallon tank-up.

Another consideration for off-the-track voyaging is food-carrying capacity and arrangements. Although seafood can add to your supplies, you'll find few shops in the northern reaches of Newfoundland, up the Amazon, or on the west side of Vancouver Island. So you'll want to be able to carry enough not only for your voyage out, but also for an extended stay in isolated anchorages, plus supplies for your voyage back to reprovisioning ports. Since fresh produce will last longer in higher latitudes, you can carry enough to last three or four months at a time. But you must find out-of-the-way places to store it. During tradewind passages, we usually use the forward bunk, which becomes redundant at sea. But in higher latitudes, we spend far more of our time at anchor and don't enjoy moving baskets of produce from one bunk to another each time we go to bed. We use our chain locker for much of the extra 50 pounds of potatoes, 30 pounds of onions, and 70 pounds of fruit we carry. Our chain locker is fully open, so it has excellent ventilation to keep produce fresh. If you cannot use your chain locker, consider baskets under the deck or hammocks in a less-used compartment.

A final word of advice for those who plan to explore isolated anchorages. Invest in canned and packaged delicacies, and don't begrudge the extra weight and storage space they require. Spend the extra money for those fancy things that will spice up a meal when your fresh produce has dwindled away: artichoke hearts, capers, sweet black cherries, plum puddings, canned Brie. The initial cost might shock you, but remember that you'll be spending nothing at all during the weeks while you are exploring far-off places, and good eating is the personal comfort you can improve most easily by simple planning before you set sail.

This ability to create personal pleasure is very important as you voyage farther into the variables. You'll be spending more time on your own and probably more time waiting for the right weather pattern to form, the right tides to begin. This leads to another similarity we find in all off-the-beaten-track voyagers – the ability to entertain themselves. Some are avid readers, some love to hike and explore ashore no matter what the weather conditions, some study language or music, others practice guitar, trumpet, trombone, or flute. Still others are carvers or weavers. But all are people who, though aggressive enough to have earned the funds to buy or build a getaway boat, have an underlying patience that allows them to settle in for a week or a month of quiet time with the boat and the majesty of a completely secluded anchorage as their idea of perfection.

Yes, the tradewind routes are used by far more voyagers than they were 25 years ago, when we were one of only 14 yachts to transit the Panama Canal in either direction during an entire year. But as Susan Hiscock wrote in one of the last letters we exchanged, "Cruising people are getting ever more enterprising and hardy, with our friends the Ponces in *Damien* and the Carrs in *Curlew* visiting the Falklands and on to Antarctica. Ernie and Val Haige are leaving Australia bound for Canada by way of Tasmania and New Zealand." Yes, cruising sailors are still finding new and interesting destinations where the attractions near shore and farther inland are amazingly different from those found in tropical seas. Yet these high-latitude routes probably will never be considered crowded.

Bill and Pam Kellett, voyagers we first met when they were on board Ed Greeff's *Puffin*, the only other North American yacht to cruise the Baltic in 1974, wrote of their wonderful adventures along the shores of Finland and into the just-opened ports of eastern Germany, and said, "During our entire summer (1992) we only met four other North American cruising yachts, and all of us were thrilled by the warm treatment we received." Yes, the adage a Swedish voyager told us back in 1969 still holds true: "The colder the climate, the warmer the welcome."

CHAPTER
19

CONQUERING FEAR: GAINING CONFIDENCE ON A WINTER PASSAGE

I was furious. The blinking jib was wrapped twice around the headstay. The boat was rolling, the 20-foot-long whisker pole was banging against the stay, and I couldn't keep the flashlight directed on the twist to help me figure which way the sail had wrapped. It had been a lousy watch from the beginning. Larry hadn't been sleepy at 1900 because we'd had one of those sailing days that seem to hype you up, get you counting your blessings. So we'd chatted until 1930. "Okay, that's it. If you want your full three hours off, it starts right now," I'd said in a half-serious, stern voice. Then the wind went fluky. Each time the sails slatted, Larry's eyes fluttered open. I tried adjusting the wind vane, putting shock cords on the tiller, oversheeting the sails, hand steering – anything to keep the boat quiet so he could get some sleep. I really didn't want to be working on deck. I'd discovered a new author and would have preferred being below, book in hand, checking on deck every 10 minutes. But Larry needed sleep, and nothing bothers him quite so much as slatting, banging sails.

The wind veered to that impossible spot, 35 degrees aft of the beam. As the boat surged off each wave, the damned jib would blanket just for a second, then BAMM, it would fill, clunking against the fairleads. Through the open hatch, I'd see Larry's eyes flutter.

"I'll set the g--d--- pole and run off for a while. If the wind backs any more, we'll need the pole anyway. If not, we can reach up in the morning," I mumbled to myself as I planned a super-quiet pole raising. I set the vane to run off dead downwind. I eased the jib to give me lots of sheet so I could pull the pole down its track on the mast. I went forward on the rolling deck and clipped the weather sheet into the pole end, then grabbed the pole downhaul. Nothing much happened. Back to the cockpit for a flashlight. Ease the leeward jibsheet some more so the sail is almost flying free. Back to the pole downhaul – pole up, head for the cockpit. Boat lurches – sail flogs – before I reach for the sheet and get some tension on it, it's twice around the headstay. I try winching the sheet, then loosening it. I try running by the lee. Finally, I wake Larry and, while he pulls on some clothes, I tie a halyard tail around my waist and go out to the end of the bowsprit. Then I jerk the sail free, guided by the light Larry is now shining on the jib. He grabs the sheet as soon as the sail is unwound, and a minute later, we are running wing-and-wing over a much smoother-feeling sea, the vane perfectly in control, the breeze fresh and fair. Larry is chuckling, "You looked cute out there fighting that sail. But aren't you cold without any pants on?" I didn't particularly care about looking cute. I just wanted him asleep, and now I knew – to be fair – I owed him another half hour in the bunk before I got to climb in.

As I fine-tuned the vane, coiled the lines, and calmed down, I considered ways I could have avoided the snarl. I could have run a bit higher as I put up the pole, worked a bit faster. Then I thought back to the far less solvable problem I'd faced over the past two weeks, and tonight's glitch came more into perspective. At least it had been something physical, curse-able, easily fixed and soon to be forgotten.

Two weeks earlier, the alarm clock woke us early after a laughter-filled party with a dozen friends on a farm nine miles from our home base in New Zealand. The voyage from our wharf to the anchorage below their hilltop Mahrangi River home on the northeast coast of New Zealand had been the first step of our voyage toward Australia. The morning forecast said, "Strong wind warning, SW to W, 20 to 25 knots, some gusts to 35." That was less than perfect for the second step of our voyage, but since we would have a beam reach northeast for 60 miles to our clearance port, and we would always be in the lee of the land, we decided to go for it. I cleaned up below as Larry hanked our 100 percent reefing jib onto the headstay. "We'll reef it down when the wind freshens; right now we'll need it," he called to me. I flaked the chain into its locker as he cranked it in, then went on deck to help set the pole as we ran away from shore. As soon as the sails were settled, and a bit of anchor mud washed off the foredeck, I went below to record our departure time in the log. The morning chill caught at my fingers as I pulled off my sailing mittens. The pen on the chart table rolled away from my grasp as I turned to the correct page in the log. I got a strange dizzy feeling as I started to write, "June 25th, 0800 set sail...." I sat down on the settee, my head against a

All of the preparations for this voyage reminded me that we were going to face heavy winds.

cushion, and cursed, "You can't be seasick yet, we're still in the river; there's less than two feet of wind chop." I poked my head out of the companionway to get some fresh air. The wind was already fresher and we were running at close to 5 knots. My head began to throb, and I could feel the clamminess of growing seasickness – or was it fear? This was the first passage of a midwinter voyage across a sea notorious for boisterous winds and sudden gales. This *was* my first voyage outside the Hauraki Gulf and into open ocean in two and a half years. Almost every day for the previous five weeks, there had been reports of storm-force winds 300 miles south of us.

A short while later, I helped Larry jibe the boat, and as we reached up in the lee of Kawau Island, 25-knot gusts convinced us to drop the 100 percent jib and reef it to its working-jib configuration. A cross swell set the boat dancing a bit as she reached quickly toward the north. "I'm going to put my head down for a minute," I told Larry as I climbed below. "Your first-day-at-sea stomach," Larry commented, "You'll soon be over it."

But I lay there feeling horrid, slowly accepting that it might be fear, not motion, at the bottom of my problem. But fear of what? I thought back over the previous month of preparations. I'd inspected every inch of the boat inside and out before we'd loaded the cruising gear on board, after two years of local racing and gunkholing. Both Larry and I had done a complete inspection of every inch of the mast and rigging. The boat was well proven, well outfitted – in fact in some ways, almost over-outfitted. Besides the storm trysail that was now hanked onto the base of its own track, we carried a brand-new spare mainsail and staysail, since our working sails were almost five years old and looked a bit tender. Our lockers were full, we had lots of warm clothes, and, luxury of luxury, we had two complete sets of foulweather gear. But – I then began thinking of the preparations that are a vital part of prudent offshore voyaging. Inspect and repack the abandon-ship kit. Inspect and oil the flare pistol. Refurbish the emergency medical kit. Check the EPIRB signal and make sure the batteries are good. New batteries for the man-overboard strobes, lock-downs to keep the cabin floorboards and bilge contents from getting loose in a knockdown – nearly everything reminded me of potential dangers. Even the purchase of spare mittens was a reminder that this would be a rough and cold passage. What a contrast to preparing for more normal modes of travel toward sunny climes and skin-diving locales. Every bit of preparation for those trips was positive – pack the sunglasses, suntan lotion, lots of good books. I'd done the final preparations for a few dozen ocean crossings. I'd checked all of the emergency gear then. I'd never experienced this feeling of fear. "Why this time?" I questioned myself.

The wind began increasing, and *Taleisin* roared through seas that were now reaching 5 feet (1.5m) in height only a mile and a half offshore. We cleared the channel to the north of Kawau Island and fell into a light-wind patch at Cape Rodney. For half an hour, we reached along with our working jib, staysail, and full mainsail. Then, as we came clear of the high cliffs and began reaching across the wide bay toward Whangarei, the water ahead became streaked with blown spume. Larry opened the hatch a few inches and called down, "I'm going to drop the jib. I'll lash it down on the bowsprit; probably sail out of the wind as soon as we pass the next headland." For 10 minutes, I lay and listened to him working on the foredeck, then moving back to the cockpit to sheet in the staysail. *Taleisin* still reached along at full speed under the reduced canvas. Two hours later, Larry slid open the hatch and called down, "Better put on your foulweather gear and help me get the jib off the bowsprit."

I struggled into boots, jacket, foulies, and stocking cap and scrambled up on deck, feeling woozy and horribly clumsy as the boat lurched and bucked. Forty-five-knot gusts heeled us as the seas grew across the three miles of fetch to reach almost 9 feet (2.8m) in the current-swept shallow water. We didn't want to lose ground by running off to make it easier to take the jib off the bowsprit, so constant sheets of spray flew across us as Larry unhanked it and I pulled the unruly, soaking mass inboard. I helped Larry set a reef in the staysail, along with the two in the mainsail, and then we started working inshore toward smoother water. I sat in the cockpit, ducking spray, while Larry adjusted the self-steering vane. He was grumbling when he sat down next to me. "Should have known better. Should have taken that jib right off the bowsprit while we were in calm water. Guess I'm a bit rusty after all this gulf cruising." But as he settled in and watched the boat bash through the waves, I could see that the whole wild scene seemed to excite him. "Look at how she's moving; she's great, isn't she?" he called in my ear as we sat side by side. "I think we can get a better angle on these seas if we tack. Then we can work in toward smoother water. Check the chart and see if there are any dangers near the beach. If this keeps up, we can anchor in the lee of the land somewhere for the night."

I went below, pulled off my gear, and tuned the radio. "Gale warnings for all exposed areas. Gusts to 50 knots." My seasickness/fear was still there. Even four hours later, when we lay anchored 300 yards off the beach in surprisingly calm conditions, I still didn't feel much better.

By morning, the wind was down to 25 knots, and we had an amazing sail along the shore toward Whangarei, escorted by a pod of 8-foot-long dolphin. We anchored in a secluded, soothing bay seven miles from the city and hitchhiked in to buy our final provisions and duty-free stores. We did some last-minute re-storing, and each evening for five days I rowed to a little pub a mile away. There I'd buy the daily paper to check the weather map and track a huge high-pressure system that was slowly moving along the south of Australia toward the Tasman Sea. And each day my mind explored my fear. I finally began to talk about it with Larry. "What is different this time?" I asked. "I've been out in some pretty bad storms. We've sailed across the North Sea in winter, down through the gales of the Red Sea and the storms of the Bay of Bengal – why now?"

"We're both a bit rusty at passagemaking," he reminded me. "Besides, the Pilot Charts do show a pretty negative view. They predict a 7 percent chance of gale-force winds for the first 400 miles. They show wave heights above 12 feet for over 20 percent of the time all along our route. The pilot

We reached along for several days with only the storm trysail and staysail set.

books predict even higher storm percentages, and Susan and Eric Hiscock have been across the Tasman seven times and they said they'd never had fewer than three or four days with gale-force winds." Larry was right. We'd encountered our share of blows on other passages, but never before had we set out knowing the odds were against us. And what was worrying me? I knew the boat and Larry could take it. But I also knew, with my allergy to seasickness remedies that I'd be seasick for at least a couple of days. It often hit me in heavy weather. I knew I wouldn't be able to hold up what I felt was my fair share of the work of running the boat. I'd be dependent on Larry and, in a way, reminded daily of my small size and lack of physical strength as basic necessary chores became endlessly energy-consuming.

The high-pressure system moved toward New Zealand. The associated frontal troughs swept across us, and after five days we realized we could be stuck for a month or more waiting for perfect weather. If we wanted to get to Australia before the hurricane season, we'd have to calculate our risks and take our lumps. So we set off with three days' worth of meals ready to be heated and served, *Taleisin* as ready as she'd ever be.

Less than 12 hours out, we hit gale-force winds. The storm trysail came out of its bag and a simple change of the main halyard had it pulling us along on a close reach, its short luff cutting the heeling pressure of the growing wind. Eighteen hours out, we dropped the staysail and lay hove-to in storm-force winds; the trysail with its short hoist and long foot kept the sail area low and well aft and held *Taleisin's* bow up, so she lay quietly. The trysail definitely worked better than the triple-reefed mainsail had on *Seraffyn*.

Those first few days at sea were uncomfortable and cold, but I'd had my minor triumphs. In spite of a few visits to the lee rail, I'd stood my wet watches, hand steering and feathering the boat into the wind through the heaviest gusts at the front of each squall, then letting the wind vane steer until the next black squall cloud overtook us as we close-reached away from the land to gain a good offing. I'd heated and served Larry's meals, though I hadn't shared them. I'd recorded changes and barometer readings in the log and advanced our DR on the chart, in spite of my complete lack of interest. I'd helped Larry adjust the boat so she lay hove-to properly.

Gradually, my fear eroded as I felt the boat lying securely, lifting surely to each sea that rolled toward us. I was able to sleep despite the storm that roared outside. Then, as the winds abated enough so we could again set sail, my confidence grew. I felt *Taleisin* battle westward without a creak or groan, stiff and dry under her staysail and trysail. As each day passed and I slowly grew more attuned to the heavy motion, the words of the well-loved English voyager Peter Pye came to mind, "If you want to be a sailor, you have got to go to sea."

How right he was. It is fine to begin a sailing career by avoiding strong winds. It is okay to gain experience with gales gradually, as we did in *Seraffyn*. But to truly trust myself, to have complete confidence in the boat on which I sailed, the man with whom I sailed, I had to make my winter passage. I had to go to sea.

Our 1,350-mile Tasman Sea passage, in 1988, took $11^1/2$ days, during which we were hove-to three separate times for a total of 17 hours. We reached and ran with Force 7 and Force 8 winds for eight days, reached in Force 4 to Force 6 winds the rest of the time. The only mishaps of the trip were a sailbag washed overboard (we hadn't stowed it where it belonged) and a plate of stew overturned on the velour settee upholstery.

CHAPTER
20
INTIMATE ENCOUNTERS: THE BONUS OF CRUISING

I didn't learn to play the clarsach. I never conquered the Hebridean backstep. But each day I spent at the Feis, a two-week summer workshop and celebration of Celtic arts, music, and language, found me surrounded by schoolchildren, their parents, and musicians from the Highlands and islands of Scotland. Each evening was filled with memorable music and insights into the realities of life in the windswept corner of the world called Castlebay, Barra.

When Larry and I had set sail from southwest England with plans to explore Scotland's western islands, our heads were swimming with ideas for the best spots to visit in this maze of islands, lochs, and waterways. We'd been lent 45 charts and six cruising guides to help us explore an area that is only about 60 miles wide and 200 miles long. But the unbelievable complexity of islands, tides, history and culture we encountered was daunting. For more than a month, we tried to sample as many as possible of the seemingly limitless supply of anchorages, villages, and pubs. The sailing, in spite of occasional stormy days, was surprisingly good, the people were kind and friendly. Pubs featured excellent meals and even better samples of single-malt whiskies from small local distilleries. Stunning vistas greeted us every time we ventured to any headland or hilltop. But it wasn't until we sailed into Barra and used *Taleisin* as our home base instead of as transport, until we joined in the Feis, that we felt we'd broken the barrier as "tourists" and actually made friends and tasted and felt the real life of Scottish islanders.

When we look back over three decades of voyaging, it is the time we spent being involved with local people – sharing their lives and concerns for a week, a month or a season – that we most often recall. Other long-

Anna not only took care of us cruisers on St. Helena, but told us of the history and romance of her island home.

term cruisers confirm this. It is rarely "the most beautiful anchorages in the world" that long-termers talk about, but rather the intense cross-cultural encounters that could only happen because we, or they, arrived on that wonderful spacecraft called a cruising boat with the time and facilities to stop and join for a while.

I can almost hear potential cruisers thinking, "It is easy for you to have great encounters. You are always going off the beaten track. But I am going to gain my sea legs along the tradewind route, where local people are already overwhelmed with visiting cruisers." Don't make this assumption. Special encounters can happen anywhere, but there are a few tricks to making them more likely, ways to make sure communication leads to invitations, ways you as the visitor can make sure you do not erect any barriers.

Probably the biggest barrier to memorable encounters is the singlemindedness that got you out cruising in the first place. You set goals, made a schedule, and stuck to it. Now you are bound off cruising; everything in your training, every friend or family member with whom you communicate, keeps pressuring you by demanding, "What is your schedule?" To have interesting encounters, you have to keep any schedule flexible. When we sailed into the rock-strewn anchorage at Cashla, 40 miles from Galway, Ireland, we planned only to stop for a night's sleep before pressing on northward. An ancient-looking, black-hulled open workboat sailed in to share our anchorage. Larry rowed over to look more closely at this 100-year-old Galway Hooker and was soon chatting with the two fishermen on board. "We'll be racing against a dozen other hookers in the next bay at the weekend," I heard one of them say. "How long you staying around?" Larry came back to tell me, "Those fishermen were shocked when I said we'd stay around to watch them race. Said 20 yachts a year anchor here, stay one night, and leave. We've been invited to crew with them if we want." That changed our whole summer. Instead of visiting all of the western Irish islands and then sailing over the top and down the Irish Sea, we raced and partied with the crews of 22 different hookers as they sailed from village fete to village fete, from regatta to regatta, for a summer full of Guinness, Irish humor, and heartwarming memories. That reinforced a lesson we'd learned when we first set off cruising. When someone you meet asks when you are leaving, don't say, "Tomorrow." They'll feel there is too little time to get to know you, that you wouldn't be interested in joining them for a visit to their home the next day. It is far better to leave open the doors to friendship by saying, "We're in no hurry, we're enjoying ourselves here."

By choosing to make occasional passages, by staying at sea for two or three nights a month, you'll increase your chances of meeting people. It is possible to voyage from San Francisco to Panama with only one or two overnight hops. But doing that means getting up early, pulling up your ground tackle, setting sail for 10 hours or so to cover 35 or 40 miles, working into a new anchorage or dock, and bedding the boat down – only to get up and go again the next morning so you can be in a town to get provisions before the weekend, do the laundry and top up water and fuel tanks. The 2,500-mile journey itself will fill at least 60 to 80 days of the intercyclone season. Instead, if you make a 300- or 400-mile passage every month, you can reach the same destination with only 18 or 20 days at sea and save time and energy for getting involved with local people. There were three of us who set sail at the same time from San Diego back in 1985, planning to head straight for Turtle Bay, 350 miles to the south. About 20 other cruising families planned to day-hop along the coast. Steve Brown on *Southwind* and the two of us on *Taleisin* arrived and anchored three days later. During an evening stroll ashore, we met a woman who was trying to plant some flowers in her windswept, sandy front yard. This led to an invitation to the local fishing co-op's anniversary party and dance, which led to all of our becoming involved with the local children's games and excursions for four days. As we were preparing to set sail six days after arriving, half a dozen of the cruising boats we'd last seen in San Diego filed in, their crews telling of not having to stay out even one night. Each was hoping they could get fresh food the next morning and be underway before 10 a.m.

Just as this desire to avoid sailing at night can leave you too tired to meet local people, so can the desire to see everything. There is an underlying competitive spirit among sailors. I even hear myself greeting someone just in from a cruise, by saying, "Did you stop at my favorite spot? Oh, what a pity – you really missed out." Accept it right from the start: No matter how long you have for a cruise, be it two weeks or two years, you are going to miss lots of interesting places, lots of stunning anchorages and vistas. Not only is time against you, but weather conditions could make someone else's favorite destination untenable just when you are approaching. This happened as we were crossing the Indian Ocean from Cocos-Keeling Atoll toward South Africa. We'd heard rave reviews about the uninhabited coral atolls of the Chagos Archipelago from friends who'd spent almost a month gorging on lobster, fish, and fruit in solitary tropical splendor two years earlier. Constant squalls, visibility often limited to less than a few hundred feet, and near-gale-force winds drove us toward these islands for six days. Every forecast we could get on our shortwave radio indicated that the gloomy, squally weather would persist because of a series of developing lows just north of the equator. Finally, we decided it was foolish to risk running downwind into reef-strewn waters with bad visibility, even if paradise were at the end. So we diverted south toward the small island of Rodriguez, a place about which we'd heard little. There we found ourselves the only visiting yacht in a warm and friendly village where a fishing family taught us how to sail and pole lateen-rigged pirogues over just-submerged coral reefs.

As enjoyable as cruising in company can be, it definitely makes meeting local people far more difficult. A rally can be a great experience, rather like being part of a friendly, movable yacht club. But because schedules and events are organized long before you arrive in each port, you will have no time, or social need to get involved on shore. Less obvious is the fact that cruising in company with even one buddy boat cuts you off from those on shore. You arrive in port with prearranged plans to have dinner or to rent a car together and go exploring. You feel socially included so have little time to look toward local people for the interest and entertainment needed to round out your life. Another point to consider is that local people are more willing to invite a couple home for coffee than two or three couples. They assume a group of people can't be lonely, or they simply don't have space or (in some cases) the extra resources to offer cake and coffee to six or eight people. I've seen this from both sides of the picture. When we lived at our home base in New Zealand, we tended to invite the crew from lone overseas yachts anchored in our cove to come ashore for a shower or a cup of tea. But if two or three yachts arrived at one time, we just didn't feel we could offer hospitality to a crowd.

One spring, we cruised in company with two longtime friends for six weeks in the Spanish Balearics. Great impromptu races ensued, evenings were filled with crazy card games, there was lots of sharing of boat maintenance. But the day after Richard and Susan had to return to a city because of money mix-ups, we rowed ashore and said hello to a local Spanish sailor on his 24-foot (7.3m) daysailer. After we spent two enjoyable days in the company of Juan and his family, he admitted, "I did want to invite you to come to my house as soon as I saw you sail in, but I could see you were too busy with your friends."

How can you have the best of both worlds? We try to arrange loosely framed rendezvous with other cruisers – preferably during winter refit time, or at a deserted anchorage or island we have heard about somewhere farther along our cruising route. Then we go off in our own direction for a month or two. These rendezvous with friends turn into wonderful reunions, as we all arrive eager to catch up with each other, full of fresh tales to share – at a time and place where meeting local people would not be such an important priority.

We became good friends with Niki Perryman and Jamie Morrison, two young Australian racing sailors-turned-cruisers, when we all spent a winter in southwest England. They too were bound toward Norway. But, instead of going in company, a tempting prospect, we agreed to meet at Risor, Norway, for the wooden-boat festival. "If we are not going to be able to meet up, if we find it too much of a push, we'll send one postcard to Risor and one to your regular mail drop," we all agreed. They went east around Britain, we went west around, and with no communication for three months, we arrived within two hours of each other for a happy reunion and tales to share of people we'd met along the way. Eight days later, we went our separate ways, having planned a rendezvous for another country, another season.

Once you've made the decision to open yourself and your sailing schedule to chance encounters, there are ways to increase opportunities, even in the most crowded cruising areas. By planning your arrival to coincide with some special local event, such as a town fete, a music festival, or a classic car-rally, you'll expand your potential. How do you learn about these events? For wooden-boat sailors like ourselves, it is easy: *Classic Boat* magazine and *WoodenBoat* magazine list them months in advance. For mainland United States sailing events each summer, look to *Sail* magazine in May, with updates each month throughout the summer. But for nonsailing events such as cultural festivals, your best bet is to write to the information offices at the embassies or consulates of the countries you plan to visit. They have extensive calendars of events, and if you mention a special interest, they may have a directory that can help.

We first met Jim and Lynne Foley on their Valiant 40 *Sanctuary* in the Azores. When we rendezvoused in Cork, Ireland, four months later, they made us green with envy by telling about a storytelling festival they had joined on an island in the southwest of Ireland. For a week, they lay in a tiny harbor along with a few fishing boats and two Irish yachts and spent each evening around an open fire or at the local pub listening to storytellers from 10 different countries. We had sailed within 10 miles of the festival, unaware of its existence. Lynne had found the information in a brochure sent out by the information office at the Irish Embassy in Washington, DC.

If you don't write ahead, go to the local information office as soon as you arrive in a new area. But if your goal is meeting local people and forming new friendships that will fill your season after the festival is over, visit mostly smaller festivals. It's more likely you'll make friends at the Mardi Gras celebrations in a small island town like Guadeloupe, than those in Rio de Janeiro.

Cruising out of season is another way to increase your chances of meeting locals. It also helps to choose smaller villages and towns rather than big-city destinations. When we have wanted to visit big cities, we've found it far more hospitable to choose a harbor or marina in a nearby town, one with good rail or bus connections, and commute. Folks at the Gordon's Bay Yacht club, 30 miles from Cape Town were delighted to have a relatively rare foreign visitor and immediately drew us into their lives and club activities. Two months later, when we arrived in Cape Town, we found that the sheer size and big-city hustle-bustle precluded easy encounters. The large number of visiting yachts at the local club lowered our chances of getting to know the people who lived there.

A few other tricks we've learned from other cruisers include using your own special interests to get in touch with the local scene. One used her painting as an introduction – she joined local art classes in Venice, Barcelona, and elsewhere. Another contacted the photo club; a third contacted folk-music clubs. A less typical, but highly successful, local contact was praised as the reason one woman friend, who suffers terribly from seasickness, keeps cruising, "I'm in AA and go to meetings everywhere we cruise. We have new friends within a day after we arrive in any port." Two singlehanded friends go to church wherever they visit. They are not particularly religious, and rarely go to the same denomination church as they might in their own town, but they say it is a great way to break the ice in smaller towns. Jim and Lynne Foley are jewelrymakers, and they visit colleges, offering to give a class on working with gold, using special methods Jim developed. Instant introductions. We enjoy local yacht races. Every place we've joined in, we've stayed longer than we originally intended. This is especially true when we choose to be at smaller sailing clubs rather than the larger yacht clubs in each area.

People with children have it easy. By approaching a local school and asking if your children can join in for a few days or a few weeks, you've opened the first of many doors.

The list can go on and on. But once you've found ways to open those doors, here are a few last tips for keeping them open. Try not to look at language as a barrier. We do have a useful if limited understanding of Spanish, but we have found people eager to practice their English in each of the 66 countries we have visited. We carry a translation dictionary and have it handy so our guests can use it, too. We have, at times, bought cassette tapes of "French for tourists," or "Portuguese for tourists," and used them to fill some of our passage time as we approached a new destination. In every case, we have found it pays to learn a few local words or phrases as soon as possible. Even where English is the native language, there can be special local salutes or greetings that will help you make friends. People love to be greeted and thanked in their own language. The Irish grinned with pleasure each time we used their local drinking salute. The Scots and Norwegians reacted the same way.

To overcome any shyness you might have about meeting new people along the way, it is important to remember that most people are curious about visitors - wanting to know why they came, where they came from, who they are, and whether they like what they see. But, even more important, most people enjoy talking about themselves. We arm ourselves with questions whenever we are in a new place. As we approach local immigration officials, we ask, "What is your favorite pub? What

Soon after we met Mara and Helio at Brachuy, 200 miles south of Rio de Janeiro, we found ourselves brought right into their lives and homes. By the time we set sail five months later, it was like saying goodbye to our family.

should we see while we are here?" We ask local fishermen, "Which boatyard is the most careful? Where do we find bottom paint, parts...?" Any question can serve as an opener, and as soon as the conversation gets going, we ask people to tell us about themselves, about what is happening in their homes. That is why we suggest that as soon as you arrive, try to read a local paper. Then you'll have a few ideas for questions you can ask local people about the events affecting their communities. This will serve as a good opening gambit for conversations. Carry photos of your home and family, plus a few books about your own country, to show people you meet. Our boatbuilding photo album has been an icebreaker when people with limited English came to visit. A photo book of your own country can do the same.

Be willing to show people through your boat and offer to take them sailing. Nothing will repay their hospitality quite as well as a chance to see how your world works.

Keep on hand a small supply of handicraft-type gifts from countries and ports you have visited plus some wrapping paper. That way, if a new friend invites you to go right home with him because it's his child's birthday, or if you wish to ensure that his wife doesn't feel too invaded, you will have something to take along. A picture of you on your boat makes a nice card to go along with that gift or a bottle of wine.

When we first started out cruising we often were the only yacht in ports we visited, so if we wanted to talk to someone besides each other, we had to look on shore. By 1997, even in the isolated Outer Hebrides, it was rare to find an anchorage without a sailboat in it. But those yachts were owned by Scottish sailors from the mainland, and we saw only one other international-flagged vessel. We could have spent the whole summer enjoyably socializing with those Scottish sailors and still felt like we'd been to a foreign country. But if we had made that choice, enjoyable as it might have been, we would have risked visiting the Outer Hebrides without actually experiencing them. I'd never have joined the hilarity of the local baby-judging competition and heard the kilt-clad judge ask, "Is his father as bald as this one?" I'd never have had the chance to try to play the sweet-sounding miniature harp called a clarsach, nor would I have headed down the rocky hills of Castlebay, Barra, with the local women who had shared another afternoon of Hebridean reels, backsteps, and infectious laughter.

CHAPTER

21

COST-EFFECTIVE, SAFE WAYS TO LEAVE YOUR BOAT AS YOU EXPLORE FARTHER AFIELD

We'd been underway less than five months on *Seraffyn*. It was our first extended cruise and the only thing we owned in the whole world was this 5-ton Lyle Hess cutter we'd built with our four little hands and $4,000 we had tucked away in a term deposit as a safety net, plus cash to last another three months of cruising (about $900 back in 1970). Our plans were to beat back to California against the 25-knot northwesterlies to find work if we couldn't somehow replenish our cruising kitty within the next month or so. This option did not sound terribly interesting as we sat comfortably under our sun awning nibbling the last of the fresh steamed clams from our morning's foraging in the mangroves a mile from where *Seraffyn* lay at anchor. The solitude of our afternoon was shattered by the sound of another boat motoring around the point. "You Larry and Lin?" called the skipper. "Lee over in La Paz said you guys did some delivery work. Come on over and have a drink and a chat."

Three hours later, we were back in our own cockpit feeling pretty excited. If we accepted his proposal, we could top up our kitty for another seven months of Mexican cruising. We'd get a free trip home to visit friends, too. Then it hit. To deliver another man's boat meant we'd have to leave our child-substitute, the most precious possession we had, in a foreign country that had no marinas, yacht clubs, or formal yachting facilities.

Our night-long emotional debate set the tone for the rest of our cruising life. Larry summed it up by stating, "Tonight we have to decide who owns whom." This is a decision most cruisers will have to make someday, whether they are leaving their boat for a long afternoon and evening to go sightseeing on the far side of an island or are on a month-long cruise and have to rush home to handle an emergency. Learning how to ensure your boat's safety can help you feel like we do – that you own your boat, not the other way around.

Not all cruisers make the same choice. We met a well-known couple who never spent a night away from their beautiful 32-foot (9.8m) cutter in 20 years of foreign cruising. "It was not what I wanted," the woman admitted, "but Chuck said he couldn't take the strain of thinking the boat could be dragging or a ship might bash into us when we were away. It's so much work to build a new boat." Only a few years ago, a Dutch couple near whom we moored at Cocos-Keeling Atoll in the Indian Ocean turned down a chance to join a fun birthday party at the magnificent 100-year-old mansion house 5 miles from their anchored boat because they never left it at anchor without one of them being nearby at all times. Other people have cut deeply into their cruising kitty to pay for "the only marina berth available" while they flew home to take care of business – when they could have left their boat just as safely lying on their own anchors at a fraction of the cost.

Boat safety comes through a combination of thinking ahead, having a plan (or maybe plans A, B, and C), and carrying the gear and tools to implement your plans. You can learn the procedures by thinking through and instigating your ideas during short-term absences in familiar waters.

There is less risk (by insurance actuarial tables) in leaving your boat on its own for a week than for a month or more – simply because it is easier to guess at the type of weather your area will experience, there will be fewer other boats passing by, and potential thieves are less likely to notice that she is unattended. But even for one night on shore, we would not leave our boat alone on a mooring or at anchor in an open roadstead. Even in tradewind areas, abnormal onshore winds can happen. (Witness the infamous Cabo San Lucas story, where 29 boats were driven ashore in just this type of situation; see *The Capable Cruiser*, chapter 27.) *View with suspicion any anchorage with less-than-perfect 360-degree protection.*

If there are several equally protected places to moor your boat, choose the one that gives the best protection against theft. An unguarded marina would give easier access to your boat than a mooring out in the open, where an intruder would be more visible. In areas with security problems, such as the north coast of Brazil, choose a locked marina with night-time security patrols.

Mooring or marina, try to be near live-aboards. Marina operators worldwide say a 5 percent contingency of live-aboards can cut theft and other problems. We saw this truism in Fremantle, Western Australia, when we moved ashore for a month. A 45-foot (13.7m) racing yacht exploded into flame at 0100. By the time the fire brigade arrived, half a dozen live-aboard sailors had the blazing vessel out of its berth, clear of

Figure 21-1.
Two- and three-anchor mooring setups, using ship's gear.

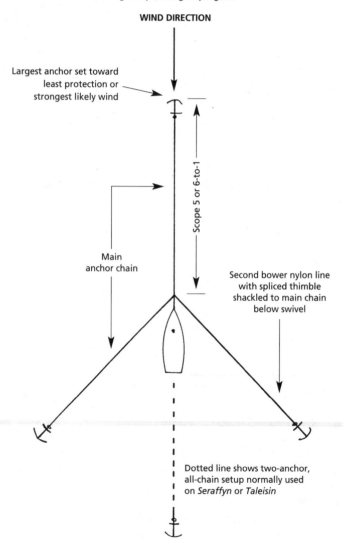

WIND DIRECTION

Largest anchor set toward least protection or strongest likely wind

Scope 5 or 6-to-1

Main anchor chain

Second bower nylon line with spliced thimble shackled to main chain below swivel

Dotted line shows two-anchor, all-chain setup normally used on *Seraffyn* or *Taleisin* other boats, and secured so it could not drift down onto *Taleisin*, only 60 feet (18.3m) to leeward. Try to choose a berth away from frequently used bareboat chartering fleets, sailing schools, and sail-training vessels. This will cut down on the chance of collision.

You can use your own ground tackle to set an excellent mooring. If you do this, look for a space with lots of swinging room, well away from the main channel and any racing marks. In areas known for strong winds from one specific direction, try to be the windward boat. If a neighbor's mooring pendant fails or his anchor drags, you will not be in his path of destruction. In fact, we try to do this whenever we anchor, even for an afternoon.

Be skeptical about using anyone's mooring without inspecting it right away. We once woke up 5 miles downriver, *Seraffyn* still attached to the chain of the mooring we'd been assured was "professionally set only four months ago." We've risked insulting mooring owners in many parts of the world by lying to our own anchor until we could dive and check the mooring. The results of these inspections have reinforced our resolve. Three out of five had defective or badly worn components, the most common of which was unseized or rusted shackle pins. We carry a few spare $5/8$-inch galvanized shackles for such occasions (see Fig. 21-4).

For short forays, we usually set a second anchor and ask someone on a nearby boat to row over and check our "baby." In theft-prone areas, we pay someone to sleep on board. The 16-year-old son of a Canadian cruising family was delighted to earn $5 a night this way in La Paz, Baja California. Thus, we could enjoy five carefree days mingling with California gray whales in the lagoons 400 miles away on the Pacific side of the peninsula with old friends from Mexico. Our caretaker also helped by alerting other sailors who would otherwise have anchored too close and fouled *Taleisin's* ground tackle.

Two final important items before you leave your boat: If possible, remove signs of electronic gear from on deck, and don't discuss your departure on any radio transmission. Remember that many people can be tuned to the same channel. In Mexico, we listened while cruisers broadcast their holiday plans to the people who would be watching their boat. Two hours later, at the shipyard, the local workmen told us about translating this broadcast. "Good thing this isn't Carnival time," one said. "Some of the fishermen who come then aren't as honest as we are."

In some ways, leaving our boat for extended periods can be less hassle than preparing it for short excursions. Longer forays are rarely spur-of-the-moment, so we have more time to make choices and can spread

Figure 21-2. *Setting* Taleisin's *two-anchor mooring.*

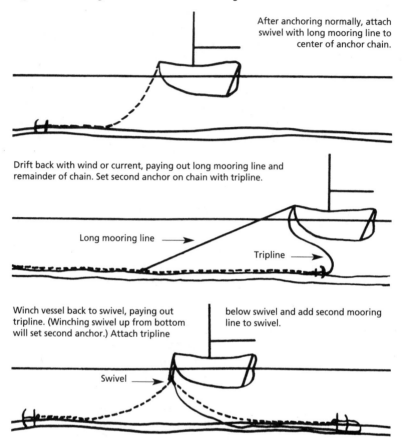

After anchoring normally, attach swivel with long mooring line to center of anchor chain.

Drift back with wind or current, paying out long mooring line and remainder of chain. Set second anchor on chain with tripline.

Long mooring line ⟶

Tripline ⟶

Winch vessel back to swivel, paying out tripline. (Winching swivel up from bottom will set second anchor.) Attach tripline

below swivel and add second mooring line to swivel.

Swivel ⟶

Lower swivel into water to below depth of keel and secure both mooring lines with well-attached chafing gear.

the closing-up chores over a week or two. By then, we know more about the local situation and can choose our "preventive insurance" methods with more confidence. Before you choose among a mooring, your own ground tackle, a marina, or dry storage, certain major concerns need to be addressed while you prepare to set off for four or five months back home. First, no matter how attractive it may seem, *avoid* leaving the boat in any area subject to cyclones during, and a month before and after, the cyclone season. Even in the best marina, your boat can be sunk by wind-driven tidal rises that commonly reach eight or 10 feet above normal and have been known to float marina pontoons right off their pilings. Flying debris can cut through running rigging or worse, and even the most dedicated caretaker may not be able to attend to your boat at the height of such a storm. If you have no other choice, assume there will be a cyclone during your absence and prepare your boat for the "worst case scenario" before you leave. In areas with extreme catatonic winds, such as around New Zealand's Cook Strait, Cape Town in South Africa, or Southern California, avoid berths with more than one-fourth mile of fetch (open water) to windward. The floating dock we used after launching *Taleisin* in Newport Beach, California, was literally torn apart in a Santa Ana wind that gusted to 90 knots across three-fourths mile of open water. Fortunately, our 65-pound, three-piece Luke anchor, kedged out to windward, held us and the dock until the wind diminished.

Deep, narrow river gorges in areas prone to rain squalls can flood. This happened in the Kerikeri River in New Zealand. Friends gave us firsthand accounts of more than 200 boats being damaged, lost, or driven downriver when a once-in-25-years flood raised water levels in the steep-sided river 20 feet and pulled out moorings, wharves and pilings.

Figure 21-3. *The swivel-and-shackle arrangement used when we left* Seraffyn *on two anchors at Pichilinque while we delivered a yacht north.*

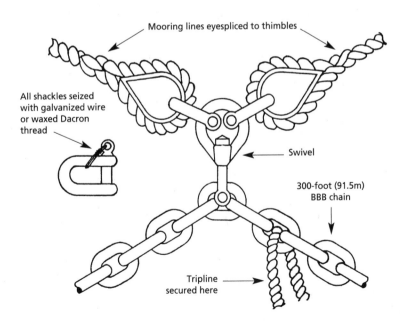

Figure 21-4. *A, B, C, D of checking a typical swing mooring.*

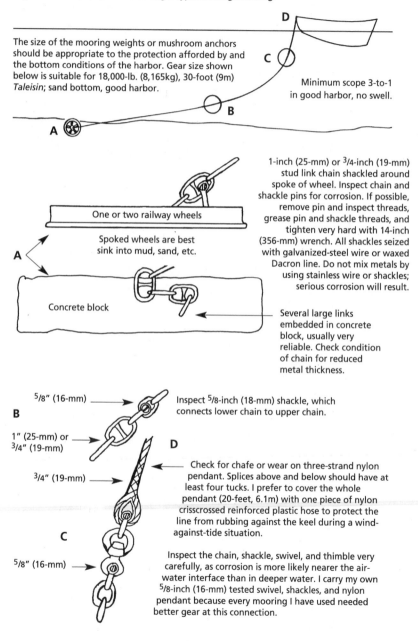

The size of the mooring weights or mushroom anchors should be appropriate to the protection afforded by and the bottom conditions of the harbor. Gear size shown below is suitable for 18,000-lb. (8,165kg), 30-foot (9m) *Taleisin*; sand bottom, good harbor.

Minimum scope 3-to-1 in good harbor, no swell.

One or two railway wheels

Spoked wheels are best sink into mud, sand, etc.

A

Concrete block

1-inch (25-mm) or 3/4-inch (19-mm) stud link chain shackled around spoke of wheel. Inspect chain and shackle pins for corrosion. If possible, remove pin and inspect threads, grease pin and shackle threads, and tighten very hard with 14-inch (356-mm) wrench. All shackles seized with galvanized-steel wire or waxed Dacron line. Do not mix metals by using stainless wire or shackles; serious corrosion will result.

Several large links embedded in concrete block, usually very reliable. Check condition of chain for reduced metal thickness.

5/8" (16-mm)

B

1" (25-mm) or 3/4" (19-mm)

3/4" (19-mm)

C

5/8" (16-mm)

D

Inspect 5/8-inch (18-mm) shackle, which connects lower chain to upper chain.

Check for chafe or wear on three-strand nylon pendant. Splices above and below should have at least four tucks. I prefer to cover the whole pendant (20-feet, 6.1m) with one piece of nylon crisscrossed reinforced plastic hose to protect the line from rubbing against the keel during a wind-against-tide situation.

Inspect the chain, shackle, swivel, and thimble very carefully, as corrosion is more likely nearer the air-water interface than in deeper water. I carry my own 5/8-inch (16-mm) tested swivel, shackles, and nylon pendant because every mooring I have used needed better gear at this connection.

Generally, larger yacht clubs and marinas tend to be more accident-prone than smaller ones. Smaller clubs have fewer foreign visitors, so you'll be more likely to get a little special attention.

A final important point to remember when you are looking for a place to leave your faithful pal is to choose the place, port, or mooring method that is best for the boat, not the one that gives you easiest access to the airport. We learned that by not considering ease of access, we have found safer and less expensive places for the boat. The marina in Palma, Mallorca had easy access to the airport but would have cost $250 a month while we made a four- month delivery trip to the United States. Instead, we chose theft-free Andraitx and put *Seraffyn* on a mooring we set ourselves, then we hired a nearby caretaker for $60 a month. The cost of getting to the airport was less than $100.

Your hull material may have an effect on your choice of mooring, marina, or dry berth. We definitely prefer leaving wooden-hulled *Taleisin* on a swing mooring. Since she will expose different parts of her hull to the sun during different winds and tides, the UV deterioration of paint will be less. Furthermore, the drying effects of the sun will be less likely to cause local shrinkage and cracking, important on any wooden hull, carvel-planked, multi-skinned, or sheathed. (This is also important on epoxy-bonded composite hulls, as exposure to heat can promote delamination.) Even a metal or glass hull will benefit from the improved interior ventilation of swinging to the wind and tide. Your ventilators can be turned forward to catch the breeze, and the boat is clear of other boats and buildings that would block free airflow in a marina berth.

If a boat is in a collision on a mooring, she can often move away from the blow to minimize damage. If she's tied tightly in a marina, the opposite is true. Furthermore, you can inspect every inch of a mooring, using a simple mask and fins, and replace suspect portions inexpensively. This wouldn't be possible in a marina, a much more complex structure. (And even marinas can fail – three marina pontoons in Hout Bay, South Africa, broke loose during the winter of 1995, destroying several yachts.) With one or two mooring pendants covered with plastic hose and led through bow rollers onto winch drums, or bitts designed to take anchor strains, there is less risk of chafe or stress to gear than there is with six or eight lines leading through various fairleads and to various cleats, as would be the case in a marina berth. It is also easier for your hired caretaker (see below) to inspect just one or two mooring lines and catch potential problems. Furthermore, when your caretaker goes out to check your boat, he or she probably will spend a few minutes on board and

Taleisin carried us to South Africa, but only by finding a safe place to leave her, then securing her well, were we able to go off to explore the Kalihari desert and meet members of the amazing Bushman race who live there.

take the time to secure a loose halyard or sail cover. In a marina, the same caretaker could be tempted to take a quick look, then hurry on to a sailing date.

Access for thieves is harder when your boat is out on a mooring – they have to locate a boat to board yours. On the other hand, where small fishboat traffic is frequent, the opposite could be true. Some theft has also resulted from foreign cruisers on a shoestring budget being too easily tempted by moored boats that look deserted.

Using a mooring or setting your own gear as a mooring definitely cuts costs and opens up a lot of potentially less-developed storage locations, but to make it even safer, hire what we call "active insurance" – a caretaker to inspect the mooring lines, wash down the boat twice a week, and open it once a week for airing and bilge inspection. If you are in an unrecognized or nondemarcated mooring area, have the caretaker light an anchor light nightly. This keeps the boat from appearing deserted and makes it legally free of responsibility, should there be a collision. When we look for a caretaker, we try to choose one who can do something to solve problems should they occur. In South Africa, we paid a monthly fee of $60 to Roger Clancey, a professional diver and boatbuilder with his own workboat who lived aboard about 300 meters from *Taleisin*. He kept his workboat *Spanner* tied alongside, so he could get to our boat quickly if necessary.

It really does pay to make this caretaker arrangement a professional one. Accepting the kind offer of free help from a new friend or a cruising buddy could be a poor way to save money. In a nonprofessional arrangement, when things start going wrong, your chum naturally will take care of his boat first, yours second. But a professional has his local reputation to consider.

A guarded marina berth is probably the best choice in high-theft areas or where cost is not a factor and UV damage and heat are not too high a risk. But if possible, try to moor away from boats with heavy arrays of electronic gear and/or permanently rigged shore-power cables. Chances of electrolysis can be increased in these close quarters.

To make sure people in adjacent berths do not uncleat your lines, use unsplit nylon-reinforced PVC hose on each line. Run it through the base of each cleat on the dock and tie it with a snug bowline, then adjust it on the deck of your boat. The only way someone can untie it is by boarding your boat.

Before you leave your boat, look at the mooring-line arrangements used by well-maintained local boats. If they have specialized snubbing gear, such as chains and weights, rubber bungees, or doubled-up lines, invest in similar gear for yourself. A marina that looks wonderfully calm during one weather pattern can be subject to heavy surge during another.

For fiberglass- or metal-hulled cruising boats, dry storage could be the most economical choice. Steel or alloy boats will be less prone to corrosion and electrolysis when they are out of salt water. Fiberglass hulls can have a good, long dry-out period to delay or even prevent the moisture absorption that can lead to osmosis. The cost of lifting the boat out of the water can be covered by planning your yearly bottom painting for your return. But before you are tempted by an onshore berth, look at the worst-case figures for high tides and storms in the area. If the storage yard is on a large bay and only a few feet above high water, it could be awash in a storm. This happened to us in England, where once-in-300-years tides combined with extreme storm winds to send 4-foot waves through the boatyard where *Seraffyn* was stored for the winter. When there is a choice between a storage yard exposed to potential waves and one farther up a backwater or on higher ground, choose the higher ground.

As we suggested in chapter 14, ask the yard manager to place your boat out of the normal working area of Travelifts or boat-moving gear,

We spent seven months exploring the most isolated areas of Namibia, Botswana and Zimbabwe using a four-wheel-drive camper we outfitted in South Africa. This safari, is, to date, one of the most memorable times of our cruising life.

bow-to the strongest expected winds and preferably next to low-center-of-gravity powerboats or multihulls. Finally, no matter how secure the cradle chosen for your boat looks, no matter what assurances the yard personnel give you, inspect the cradle system yourself and add extra supports for insurance. You might notice the cracked weld or the worn, corroded bolt that a less-interested person could miss. Research cradle design and boat-support methods to know what to look for – not only when you plan to store your boat for long periods, but for each haulout you need during normal sailing.

Once your storage choice is made, you can begin the final preparations. In poorer countries, where one piece of boat gear could represent half of a man's salary for the year, consider finding someone on shore who is willing to lock up your gear in a garage or basement. Of greatest concern should be easily fenced electronic gear and inflatable dinghies. Then tell everybody and make an obvious display of removing your gear from the boat. Decommission your boat, removing not only deck hardware or lines that could tempt others, but also canvaswork such as dodgers, seat covers, solar panels, deck-stored sails and especially roller-furling sails. This will cut down on damage induced by months of sun and wind and also present less windage for gales or storms. Tie extra lines around your mainsail cover to keep it from flogging and chafing. Consider lashing a heavy-duty canvas cover over the boom and out to the toerails as a tent to cover varnish or paintwork on your deckhouse. We find that synthetic carpet, fuzzy-side down, makes a perfect long-term protector for varnish work on boomkins and bowsprits. We lash it in place securely with nylon twine.

The final step for long-term, no-hassle foreign boat storage is to check the legalities with customs officials. Also check with immigration officials about re-entry for yourself. A word of warning from another cruiser saved us a lot of problems. We had a new re-entry visa added to our passports, explaining that we were returning to a yacht in temporary storage in South Africa. Without that visa, we would have had to post a repatriation bond of almost $3,000 to get back to *Taleisin* after our four-wheel-drive safari into the wilds of Namibia, Botswana, and Zimbabwe.

Also, carry a copy of your entry documents to prove you own the boat and that it is "under bond." A copy of our European Customs clearance solved all problems when we were returning to *Taleisin* after a six- month working visit to the United States. Ticket agents at Los Angeles Airport would not let us board the flight to London until we showed them this document – proof to them that we had a means of leaving England when our visit ended.

Though the planning necessary to leave your boat for long periods sounds daunting enough to make you say, "Better to sail the boat home, then come back by plane," don't be put off; don't let your boat own you. Once you've tried it, you'll find it is logical and not too tedious. Twenty-six years ago, back in Mexico, we learned to leave *Seraffyn* and we've used that knowledge to leave *Taleisin* and forget about her, knowing we've put our money and time into prevention instead of spending it to cure problems that cropped up later. The ability to leave our boat to venture inland lightheartedly has added tremendously to the personal freedom that is the special charm of cruising.

NOTE: Over the past three decades, we've left first *Seraffyn*, then *Taleisin*, in 19 different countries. Our absences have ranged from two or three days in the Dindings River of Malaysia to seven months in South Africa. Not once has either boat suffered from any theft or damage other than some chafed paint from the lines securing our canvas covers.

HANDS ON: UPGRADES AND IDEAS FOR THE BOAT YOU OWN NOW

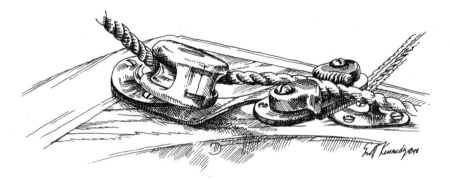

WE'VE NOTICED THAT THE MOST CONTENTED, successful long-term voyagers are those who take a hands-on approach to maintaining and upgrading their cruising boat. It is not only low-budget cruisers who come to enjoy using their own skills to maintain and build new items for their boat; we've seen high-powered executive types, on custom-built 50-footers (15.3m), completely hooked on doing the varnishwork themselves, or in creating some simple new item for their own boat. An amazing number of previously unhandy first-time cruisers eventually find they want to install a workbench on board so they can progress to doing more of their own upgrading, their own maintenance.

In today's computer-driven world, many of us feel we are losing the use of our own hands; we lament that handcrafting skills are being lost. But once you get afloat, you will have the time (and often the need) to upgrade your boat using your own skills. Start by trying some of the simple ideas shown in these chapters, and we're sure you will grow to feel comfortable fixing more and more of the gear you have on board. Each skill you gain helps you control costs as you cruise. You may even find you can earn extra cruising funds as we have done, by using ideas shown in the last two chapters of this section.

CHAPTER

22

BY THE MARK

Fresh, gusty wind; long day of sailing; exciting but tiring dusk entry through a range of leading lights into a safe but crowded harbor. Pick a spot and get that anchor down, set the anchor light; dinner is sizzling in the oven and wonderful aromas drift into the cockpit.

It is dark by the time you take a tour of the anchorage and choose your spot. "Come on up and help me get the anchor set; it won't take five minutes," you call to your partner. Your boat positioned just where you want it, you give the signal: "Let go that anchor, we're in 35 feet of water. Snub the chain when you reach 180 feet."

A gust catches your bow and chain rumbles with increasing speed, out the hawsepipe and over the bow roller. In the dark, it is difficult to judge distances, and you call, "We seem to be getting pretty close to the boat astern of us. Got full scope out yet?" Your partner calls back, "Not sure; didn't see any of those marks you painted. I'll stop the chain and get a better flashlight."

Chain snubbed, the next gust hits and you begin dragging. Before either of you can let out more chain, you are too close to the other boat. So, you'll need to lift the chain and anchor so you can move back to the right spot to do it all again. As the chain comes up, you find you only had about 80 feet out when your partner went to find the flashlight. Reason? The paint at the 60-foot mark has mostly flaked off. You maneuver back into position and do it right this time. But dinner is overcooked, and both of you are grumbly, forgetting that the rest of the day had held fine sailing – all discounted because of what is only one small pre-cruise detail, marking your anchor chain or anchor line.

Knowing exactly how much line or chain you have let out of the locker seems of little importance when you are at the dock. But the above scenario is one we've seen reenacted time and again, one in which we've been unhappy participants a few times ourselves. In fact, it is probably the main cause of dragging anchor, as without easy-to-observe markings, it is difficult to know if you've let out the five-to-one scope your anchor needs with chain, the seven-to-one scope it needs with line, so it can work at full holding power.

It took a lot of experimenting for us to find durable, simple ways to mark both our anchor chain and the nylon line that makes up our second bower. The criteria for good bower markings is that they must be easily visible in daylight or with a flashlight at night. Better yet, especially on line, the marks should be easy to feel as they glide through your hand. In all cases, the marks should be easy to tally so you know at a glance the difference between 20 fathoms and 40 fathoms. The numbering system we finally evolved allows us to end-for-end either nylon or chain to spread the wear without re-marking the chain or line or rememorizing a now-backward numbering system.

Our chain-marking system evolved along common routes. Years ago, we painted some links with a code to mark every 5 fathoms. The paint flaked off within three months of cruising use. Then came galvanized seizing wire – three turns on the chain link marking the fifth fathom, two links with three turns of wire to mark the tenth fathom. These markings lasted, but they didn't show up well, day or night, unless the chain was eased out slowly. Then came store-bought plastic markings. The cathead on the anchor windlass ripped them off one at a time. Final solution: short lengths of $1/2$-inch wide flat, tubular nylon webbing sewn around the appropriate chain links, with a one-inch tab sticking out like a little flag. The flag cannot be much longer or it will jam in the cathead; if it's

Chain marking

shorter, your flashlight can miss it. The stitching must be strong. We use four or five turns of doubled Dacron sailmaker's waxed twine, knot the ends, and heat-seal them. (We also heat-seal the ends of the tubular webbing to keep it from fraying with use.) We've found that these markings last as long as the galvanizing on our chain – or about 30 months of cruising and lying to the anchor 90 percent of the year. They are easy to see and easy to feel at night. Finally, they are easy to remove when it is time to regalvanize the chain.

Our line-marking system evolved similarly: Cloth markers and store-bought reinforced plastic markers all ripped off as we winched in the line. If they didn't rip off, they caused a jam on the winch as turn lay tightly against turn on the drum while we cranked in the line. Nylon webbing tabs didn't work here, no matter how short we made them. Then we found dark blue polyester fishnet mending line (0.75mm diameter) in a fisherman's supply house. Larry made tight sailmaker's seizings at the appropriate intervals, using the same numbering system as we do for chain. Since line does not have the same logical spacings as chain, he chose to put each of the seizings 1 to $1^1/2$ inches apart wherever they were used in multiples. Now, day or night, the contrast in colors makes the markings easy to spot. Even better, because of the completely different textures created by the seizing lying across the nylon line, we can feel the marks as they slide through our hands, so we don't have to fumble with a flashlight as we set the ground tackle.

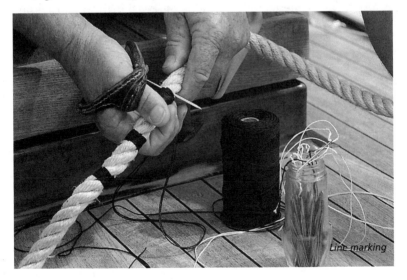

Line marking

The actual numbering system we use is based on fathoms and follows the pattern shown for our normal-length warps of 300 feet or 50 fathoms.

MARKING SYSTEM

0 (anchor attached)

5 fathoms	30 feet (9.2m)	1 mark
10 fathoms	60 feet (18.3m)	2 marks
15 fathoms	90 feet (27.5m)	3 marks
20 fathoms	120 feet (36.6m)	4 marks
25 fathoms	150 feet (45.8m)	1 mark
30 fathoms	180 feet (55m)	4 marks – striped
35 fathoms	210 feet (64.1m)	3 marks – striped
40 fathoms	240 feet (73.2m)	2 marks – striped
45 fathoms	270 feet (82.4m)	1 mark – striped
50 fathoms	300 feet (91.5m)	bitter end of chain bower secured inboard to 50-foot (15.3m) snubbing line

In other words, we put a nylon tab on each of two links at 10 fathoms. At 40 fathoms, there are also two tabbed links, but the tabs have stripes down their length. The stripe is added with a black marker. The ink is indelible and lasts even in salt water.

The reason for the ascending, then descending marking system is twofold: It cuts the tedium of sewing on a geometrically increasing number of tabs or seizings and, more important, when we notice that the galvanizing at one end of the chain is getting a bit dented or showing spots of rust, we switch the anchor to the end that has lived most of its life in the chain locker. This usually gives us an extra year between expensive (and hassle-laden) jaunts to the galvanizer. End-for-ending is also important for spreading the chafe that shortens the useful life of your nylon anchor rode. When you switch ends the numbering system reads just the same.

A simple problem, a simple solution. But that is one of the nicest aspects of pottering around in boats. It's a small job you can do with your own hands at little cost on an otherwise-boring rainy day. A week, a month, or a year later, you'll bless those busy quiet hours as the easy-to-spot bower markings slide over the roller to help you set the proper scope so you can quickly get out of the howling wind and lashing rain to enjoy the warmth of your cabin in a secure and friendly anchorage.

CHAPTER
23
THE BETTER BUCKET

It is such a simple chore, lifting water from the sea. Seems like any old bucket should work. But at sea, nothing is ever that simple. You've just caught a glowing, leaping, 18-pound mahi-mahi (dorado). Your luck holds and you land it flapping, glorious gold and royal blue. The battle over, the fish subdued, reality hits – blood and scales litter the battlefield. You are moving at 6 or 7 knots and you want to sluice the decks with salt water quickly before the sun turns scales into sequins that will stick like barnacles all along your side deck. You grab your plastic bucket with a rope spliced around its metal bail, but when you toss it overboard, it skips and bounces and refuses to dip its brim. Five tries later, it finally fills and almost jerks you overboard. If the bail doesn't pull out, the metal handle quite often scratches your topsides. We know the drill, because we've tried all sorts of buckets over the years. Canvas ones with wooden bottoms are designed so the wood floats to tip the rim – great, but in a seaway, the wooden bottom swings wildly as you pull the water on board and thumps threateningly against everything in its path. So get rid of the wood, but then the rim won't dip and scoop up water. After a dozen years of trying, we think the perfect deck bucket has evolved, one that can be made by hand in about an hour or two. For materials, you'll need $1/2$ yard of sail-cover cloth (Sunbrella or the like), 3 yards of $3/8$-inch or $1/2$-inch line (new or used, three-strand or braid), and 2 or 3 ounces of lead (fishing weights or old wheel-balancing weights will do).

To make the bucket, form an 8-inch (20.3cm) diameter grommet using 28 inches (71.1cm) of line. You can make a proper longspliced grommet, or simply overlap the line and stitch it together to form a circle (Fig. 23-1). Next, fold a 27-inch-by-20-inch piece of fabric, as shown in Figures 23-2 and 23-3, and stitch the end together. You can use a machine, but it's just as fast to hand-stitch the material using a running stitch and waxed sail-repair twine. Open out the tube and fold it through and over the rope grommet, with the raw edge of the seam hidden from view in what are now the double sides for your bucket. The double-layered sides help hold the water even as the canvas ages.

Figure 23-1. ROPE RIM. *Step One*

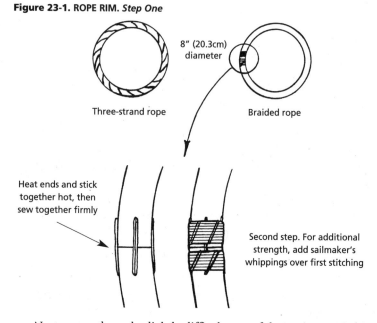

8″ (20.3cm) diameter

Three-strand rope

Braided rope

Heat ends and stick together hot, then sew together firmly

Second step. For additional strength, add sailmaker's whippings over first stitching

Next comes the only slightly difficult part of the project – stitching in the double bottom. In sewing parlance, you pin one edge of the bottom fabric to the sides of the bucket. Ease the sides and bottom together, working slowly around and pinning it every inch. Use spare sail needles if your regular pins are too short. When you are halfway around, start from the opposite direction. The fabric will have puckers in it, and you may have to re-pin it two or three times to get it to lie nicely. But once you sew the double bottom to the sides and turn the bucket right side out, the final product will look and work fine.

Figure 23-2. BETTER BUCKET CONSTRUCTION. *Step Two*

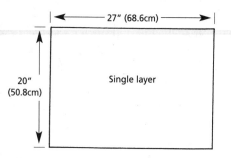

27″ (68.6cm)

20″ (50.8cm)

Single layer

Figure 23-3. *Step Three*

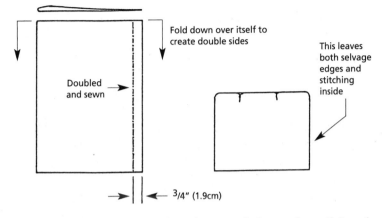

Fold down over itself to create double sides

This leaves both selvage edges and stitching inside

Doubled and sewn

3/4" (1.9cm)

Next step is to run a line of stitching just below and parallel to the rope brim (Fig.23-4) to hold it in place.

To fit the rope bail, form two small grommets out of 1/16-inch nylon three-strand twine and stitch them on each side of the bucket. This works better than metal grommets, as there is nothing on the bucket to scratch topsides or varnishwork on deck. Just before we splice the rope bail onto the bucket, we add the secret ingredient.

Melt the 2 ounces of lead in an old tin can. A stove burner works fine for this, but make sure the tin and the lead are absolutely dry before you begin the meltdown, or the lead can blow all over the stove. Pour the

Figure 23-4. *Step Four*

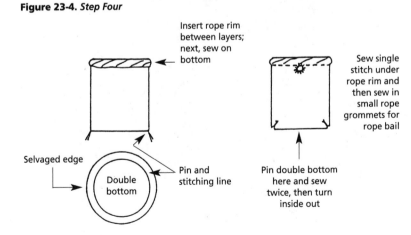

Insert rope rim between layers; next, sew on bottom

Sew single stitch under rope rim and then sew in small rope grommets for rope bail

Selvaged edge

Double bottom

Pin and stitching line

Pin double bottom here and sew twice, then turn inside out

melted lead into a big soup ladle or a beer can to form a slightly rounded, pancake-like shape. When the lead is cool, it will drop right off the ladle. Now drill a hole on each edge of this weight, using a heated sail needle or awl or a small drill. Then sew the weight inside the bucket – just below the rim and midway between the grommets for your bail.

Splice a short, three-strand rope bail in place, or tie a handle onto the bucket using bowlines if braid is your rope choice. Then splice or tie 8 feet (2.4m) of line onto the bail as a hauling line. We prefer three- strand

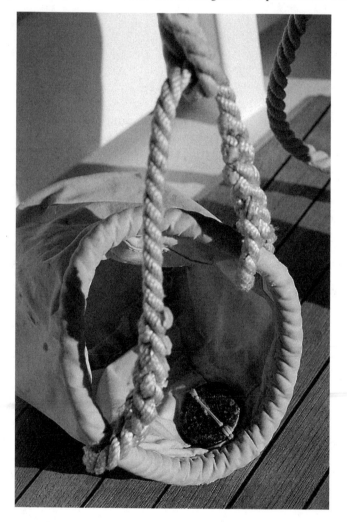

line for the hauling line of the bucket, as its natural finger-holds make it easier to grip. We also like to use line that is $7/16$-inch or $1/2$-inch in diameter, as it is easier to grip than smaller-diameter line.

When you are sailing fast, clove-hitch the inboard end of the hauling line on deck, just in case the bucket is jerked out of your hands. The lead-weighted bucket will tilt and fill on the first try, whether at anchor or sailing at speed.

Nothing on the bucket can scratch or dent the topside finish, and the bucket squashes flat for storage. Don't be tempted to make it much larger than the given dimensions, or it becomes too heavy to pull on board when you are moving fast.

The Better Bucket makes a perfect gift for a friend's boat launching. And if you keep your boat on a swing mooring, far from a dock hose, the easy-to-use bucket makes it far easier to remove birds' messy calling cards. The final reward: You'll smile with satisfaction each time you use something you made on board with your own hands.

CHAPTER

24

KEEP IT FLOWING

Most of us are familiar with houses where clothes and kitchenware are all neatly hidden behind doors, so it's not surprising that our first reaction is to try for the same organized appearance afloat. Unfortunately, on a cruising boat, this is exactly what can promote mildew, rusted canned food, short-lived produce, and sometimes even hull damage. A flow of fresh air plus good drainage is vital inside your boat. After you make sure there is sufficient ventilation coming into the boat, you must make sure air can keep moving. This means reconsidering the way you look at lockers and doors. So if you are planning a new interior for your boat, modifying parts of the one you now own, or just trying to cut down on mildew problems, some of the following ideas could help you improve airflow.

The open plan forward cabin

One of the best ways to provide for free airflow is to avoid cutting up your boat into compartments. Every separate compartment makes your boat appear smaller and restricts ventilation. On *Taleisin*, we eliminated the top half of the chain-locker bulkhead. The 275 feet (83.9 m) of anchor chain flakes into an area well below this partition, and all you can see when you look forward is the downpipe for the chain. Without doors or bulkheads, this area is easily accessible for other uses. Instead of looking like it measures 7 feet (2m) long, the forward cabin appears 10 feet long, and air can flow easily from the forward vents through this whole area. To keep mud or salt water inside the chain locker, we hook in place a Dacron spray curtain when necessary.

The use of curtains instead of doors can increase ventilation throughout your cruising home. As a bonus, curtains are less costly, simpler to build and install, lighter in weight, require less hardware, and can be more easily maintained than doors. They require less room to open and are quieter as they deaden sounds instead of creating rattles. They can be changed inexpensively to revive the decor of your boat. On smaller boats, space limitations could make curtains your only logical choice. But even on larger boats, curtains can work well. On board *Gipsy Pearl*, a handsome 40-foot (12.2m) ketch built by Paul Procter, substantial, luxurious curtains form the doors for his two forward cabins and the head. To keep air flowing, Paul set his brass curtain rods about 5 inches (12.7cm) below the tops of the openings and cut the curtains so they hang the same distance above the floor. The curtains can be left slightly open to let extra light or air into the cabins yet still provide adequate privacy. This is definitely an advantage over solid doors, which cannot be left partially open at sea or in port.

Curtains can also work like two-way doors, at little cost. Instead of having a solid door for our hanging locker, Larry secured two hooks, 2 inches (51-mm) below deck level, just inside the framing for the locker. I made a simple curtain, hemmed top and bottom, using the same dark-green velour we use for our cabin cushions. A length of shock cord, with a loop at each end, acts as a curtain rod inside the top hem turnover. A white, 3/16-inch (4-mm)-diameter, three-strand line with eyes spliced to each end secures across the curtain halfway down. This keeps it and the clothes from swinging in a seaway and also acts as a tieback for the curtain. If you install a third hook across the companionway from the hanging locker, this same curtain can close the passageway between the forepeak and the main cabin. The shock-cord loop simply unhooks from the forward end of the locker and swings across to hook on the far side of

Figure 24-1.

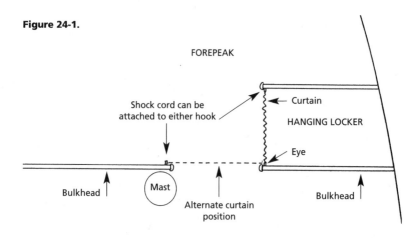

the companionway. Inexpensive, yet effective, the curtain adds a softness to the forward cabin that a solid door would not, and air can circulate into the hanging locker at all times. (See Figure 24-1.)

For those who prefer, ventilation can be provided by correct door

Figure 24-2.

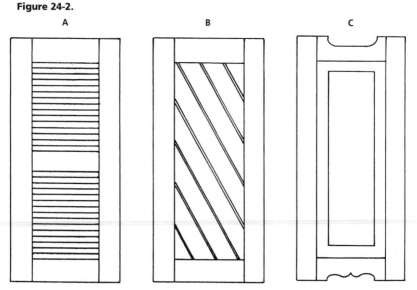

A	B	C
Louvered door Additional center rail strengthens louvered panels	**Diagonal slats** **with 7/16-inch (11-mm) gaps** This is a strong easy-to-build door	**Raised-panel door** Two types of vents you can sabersaw into the rails

design. Cane-centered doors look handsome, are lightweight, and provide excellent ventilation. Unfortunately, they are not particularly strong, so they should not be used for larger doors that could be subjected to the thump of crew being tossed at sea. The same can be said of fully louvered doors (Fig. 24-2a), which have the additional drawback of being hard to clean or refinish. Other ventilating-door options are shown in Figure 24-2. Our favorite probably is the door found in some older Concordia yawls (Fig. 24-2b). If you have solid doors now, you can cut away a portion of the top and bottom in a handsome sweep, as shown in Figure 24-2c. This will weaken the door only slightly, and it will provide good airflow.

If you are fitting out a new interior, providing proper ventilation to clothes-storage areas starts with open-spaced hull ceiling. Most production boats are built with separate liners forming the fronts and tops of lockers, while the hull forms the back. This is economical for the builder, but whenever water temperatures are significantly lower than interior temperatures, condensation will spring up below your boat's waterline and soak into anything in contact with your hull. So any clothes lockers at or below water level should be fitted with a ceiling set on small frames to provide about $3/4$-inch (19-mm) of air space between the hull and clothes. The slats should be spaced $1/4$-inch(6.4-mm) apart. Not only will this open-style ceiling provide ventilation, but if your deck or hull develops leaks, the water probably will flow between the hull and the ceiling, so your clothes will stay dry.

For food lockers in which ceiling would take up too much space and also be difficult to keep clean, we've found an excellent solution at a plastics supply house. (It is also available at marine stores specializing in gear for large sportfishing boats.) This heavy-duty plastic, open-weave $1/8$-inch (3.2-mm)- thick screenlike material is designed to cut down on rattling caused by vibration. We've cut this matting to fit every food locker and also to fit under pots and pans stored on shelves under the galley sink. With the mat in place, few cans have rusted, the hull finish is protected, and minor spills drain under the provisions. The matting can be handwashed or run through a washing machine and dryer.

To get air into any lockers without ceiling, nonstructural bulkheads that form their ends can be built of slats with $1/2$-inch (13-mm)-wide air spaces. We use this system for the sides of lockers and the ends of pilot berths. Our policy is, if there is no reason to close it off, leave it open. Even with structural bulkheads, limber holes big enough to get a finger through should be provided at the lowest point and next to any framing that could stop the downward flow of water. If water can't flow out, air can't flow in. Once when we were delivering a new boat from Florida to its owner in Puerto Rico, we had stored our portable shortwave receiver in the "waterproof" hanging locker. After two days of bashing against the Gulf Stream, we opened the door to find our radio half-submerged in salt water. The bottom of the locker was watertight, but the deck above it had leaked. This sealed bottom was not only a water and air trap but also a surefire recipe for mildew.

On a boat with deckbeams, it makes sense to stop the fore-and-aft faces of storage lockers just below the beams. This makes fitting joinery easier and helps with ventilation. The same is true of cabinets fitted in boats with a deck liner. There is no reason to carry the faces right to the top, and fitting will be far easier. Handsomely designed but open-fronted dish-storage racks help keep air flowing. Even more important than dish racks are book racks. Books love to mildew. Yet by building book racks that allowed air to flow in back of the books as well as beneath them, we've been able to carry some of our favorite books for more than 25 years with no major deterioration. Figure 24-3 shows an easy-to-build, easy-to-install book rack such as we use.

During long passages, hard vegetables such as onions, garlic, potatoes, and squashes last twice as long in baskets stored in open areas. So instead of enclosing the locker under our stove with a curtain or door, we've learned to keep it tidy and now enjoy seeing baskets full of fresh provisions. Other sailors accomplish the same thing by using hanging

Figure 24-3. VENTILATED BOOK SHELF

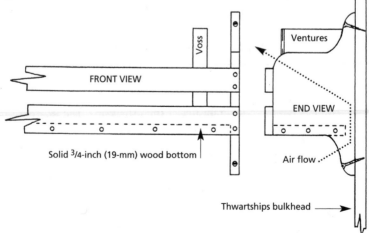

FRONT VIEW

Voss

Solid 3/4-inch (19-mm) wood bottom

Ventures

END VIEW

Air flow

Thwartships bulkhead

nets slung just below deck level to hold fresh produce. This is an excellent idea as long as the nets swing well clear of any obstacles. A new voyager told us a gruesome story. She climbed into the forepeak to retrieve some fresh fruit from one of five hammocks slung below the deck. Instead of fresh, sweet, fruit she found that three days of boisterous sailing had pounded everything to a gooey, oozing pulp against the side of the hull. After that incident, she moved the hammocks so they could swing freely in the center of the forepeak.

A leave-it-open policy, combined with hammocks, worked well in designing storage areas for the quarter berths of a 47-foot (14.3m) cutter Larry was upgrading in New Zealand. The quarter berths on *Sorceress* were wider than necessary for sleeping, and her owner, Peter Bailey, asked Larry to build wooden lockers against the hull to hold blankets, pillows, and guests' gear. We suggested mocking up two levels of canvas gear hammocks. Peter immediately agreed they worked better than wooden cabinets, as they were lightweight, inexpensive to build and install, fully ventilated, and soft for the crew to lie against in the leeward bunk. These hammocks provided flexible storage and a sense of openness that would have been lost with solid cabinet doors (See Figure 24-4.)

If you are trying to improve ventilation in the boat you now have, consider drilling air holes between lockers and through bunkboards or bunk faces. Think of using cedar slats instead of solid sheets of plywood for locker shelves and bunkboards. Remember that every locker needs limber holes at its lowest point. Look at your floorboards and bilges to try to picture the airflow through this area. Are there openings throughout the boat or are all of the floors fitted and screwed down right to the edges of the hull? One-inch (2.54cm) finger holes drilled right through the floorboards keep air flowing. One-inch limber holes at the low points of fore-and-aft bulkheads help it along. A final bonus with these limber holes and air passages is that you'll be able to use a bucket of water and scrub and bleach out all the lockers during a spring cleanup.

A spring cleanup is an important part of keeping mildew out of a cruising boat. Mildew spores spread easily, especially if there is moisture to keep them fed and growing. Salt attracts moisture, and every time you go inside your boat, you take small amounts of salt with you on your clothes and shoes. It is amazing how it creeps through the boat, eventually reaching every corner, no matter how careful you are. Since there is no wiring through most of *Taleisin*, we are able to empty each section and take a hose, bucket of soap, bleach, and a soft brush and scrub down everything from the deckhead to the bilge. This gets out the

Figure 24-4. CANVAS GEAR HAMMOCK FOR BERTHS

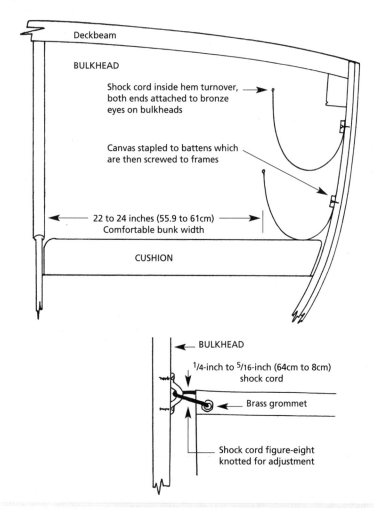

salt and virtually eliminates mildew. As we clean, we survey every inch of the inside of the boat, usually finding some redundant gear we don't need. But even if you cannot empty whole sections of your boat for an annual hose-out, a locker-by-locker washdown and inventory can help your boat and all your gear last longer and stay fresher. As you work, you'll find and clear any blocked limber holes and you'll also be able to assess the need for additional ventilation.

Although owners of wooden boats are constantly reminded that an easy flow of air inside their boats is necessary to prevent rot, airflow is just as important for every boat, no matter what the hull material. Plywood and timber used for bulkheads and interior joinery in any hull will be far less likely to rot or delaminate if all of the recesses of your boat are open to a reasonable flow of air and good water drainage. Fiberglass osmosis is known to be aggravated by moisture seeping into hull laminates from both inside and outside the boat. Unaired, condensation-prone lockers can act as moisture traps to promote the onset of the pox. We learned this from personal experience when a large blister bulged out through the gelcoat of our fiberglass tender. The source? We'd left a tiny puddle of water sitting inside the waterproof forward compartment for several months. In steel or alloy hulls, the onset of corrosion can be delayed if the insides of lockers are kept drained and dry by free air movement. Both fresh and canned provisions will last longer in a well-aired boat. As a real bonus, that favorite evening dress or sport coat you stored away while you explored the coves of the outer Bahamas, the lagoons of Baja California, or the wilds of Turkey can be pulled out fresh-smelling and ready for use when you sail into the night spots of Freeport, Acapulco, or Mykonos.

CHAPTER

25

AIRING THE SUBJECT

A crusty British sailor we met in the Azores apologized for his soggy settee cushions by saying, "If you didn't want to get wet, you wouldn't go to sea, would you?" We laughed as he explained how water came in through his ventilators. But his plight highlighted the problem facing cruising sailors. How do you get lots of air flowing through your boat without water coming in with it? This is a problem often ignored by designers and builders, probably because of the cost. But you need to consider it seriously before you move on board your boat for more than a week or two.

Insufficient ventilation will cause the inside of your boat to smell musty; clothes and sails stored below will grow spots of mildew; leather goods will sprout hairdos of mold; and, most important, your crew can grow groggy and more prone to seasickness if there is a shortage of fresh air flowing through the boat. In port, lack of ventilation can be even more serious, especially in rainy or wintry conditions. One winter night in England, we came close to suffocating on board *Seraffyn*. As soon as we mentioned this, several people showed us newspaper reports of whole families dying from asphyxiation and carbon-monoxide poisoning during high-latitude winters when they closed the hatches to keep out rain or snow, then used an open oven or barbecue to cut the chill.

So to create safety and comfort on board your floating home, and to eliminate mildew-damaged gear, first calculate the volume of air you'll need moving through your boat using the table at Figure 25-1. Then consider adding as many of the ventilation options as practical. Most of the ones described here can be home-built with a minimum of expense.

It is difficult to do actual on-board tests to determine if there is sufficient airflow inside your boat in all conditions. Ventilators that work well when the wind is blowing 15 knots, may not be sufficient when the wind is only five knots. Airflow patterns change as the wind direction changes. With the boat laying head to wind, two Dorades and a

Figure 25-1. *Sparkman and Stephens' guidelines for determining the correct number and size of Dorade vents for safe use on a racing/cruising yacht.*

The total intake area in square inches should equal beam times load waterline length (computed in feet).

Diameter of each hole	Intake area (cowl mouth
3 inches	28 sq.in.
4 inches	50 sq.in.
5 inches	78 sq.in.
6 inches	113 sq.in.

For a 35-foot (10.7m)-waterline hull with 10 feet (3.1m) of beam:
35 x 10 = 350

Therefore, a good choice of vents would be:
4 – 4-inch vents   4 x 50 sq. in. = 200
2 – 5-inch vents   2 x 78 sq. in. = 156
                     for a total of 356 sq. in.

mushroom ventilator aft could provide adequate airflow, but with the wind on the beam or from aft, the airflow could decrease dramatically. It is up to you to watch for clues which could indicate insufficient airflow. If you use oil lamps for lighting, and notice that they begin to dim when you have the cabin closed up, or when you light the burners on your stove, this indicates there isn't enough ventilation in your boat to provide for safe human occupation. If you did nothing to provide more air, you'd soon find your crew growing groggy. People who fall asleep at this point could succumb to asphyxiation. If you do not have an oil lamp and live on board during inclement weather which forces you to keep the boat closed up to retain heat, it could pay to have a candle burning to provide a warning. If the flame dims or the candle begins to smoke, open a hatch immediately – then think of ways to add more permanent ventilation.

Another clue to poor ventilation is a tendency for oil lamps, heating stoves, or even the burners on your cookstove to cause soot or smoke stains in spite of being properly trimmed or stoked. If the flames on your cookstove change color and begin burning orange instead of blue, they are being starved of oxygen. How much ventilation do you need? According to *Skene's Elements of Yacht Design*, 15 cubic feet of fresh air per minute for each person on board is an appropriate safety and comfort minimum.

To work properly, any ventilation system must include not only air intakes but also exhaust routes. As you consider increasing flow through your boat, remember that you'll need the same volume of aft-facing vents as forward-facing ones. This way, your system will work well whether running before the wind or lying at anchor.

The most effective way to increase ventilation, no matter which way the wind is blowing, is to add properly designed Dorade vents. If you install these as the original designer (Rod Stephens of the Sparkman and Stephens design team) recommends, near the centerline of the deck plan so they are less likely to be submerged in a knockdown situation, they are amazingly wave- and sprayproof, yet they let in more air than any other vent we have seen.

Dorade vents do have some drawbacks. They will snag lines and feet, take up a lot of space on deck, make a breeze sound like a gale, and turn the inside of the boat into a drafty refrigerator. To cut down on jibsheet snags, we use flexible PVC vents instead of rigid brass ones. On larger yachts, where half a dozen or more Dorades must decorate the deck, we've seen stainless-steel guardrails bolted around vents that could otherwise catch jibsheets. Properly located, these guards can add excellent handholds and strategic tie-down points for light deck gear. By turning the vent 90 degrees away from strong winds, you can cut the noise, so life below decks is calmer. The turned cowl will still provide sufficient air once the wind on deck is over 12 knots, as you can see from Figure 25-2.

Although the blast through your vents can be annoying during a cold winter evening, the seemingly expedient plan of building plugs to jam into them from below decks is unsafe. With the ventilators plugged, gases from stove burners, heaters, and human breathing, plus the consumption of unreplenished oxygen, can lead to asphyxiation. A safer solution is a damper for the inside of the vent, one designed to redirect or cut down on airflow without blocking it completely. In extreme weather at sea, we turn the cowls on our Dorades so they face directly away from wind and sea. The boat still stays aired and in spite of taking a fair share of green

Figure 25-2. *Air intake for various sizes of cowl or Dorade vents, measured in cubic feet per minute.*

Vent size	4 knots of wind	12 knots of wind	16 knots of wind
3 inches	8 cfm	29	42
4 inches	12 cfm	50	73
5 inches	21 cfm	80	112
6 inches	35 cfm	117	162

To provide for safety and comfort below decks, 15 cubic feet of air per person per minute is recommended.

water on board, none has come below through the Dorades. Some sailors carry deck plates to replace the cowls for knockdown conditions. Sparkman and Stephens does not specifically recommend carrying these plates, and we feel a heavy-duty bag tied over the cowl would probably work as well and be easier to use in extreme situations.

Low-profile vents, such as screw-down mushrooms or the more common low-vents sold in many marine stores, are helpful for exhausting stale air out of smaller compartments but you should consider them auxiliary to safety requirements. Even with the addition of solar-powered fans, these vents have a relatively low air intake. A 3-inch (7.62cm) unpowered model will pull in only 10.8 cubic feet of air per minute in a 15-knot breeze. A 3-inch Dorade in the same wind will pull in 42 cfm. Even the solar-powered 4-inch (10.2cm) version will move only 14 cfm of air into or out of your boat. But these vents are easier to install than Dorades and less costly to purchase. To keep the boat aired while it is on the mooring, a pair of screw-down mushroom-type vents aft of the cockpit can be a good addition. To air toilet areas, low vents with solar fans, mounted well inboard on the cabintop can be useful. But at sea, the solar panels on these vents can be easily blocked by sailbags, dinghies, or even coils of line, so they should be backed up by high-profile Dorades.

Because Dorade boxes are too cumbersome to fit right at the bow of the boat, we compromised on *Seraffyn* and fitted a 3-inch cowl vent directly to a deck plate. The fill pipe for our kerosene tank could be reached by removing the cowl, so this deck plate served two purposes. At anchor, the vent could be left facing toward the wind; at sea, it faced away. For rougher sailing, we tied a PVC bag over the cowl. In extreme weather, we removed the cowl and substituted the bronze deck plate. Since this vent was well forward, over the chain locker, we had no problems from the small amount of rain or spray it occasionally let in.

Once you have installed permanent deck vents to meet the minimum-crew safety standards, you'll find life on board far more comfortable if you can increase airflow still further, especially when you are going to windward in tropical weather. For *Seraffyn*, we built sliding doors in the bulkhead between the cockpit storage lockers and the foot of each quarter berth. In any but the roughest weather, we could leave the front-loading locker doors open to allow an amazing amount of air through into the aft end of the accommodations. On midship-cockpit boats and those like the Rhodes 41 with cabins next to an offset companionway, opening portlights in the sides of the cockpit can direct a tremendous amount of air into otherwise stale areas. These ports should

Figure 25-3.

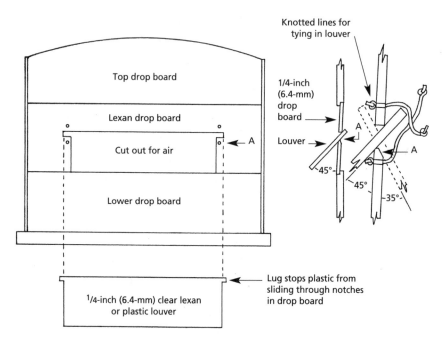

Knotted lines for tying in louver

Top drop board

1/4-inch (6.4-mm) drop board

Lexan drop board

Louver

Cut out for air ← A

45°
45°
35°

Lower drop board

1/4-inch (6.4-mm) clear lexan or plastic louver

Lug stops plastic from sliding through notches in drop board

be positioned as high as practical in the cockpit sides, so they don't accidentally act as cockpit drains. Ports on the windward side of the cockpit should be able to stay open safely in moderate conditions.

The most economical ventilation we've added to *Taleisin*, for use at sea or in port, is shown in Figure 25-3. We left this ventilating drop board in place even when we were hove-to and waiting out a Southerly Buster squall line in the Tasman Sea. (We did, however, replace it with its full-strength counterpart when we hove-to with the parachute anchor during another passage across this boisterous body of water.) At anchor or when the boat is closed up for storage on the mooring, we use this companionway-board ventilator in combination with two 4-inch Dorade vents. This allows for safe usage of a 5,800-Btu kerosene heater with a 4-inch (10.2cm) stovepipe during the winter months with two of us on board. When we have additional people below or are using more than one burner on the stove in addition to the heating stove, we find we need extra ventilation if there is less than 5 knots of wind outside. [1]

Traditional skylights were often used on larger vessels to add ventilation during moderate weather. Unfortunately, these hinged, winged hatches usually leak. Modern metal hatches have low coamings and open only in one direction, so they are not as effective for ventilation. A photograph in Eric Hiscock's *Cruising Under Sail* introduced us to an excellent compromise, a skylight-like hatch with no hinges. Instead, it has dogs at each corner with cotter (split) pins acting as hatch supports. This hatch can be tilted in any direction to catch the breeze and direct it below: on rainy days, it can open aft and act as an exhaust vent. At sea, our hard dinghy is stored upside down over this hatch, so even heavy rain will not drive under its edges. Only as we hit fresh beam-reaching weather, or boisterous windward work, do we have to dog down the hatch. At that point, the refrigerator-door gasket along its edges forms a perfect seal. This gasket – amazingly long-lasting, nonsticking, and easy to clean – can be secured in place with either contact cement or silicone sealant. It's only available from refrigerator repair shops or parts depots.

Like most offshore voyagers, we spend more than 85 percent of our time in port, and this is when a closed-up, clammy-feeling boat will get on our nerves. Here's where opening portlights come into their own as a major addition to a ventilation system. On *Taleisin*, we opted for opening 6-inch (15.2cm) diameter portlights on either side of the bow. After 15 years of use, we are delighted with them. Not only do these ports let a tremendous amount of light and air flow into the area ahead of the forward bunk, they also can be left open in port during rain storms to keep air flowing completely through the boat. To direct as much air as possible into the boat in the tropics, we add plastic flowerpots with one side cut out to act as a wind scoop (see page 285). By turning the opening slightly downward, even the heaviest rain misses the portlight opening. The outward flare of the bow means the spigot angles downward, so no rainwater is trapped and channeled inside. The ports are positioned as high as possible on the hull (3 feet/91.5cm above the waterline) so they can safely stay open when we leave *Taleisin* unattended on a mooring. There are, however, two precautions we take, as these bow ports could be potential weak spots in our hull's integrity once we are underway. First, we carry two $1/8$-inch (3-mm)-thick round aluminum plates to clamp in place should the portlight glass ever shatter. Second, we have made a

1. Proper ventilation is doubly important with a heater burning below decks, especially if, like many cruisers, you use a cockpit dodger and leave your companionway hatch slightly open during cold weather. At anchor, a dodger will cause negative pressure to form inside your boat unless sufficient ventilation is provided by Dorades or other vents well forward of the dodger. This negative pressure can cause your heating stove to backdraft, filling the boat with carbon monoxide and displacing the oxygen.

bright red pompom that secures with a shock cord to the portlight dogs when they are both closed. As soon as either port is opened, the pompom is snapped around the end of the tiller as a warning. A signal such as this is especially important if you have portlights anywhere in your hull. We witnessed the destruction of almost $30,000 worth of new electronics when a 55-footer (16.8m) with an opening hull port in the navigator's station went out on the first day of her sea trials. No one remembered to close the hull port until after the crew tried the first starboard tack in a 20-knot breeze. Hull ports amidships should never be left open when a boat is unattended at anchor or on a mooring. If the boat is blown ashore due to a broken mooring or dragging anchor, when the tide is falling, she will lay over and submerge the portlight. On the incoming tide, she could fill through the open port before she rises.

The same 55-footer had a ventilation feature – two opening ports in the transom – that could be helpful for any boat with a stern cabin. Unconventional-looking, yes, but definitely an advantage for days in port. However, if these ports are more than 8 inches (20.3cm) by 10 inches (25.4cm) we would want to carry storm covers for rough-weather protection at sea. Emergency-repair plates would also be important for any stern windows, opening or otherwise.

Figure 25-4.

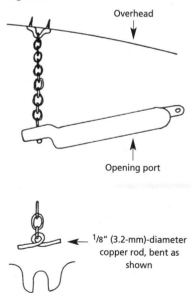

Overhead

Opening port

1/8″ (3.2-mm)-diameter copper rod, bent as shown

Although opening cabin portlights are far more expensive than fixed ports, they are worth the extra cost if you plan to spend much of your sailing time in the tropics. In selecting opening ports, bronze or stainless steel should be your first choice. Plastic portlights will tend to crack after a few years of exposure to sunlight. And their dogs sometimes snap off if too much hand-tightening force is applied. Aluminum portlights, even well-anodized ones, tend to corrode where the rubber seal seats against the metal flange. Once that flange is pitted, it becomes difficult to obtain a good seal. Look for ports with two widely spaced hinge points and at least two dogs, all of which are evenly spaced. In placing your ports, make sure they are at least 2 inches (5.1cm) above deck level. Otherwise, any water running along the deck can pour inside. (As with hatch coamings, higher is better.) To support the portlights in an open position, we use small cast-bronze anchors secured to a strap on the cabintop. Just as effective is a short length of chain with a brass crossbar attached to the deckhead by an eye strap. (See Figure 25-4.)

For tropical living, your sun awning becomes an integral part of your interior ventilation system. Not only does it keep the hot rays of the sun from pounding down on your decks, it allows you to keep portlights and hatches partially open during a rain shower.

Creating an adjustable level of airflow through your boat will take careful planning. Much of it can be done at quite reasonable cost after you move afloat. As you consider the options, remember that at sea, during extreme weather, only your Dorade vents can safely stay open. They must be adequate to provide the air you need not only for the crew but also for the burners you'll want to use to heat morale-boosting soup while you wait out the blow. Fortunately, this kind of "batten down the hatches" weather rarely lasts more than a day. At other times, you'll welcome every bit of dry air you can bring below. A well-ventilated boat smells fresher and feels drier and warmer in winter, cooler in summer. It also means everything on board will stay in better condition – from the electronics to the clothes you wear to the fresh vegetables and fruit you carry to the nonsweaty crew sharing your life afloat.

BUILDING YOUR OWN DORADE VENTS

Photo 25-1.

To catch as much air as possible, then direct it below decks while still excluding water, your vent box and ferrule (downpipe) must conform to careful design parameters. Fortunately, Rod and Olin Stephens have produced a simple formula for determining how many vents you need along with exact specifications for the box and downpipe sizes required to get the best airflow from a given cowl opening (Figs. 25-5, 25-6). In

Figure 25-5. "DORADE -TYPE" VENT BOXES

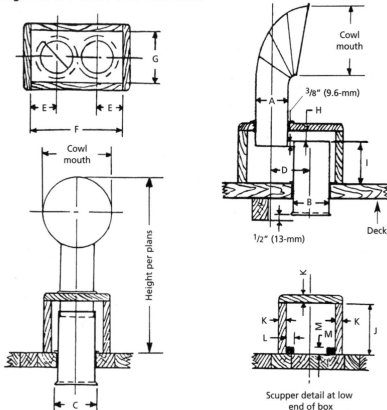

building the boxes for *Taleisin's* Dorades, Lin and I did not want to deviate from the recommended box volume, but we were concerned that the crown of our cabintop would mean the box could look ungainly. So before building it, we made a cardboard mock-up, as shown in photo 25-1. Though cowls are traditionally set vertical, we found that the box required to do this had one side almost twice the height of the other. After a bit of cardboard trimming, we compromised, angling the box top so the cowls point outboard about 10 degrees. Though unconventional, it looks quite pleasant in actual use. Once this was settled, we left the cardboard boxes in place and thought about their position for a few days to make sure they wouldn't interfere with sailing the boat or storing other deck gear.

Figure 25-5. "DORADE -TYPE" VENT BOXES *Continued*

(Drawings and table courtesy of SPARKMAN and STEPHENS, Inc. USA)

Nominal cowl size		3	3 1/2"	4	5	6	8
Clear opening cowl	A	2 3/4"	3 1/8"	5/8"	4 3/4"	5 9/16"	7 1/2"
Clear opening ferrule	B	3 3/16"	3 5/8"	4 3/16"	5 7/16"	6 3/8"	8 5/8"
O.D. Ferrule flange	C	4 1/2"	5 3/16"	6	7 13/16"	9 3/16"	12 3/8"
E TO E	D	4 3/8"	5"	5 3/4"	7 5/8"	8 7/8"	12"
E To inside box	E	1 15/16"	2 3/16"	2 9/16"	3 5/16"	3 7/8"	5 1/4"
Inside box length	F	8 1/4"	9 3/8"	10 7/8"	14 1/4"	16 5/8"	22 1/2"
Inside box width	G	3 7/8"	4 3/8"	5 1/8"	6 5/8"	7 3/4"	10 1/2"
Ferrule to underside cover	H	15/16"	1 1/8"	1 1/4"	1 11/16"	1 15/16"	2 5/8"
Ferrule height above deck	I	4 1/2"	4 7/16"	4 3/4"	5"	5 1/4"	5 3/4"
Inside box height	J	5 7/16"	5 11/16"	6"	6 11/16"	7 3/16"	8 3/8"
Box thickness	K	3/4"	13/16"	7/8"	15/16"	1"	1 1/4"
Scupper width	L	0.6"	0.7"	0.8"	1"	1.2"	1.6"
Scupper height	M	0.6"	0.7"	0.8"	1"	1.2"	1.6"

Next, as photo 25-2 shows, I made a ferrule of 4 1/4-inch (10.8cm)-diameter copper pipe purchased from a plumbing supply house. I cut a ring of copper out of 1/8-inch (3.2-mm) plate, using a metal cutting blade on my sabersaw. I then soldered it to the ferrule at the proper angle to fit as a screwing flange to the cabintop. Then I bedded the flange in place with Dolfinite compound (silicone sealant would work as well) and

Figure 25-6. DORADE VENTS

Area of cowl mouth (sq. in.)	Cowl size diameter	Minimum width and height of each	Minimum volume of box – cu.in. of two scuppers
36	3"	3"	6" x 4" 350
50	4"	4"	8" x 8" 480
79	5"	5"	1' x 1' 750
113	6"	6"	1.2' x 1.2' 1,080
201	8"	8"	1.6' x 1.6' 1,920

Courtesy of SPARKMAN and STEPHENS, Inc. USA

Photo 25-2.

secured it with number-10 wood screws. Inside the cabin, I fitted a radiused and varnished teak block between the cabin beams, with the holes for the vent cut exactly to the inside diameter of the ferrule. This is a slight deviation from dimension C, shown in the Sparkman and Stephens drawing (Fig. 25-5). I did this because it makes construction far easier while still directing airflow below deckbeam levels and also protecting the heads of taller crew members.

The PVC cowl vents we were able to purchase at a secondhand shop were not designed to extend through the top of the Dorade box to a level below the ferrule intake, so I used a teak cross beam 2 inches (5.1cm) deep, to keep any water caught by the cowl from reaching the mouth of the ferrule, as photo 25-3 shows. I added two scuppers at the aft end of the vent box. It is important to put these scuppers in the aft end of the box; if they are on the sides or the front, they will let water in as well as out.

Since the boxes were to be left bare, in keeping with our generally low-maintenance deck finish, I used a simple rabbet (rebate) joint, as shown in photo 25-4. This is easy to make, keeps end-grain checking to a minimum, and provides more gluing surface. The end grain of the top is also protected by a teak inset. Because it is rated fully waterproof, UV-proof, and highly resistant, plus excellent for use on hardwoods including teak, I used resorcinol glue for this job [2]. The tops of the boxes are

Photo 25-3.

screwed in place with four bronze oval-head finishing screws to make box removal relatively easy if necessary. Hold-downs for the boxes are simple L-brackets cut from $^1/8$-inch (3.2-mm) bronze. These are screwed to the insides of the box, which is then secured to the cabintop with long screws going through into deckbeams. On a fiberglass or molded-plywood coach roof, you'll need to use through-bolts.

I do not recommend using plywood as you would then need to paint the boxes quite often to prevent checking or delamination and keep them looking good. Dorades get a lot of knocks, since

Photo 25-4
The simple rebate joint minimizes end grain exposure. Note also the mitered insert on the box top to cover the endgrain.

they stand proud of the deck. They are also highly visible, especially if they look badly scuffed, so maintenance can be a problem – unless, as I prefer, you use bare teak. Unfortunately, wide boards of any type of wood

---

2. The vast majority of epoxy adhesives are not only sensitive to heat, but delaminate in temperatures as low as 120°F (50°C).

will tend to split, especially in hot climates. Therefore, you will need to varnish or paint the boxes if they are over 8-inches (20.3cm) high – i.e., boards are over 7.5-inches (19.1cm) wide.

A final modification that would look fine on modern boats is to use 1/2-inch (13-mm) clear Lexan for the box tops. This will give an additional circle of light through the ferrule and into your cabin, at no extra cost. A drawback to this clear top is that your finish inside the box will have to be tidy, as it will be visible at all times.

Although sailing gear, interior layout, and space constraints probably will determine where you can place Dorades, consider not only the deck position but also where the air will be directed once it goes into the cabin. On deck, the vents should be located as close to the centerline as possible, for this same reason. If they cannot be set on a raised coach roof, the cowls should have long necks to reduce the risk of water intake. The cowl opening should also be well above any hatches or life rafts, in as clear an airflow as possible. Though vents traditionally are used in pairs, a single vent over a head compartment can be helpful as long as other vents farther aft balance it, to work as exhausts. Inside, try to get at least one vent directing air close to the cook's face. This will help clear cooking odors and if the cook is prone to seasickness, it could save his or her day. Avoid openings directly onto the heads of any bunks; if your cabin is more than 9 feet (2.8m) long, spread the airflow with two pairs of smaller vents rather than a single pair of larger ones. You'll grab more air with four 3-inch (7.6cm) vents than two 4-inch (10.2cm) ones; the required boxes will be less cumbersome; and you'll get a better intake/exhaust balance if the boat must be closed up.

A final word on Dorades. Though we coil the antenna wire for the shortwave receiver inside our port Dorade vent and run its connector from the radio to the vent hole when we need it, we try not to stuff sail gaskets and spare bits of line down the cowls. After all, the whole idea behind Rod Stephens's careful design work was to balance the box and cowl volume to keep air moving. A nest of lines will ruin this flow. It's even best to avoid screens over the cowl openings. But if you find bug screens are necessary, they will reduce airflow the least if they are snapped to the insides of the ferrules.

BUILDER'S (LARRY'S) NOTES FOR THE CONSTRUCTION OF A DORADE VENT BOX

To make the copper ferrule, I first inserted the pipe into the hole in the cabintop and marked around it with a pencil. I then cut a slightly oval hole into the $1/8$-inch (3.2-mm) flange plate and slid it onto the pipe to line up with the pencil mark. Once the hole in the flange was properly shaped, I trimmed it to an equal width and drilled the hold-down holes. I then soldered it in place with a heavy bead of soft solder, using a propane blowtorch.

To fit the end-grain protection pieces at each end of the top, I scribed the shape into the teak, using a sharp penknife. The cuts were then made with a bandsaw. (A sharp sabersaw would have been second choice for the job.)

Figure 25-7 shows how the box is eventually fitted to the cabintop. I mark the wood as shown, then saw just to the side of the pencil mark. I then work down the last $1/16$-inch (1.6-mm) of wood slowly, using a drawknife or wood file to get a perfect fit.

The L-shaped hold-down brackets were cut from $1/8$-inch (3.2-mm) bronze plate; $3/16$-inch (5-mm) copper will work as well. A bandsaw or hacksaw will cut these metals easily. The strips for these brackets were cut to $1/2$-inch (13-mm) by $2^1/2$-inches (64-mm), then bent to fit. Screw holes were drilled through the metal before I bent the angles.

Figure 25-7.

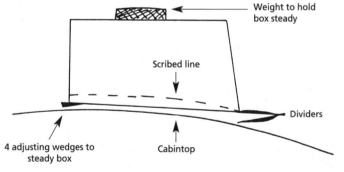

Weight to hold box steady

Scribed line

Dividers

4 adjusting wedges to steady box

Cabintop

To fit box to cabintop, scribe all four edges.
Hold the divider points vertically as you mark to
produce a line parallel to the cabintop.

CHAPTER

26

SIMPLE IDEAS FROM AROUND THE CRUISING FLEET

We always find it interesting to watch people during their first visit on someone else's cruising boat. Rarely do they say, "It changed my whole concept of boats." Instead, what they talk about with most enthusiasm are one or two ideas or items that seem so simple the owner has almost forgotten when he or she first added them to the boat. Many of the simple ideas shown here are ones we have used on board *Taleisin*. Others came from our visits on board friends' boats. Not one of these ideas is completely original. In fact, we fully expect some reader to say, "Lin and Larry stole that idea from me." They would possibly be right, for that is the way ideas spread. It is also one of the pleasures of visiting other people's boats – finding a new idea and then adapting it to your own life afloat.

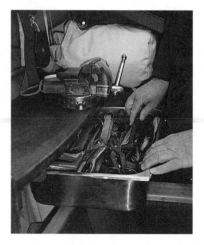

EXTRA DRAWERS

Small boat, big boat – we all could use another dedicated storage spot, another drawer. But the drawer and its framing, sides, and bottom take up a lot of space. They take plenty of time to build and, if someone else does the building, can be quite costly. We found an amazingly affordable space-saving solution at a restaurant-supply shop. The pans used to keep food warm in steam tables at buffet-type restaurants come in a dozen different sizes and depths. Made of very high-quality stainless steel, they are surprisingly affordable. To convert these pans into easy-to-clean, maintenance-free drawers, simply screw L-shaped wooden runners on the bottom side of any shelf in any locker. The locker door will keep them from sliding open underway. For the engineroom or workshop, you can install sliders under the workbench and use a simple turn knob on the edge of the bench as a stop. As you can see in the photo, Larry has installed a large, deep, steam-table tray for the tools he uses most frequently. The slide-out drawer is mounted under the workbench to serve a second purpose: when Larry is working with metal or wood in his vise, he puts an old towel over the open drawer to catch shavings and filings. This makes cleanup a simple matter of shaking the towel overboard (an idea we borrowed from a goldsmith friend).

DRAWERS THAT DROP DOWN, OR DROP-DOWN DRAWERS

This wineglass drawer only provides credibility to the rumor that one of the main reasons Lin and I go cruising is to sample the local wines. It is true, it is totally true!

We use this same deckhead-hinged design for drawers that hold our small navigation tools (such as dividers and parallel rules), for a stereo-cassette storage box, and also for our sextant. Though most of the boxes are custom-made, the sextant drawer was made by removing the top half

Our drop-down wineglass rack.

of the sextant box and using only the lower half – installed so it hinges down enough to let the instrument lift out easily. Ordinary butt hinges (all brass) are screwed to the top corner of each drawer and to the deckhead. A welded-link brass chain controls the angle of drop, and an elbow catch (woodpecker) snaphook at the inboard end of the drawer locks it in place automatically when it is pushed up to the deck.

These drawers could be used for lightweight items such as knives and forks in the galley, for small tools in the engineroom, or for magazines and reading glasses near a bunk. They can be installed anywhere you can spare the headroom.

ALL-IN-ONE: EXTRA BEDDING, EXTRA STORAGE, EXTRA PILLOW

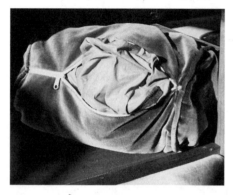

Here is an idea we saw on board a 60-foot (18.3m) power cruiser. The owner had bolster cushion covers made with a zipper at the back. Instead of having the bolsters filled with foam, he stored spare bedding in them, for those times when he had a full complement of visitors on board. We don't often have more than two visitors for the night, but as voyagers who visit both warm and cool climates, we find we need to carry both lightweight and heavyweight sleeping bags. So these storage cushions are perfect. The sleeping bags we aren't using fill them just enough so they make wonderful headrests but don't take up any storage room. When guests are using the sleeping bags, a few towels or sweaters fill the bolster cushions to provide extra pillows.

DOUBLE-USE PILOT-BERTH CUSHIONS

There is nothing like an awning-sheltered berth on deck during a warm summer's night, or a well-padded on-deck lounging area for an afternoon siesta. But what about cushions? Cockpit cushions are usually too small, but few cruising boats have room for spare lounging cushions. Inflatable mattresses sound great, but few of us have the patience to inflate and then deflate them. Solution? Have the pilot-berth or quarter-berth cushions covered in a sturdy vinyl or waterproof synthetic material. Then make slipcovers to match the rest of the boat's soft upholstery, or use coordinated toweling. The slipcovers make the bunks comfortable for lying or sitting down below and also keep the interior looking smart. Remove them and the cushions can be used on deck, even if there is salt from spray or swimmers, even if dew does happen to fall on them during the night. In the tropics, a beach towel makes the cushions comfortable for lounging. A damp sponge cleans them and removes traces of salt when they re-enter the boat. There are two hidden advantages to these slipcovers. First the pilot berths are heavily used at sea, so their cushions are likely to require more frequent cleaning than other cushions. These slipcovers are easy to remove for washing or dry cleaning. Second, even the most careful sailor will find that a heavy dollop of salt water can invade his or her cabin during an ocean crossing one way or another. Because the vinyl-covered cushions are waterproof and relatively easy to dry off, at least there will be one or two dry bunks for crew to sleep on until you reach a quiet, safe anchorage where you can dry out the rest of the boat.

DRY BUNK

A major problem among those who sail in colder waters is condensation forming under bunk cushions. The heat generated by sleeping bodies attracts so much moisture to the underside of the cushion that mildew forms. In fact, the cushion material of our most frequently used forward berth rotted. To prevent this, people who live afloat normally find they have to lift their bunk cushions daily to air or wipe them dry. Last winter, we found a solution. Called Dry Bunk, it costs only $13 for enough material to insulate two single bunks. It is a white cardboard-like sheet, made of pure cellulose about $1/8$ inch (3.2-mm) thick. According to the manufacturer, it should be aired out if it begins to feel damp. By placing this under the cushion where the trunks of our bodies lie (it's not needed at foot level), our problem has been alleviated. We have had to air the Dry Bunk about twice a month during two very wet seasons in European waters. It sure is an improvement over the previous daily care necessary to prevent mildew on my new upholstery (and the nav charts stored under the cushions).

Gerri's Dry Bunk is available direct from Gerri at 3264 Mission Creek, Cashmeer, WA 98815 USA, Fax/Tel: 509-782-2653. It is also available from West Marine Supplies.

HIDE-A-COMPASS

We found a useful and relatively simple way to hide the back of *Taleisin's* compass, which sticks through into the cabin in a very conspicuous place.

Larry built a simple mitered, deep-sided frame of teak and attached it to the cabin back with hinges. A colonial latch keeps the frame closed yet allows quick access to the compass back and frame interior. We had nonglare glass cut to fit the frame. To add variety to our interior, we made five different-colored mat boards to fit exactly inside the frame. That way, we can display a favorite photograph or sketch and change the picture from time to time. The mats store inside the frame, but it will probably be quite a while before we tire of the watercolor done for us by Roger Morris of New Zealand.

OILED TRIM

There is nothing like the lovely color of natural wood trim to set off the edges of interior joinery. And like the majority of boat owners, Larry and I decided to varnish the Honduras mahogany trim around the edges of the settees, companionways, and bulkheads on *Seraffyn*. But since this trim was in the way of traffic, right where it got bruised by everything – from belt buckles to the rivets on jeans, from cooking pots to sailing gear – keeping it looking nice meant touching it up and revarnishing it every year. This is a relatively easy task if you do not live on board, but for those who make their boat their home, it is a real hassle, because the newly varnished trim does not have time to dry properly before someone puts a hand on it.

When we built *Taleisin*, we tried another, far more successful tack. Although we used high-gloss varnish for most of her interior, we used clear, water-resistant wood oil on all of the black-walnut trim. Now, when a scratch or scuff appears, a light scrub with a plastic scouring pad (a dry one), then a wipe with a rag dipped in oil, and the trim looks like new. We use the same oil finish on the ceiling slats beside each bunk –

another area prone to scuffing. After 14 years, *Taleisin's* trim and ceiling have taken on a rich mellow sheen that gives a warm contrast to the high-gloss varnished teak, ash, and bird's-eye maple of the rest of her interior.

A PORTABLE DORADE

For many years, we carried a spare cowl vent to "someday" fit onto a proper Dorade box to add ventilation in our forepeak. Only problem is, we didn't want to have it on the foredeck all the time – only when we were leaving the boat closed up for a while. So we never could justify cluttering up the deck with the Dorade box necessary to make the vent water-resistant. Then, one day when we were preparing *Taleisin* to leave her on a mooring for seven months in South Africa, one of us got a bright

idea (can't remember who it was). I pulled out a plastic storage box. Larry installed the bronze screw plate of the ventilator in its bottom and added a small eyebolt and line as a tie-down. We placed this over the open rope pipe and secured it below decks to keep the Dorade in place. Presto – an instant in-port portable Dorade box (see

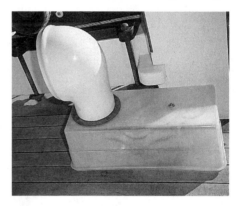

photo). When we no longer need it, the vent unscrews and stores inside the box; the box stores in an out-of-the-way locker. By adding this to our array of existing vents, plus the companionway vent (page 270), we came back to a mildew-free boat that smelled as fresh as the day we left her.

PORTLIGHT SCOOPS

When we were in Singapore, we saw dozens of ships with steel or plastic buckets sticking out of open portholes. The crews had cut out one side of a bucket to act as a wind scoop. We found this idea really useful for round portholes. We have opening ports in *Taleisin's* topsides, just forward of the double bunk in the forepeak. Not only do they let in light, but even during heavy rain at anchor, they can be left open for increased ventilation. But when the wind blows, that rain can also blow in. To stop this, we have used the Singaporean idea. We found that plastic flowerpots from the local nurseries come in the same diameters as

normal portlight openings – 6 inches, 8 inches. They cost less than $1. By cutting out a portion of the side of the pot with a hacksaw, we ended up with a perfect, cheap scoop. Turn the opening forward on a hot breezy day and it directs more air below. Turn the scoop downward, or even face it aft, and rain cannot blow in, yet the air still flows. This really is important, both in the tropics and in northern climates. With the through-ventilation, humidity does not build up inside the boat when you close the hatches or turn on a heater, nor can your stove burn up all the oxygen and threaten to asphyxiate your crew.

THE COFFEE GRINDER

No, this isn't a sheet winch, it's a real coffee-bean masticator. Why? Nothing beats the aroma and flavor of real fresh coffee first thing in the

morning, but unfortunately, it's often difficult to find freshly ground coffee as you voyage to less-developed countries. On the other hand, we have always been able to find coffee beans. Our solution was this Salter Mills grinder (model 1 or 4), made to a century-old pattern but available at very affordable prices direct or at specialized coffeehouses in major cities. Handoperated and adjustable to produce coarse or fine grind, ours is secured to the mast, right next to the stove in *Taleisin's* galley. Easy to use, it also makes a good conversation piece.

It comes from Salter Housewares Ltd., Service Dept., 211 Vale Road, Tonbridge, Kent, United Kingdom, TN9 1SU.

BUTANE HOT KNIFE

One of those don't-know-how-we-lived-without-it items we've come to depend on over the past few years is a butane-powered hot knife/soldering tool purchased from a marine hardware store for less than $30. The actual brand we chose is a Weller Portasol P-1K, which has a catalytic converter in the specialized tips to give flameless heat when required. We have the tips that convert it to a tiny hot knife, blow-torch, or soldering iron. Now, even on breezy days, we can heat-seal the ends of lines on deck. It takes care of small soldering jobs for our simple electrical system, but we seem to use it most for sail repairs and upgrades. The hot-knife tip makes it handy for cutting sailcloth and heat-sealing the edges at the same time. We also use it to eliminate the unsightly fluttering threads that occur on the edges of aging sails, or to heat-seal the sewing-thread ends as we repair seams or rings.

A word of warning. The hot knife reaches temperatures of up to 850°F, the blowtorch over 2,000°F, so make sure you have a safe place to set the tool until it cools down. We use the tray from our oven with a hot pad under it to protect the decks in case the soldering tool falls off its stand when some other boat's wake rolls through the anchorage.

The Weller Portasol is made by Weller-Cooper Tools, P.O. Box 728, Apex, NC 27502 USA

SUBMARINE PUTTY

The navy carries it on board, your children play with it, you need it for cruising. It is low-tech, and costs less than $2. We sailed without this simple item for years but wish we hadn't. What is it? Children's modeling clay, Plasticine, the colored stuff you once used to make long snakes into nice little lopsided pots. This is the type of modeling clay that leaves no marks behind on furniture – a requirement, since children spread it around so eagerly. On your boat, it will stick to wet surfaces to stop minor leaks until you can fix them, it acts as a self-conforming gasket to seal up your chainpipe, it fills gaps in the cockpit locker seat during a storm. You can form temporary nonskid rings to keep gallery gear from moving around. Use it once and you'll find it's definitely worth having on board. And you can play with it, too.

BOLT CUTTERS VS. WIRE CUTTERS

It's quite important to have real wire cutters on board. If you are dismasted, the lower ends of your wire rigging can be cut near the

turnbuckle and the wire could then be used to juryrig a salvaged spar. When we were in Sydney, Australia, well-known rigger Joe Henderson pointed out that the majority of sailors were mistaking bolt cutters for wire cutters. The difference? Wire cutters have curved cutting edges that work more like pincers than like scissors. This is a real advantage in a rough sea, as the wire cutters encompass the wire so it will not slip out of the cutters as you work. Furthermore, wire cutters cut much cleaner, so if you plan to rerig your boat before or during your cruise, it would be worth investing in a proper pair, though it will cost you three times more than bolt cutters.

AFFORDABLE EXTRA TANKAGE

We've seen people tear out the interior of their boat to increase water or fuel tankage when they set off cruising. We've seen others spend thousands of dollars on a watermaker so they could convert water tanks to fuel tanks when they faced the long trek up the Red Sea. A far less expensive (and we think logical) choice is one we saw on a 30-footer

(9.2m) bound across the Indian Ocean. It carried two flexible tanks, which were on the cabintop for the first part of the passage. When the fuel and water in these tanks were used, the tanks were rolled up and stored below. An extra advantage to this cost and space savings was that the tanks could be carried on shore for refueling in locales where it was difficult to come alongside a fuel dock.

A HOME-BUILT JAM CLEAT-TO-WINCH ARRANGEMENT

The single most satisfying item Lin and I have added to *Taleisin* since her launching has been the jam-cleat system for her double-ended mainsheet, which we rigged when we began joining two-handed round-the-buoys races. We now wonder how we sailed without it – racing or cruising – for so many years. The simple arrangement of the jam cleat in line with a sheet winch not only gives us convenient, simple mainsheet adjustments

Photos 26-12. *The in-line mainsheet jammer-to-sheet winch arrangement*

Photo 26-13. *A close-up of the S-bracket fabricated to hold the jammer.*

but also provides direct access to the unemployed windward sheet winch to give more power in fresh winds. This system eliminated the need for two mainsheet cleats, thus helping to keep the cockpit work area freer of things that could foul errant lines. Finally, it put the mainsheet control closer to the helmsman.

Although I could have purchased stock stainless-steel swivel blocks with an attached jam cleat, I chose to fabricate my own husky bracket to fit under the base of the mainsheet swivel block. This way, it not only complemented the style of the existing gear but also proved to be cheaper and neater than the sharp-cornered, lightweight, store-purchased gear available to us. The 3/16-inch-thick, 1 3/4-inch-wide S-shaped bracket also fits our basic specification for all deck hardware: It was strong enough so it would not easily bend, and it wouldn't break if someone stepped on it or a tensioned line inadvertently tweaked it.

The key to building this in-line jammer is the S-shaped bracket, for which I made a prototype from cheap, easy-to-work, 1/4-inch aluminum plate. By bolting the bracket under the swivel-block base, I could try out the system without drilling any new holes in the taffrail, so we could test the idea without leaving any scars if it didn't work well. The final S-bracket was made from silicon bronze and designed so it bolted under the swivel block and elevated the jam cleat to the height of the mortise, which is also the height of the sheet-winch barrel.

The bronze jam cleats, from Traditional Marine in Nova Scotia, are made with a round line fairlead on the front. I hacksawed off the fairleads to facilitate quick release of the mainsheet. Our mainsheet has a five-to-one purchase, so the line tension is quite low at the jam cleat. If the tension on the hauling end of any sheet, halyard, or foreguy is more direct – i.e., has less purchase – then a jammer with a positive-release lever should be used to guarantee line or sheet release when needed.

Traditional Marine, P. O. Box 268, Annapolis Royal, Nova Scotia, Canada BOS1AO, Tel: 902-532-2762, Fax: 902-532-7013.

HALYARD COIL LOOPS

We stole this idea from Hal Roth's *Whisper* and have found it is definitely worth sharing – to be sure coiled halyards stay put, to make life easier for guests who come sailing with us. We have put an eyesplice in one end of a 12-inch (30.5cm) length of $3/16$-inch line. The other end is secured around the base of a cleat on the mast. Simply pull the line through the coiled halyard and loop the eye over the cleat: instant, secure, tidy halyard coils. These coils have stayed perfectly in place through major storms. The only caveat – never secure two coils of line using the same line. We did it once and ended up with an embarrassing tangle.

A CHEAP, CHEERFUL, INSTANT AT-SEA COCKPIT COVER/AIR SCOOP

The best thing about this multipurpose cover, besides its low cost, is that it can be rigged when it's needed and quickly moved out of the way when you want to take a sextant sight, or reef or furl the mainsail. This cover can be homemade from heavy white synthetic canvas, such as Acrylon (Sunbrella), which not only is easy to sew but also has less tendency to flap in the wind. The square should have a 2-inch (50-mm)-wide tabling around all four edges. Corner grommets (either spurtooth ones or sewn rings) should be firmly secured with extra stitching or

Figure 26-1.

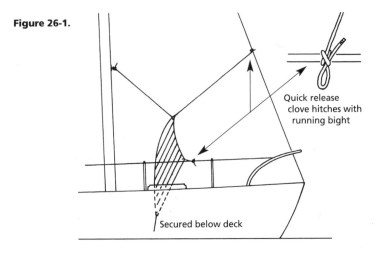

Quick release
clove hitches with
running bight

Secured below deck

webbing to spread the strains. Splice lengths of $3/16$-inch Dacron line into each grommet.

We carry two of these multipurpose canvas pieces. One is 4 feet by 6 feet (1.2m by 1.8m), the other 4 feet (1.2m) square. We use the smaller one as a simple wind scoop, to direct the wind below decks when we lie at anchor. It works almost as well as more elaborate wind scoops and catches wind even if the boat veers 20 degrees either side of head-to-wind.

The lower line is secured to the mast below decks. We attach a second line to the upper corner so one line goes to the spinnaker-pole ring on the front of the mast about 7 feet (2.1m) above the deck, the other goes to the staysail stay. By adjusting the port and starboard lines, which are tied to the lifelines with clove hitches with a running bight, we can adjust the scoop to compensate for any wind-against-tide angle that the boat might assume. It can be adjusted to catch the wind from the beam or astern and can also be used during light-wind passages. If a sudden rain shower springs up, we can untie the upper lines quickly and drop the scoop down the forehatch (Fig. 26-1).

These canvas squares have a dozen other uses on board. They can cover small on-deck paint or glue jobs in case of showers, serve as cushion protectors when engine work is going on below decks, or even act as a collision mat to help stop water from flooding into a fractured hull. Only your imagination limits their use.

LIVING CLEANER – CHAIN-SCRUBBING IDEAS

Nothing saves money more surely than choosing to lie at anchor instead of tying up in marinas. Yet we have seen people so put off by the mess created by 100 feet of muddy chain coming back on board in a river anchorage that they choose the expensive option. In New Zealand, where mud bottoms (with their wonderful holding power) are the norm and marinas the exception, we came up with an acceptable, self-produced chain scrubber by twisting together the brushes from two toilet-bowl scrubbers. We formed this into three coils and attached the brush to the boathook. By wrapping the coiled brush around the chain, and scrubbing up and down right in the water as we cranked in the anchor, we removed the majority of the mud before it could come on deck.

Then, about three years ago, we discovered a much more durable and not very expensive commercial solution to this problem. The Gunkbuster, made by Davis Instruments USA, snaps over the chain and hooks directly onto the boathook fitting, working just as our brush did. But we found that the hole through the middle of the Astro-turf bristles was a bit too large for our 5/16-inch chain, and the bristles weren't reaching between the chain's links to loosen the mud. So we decreased the hole and increased the efficiency of the scrubber by sewing a piece of 1/2-inch-thick soft foam between the plastic body and the backing of the bristles.

Davis Instruments USA, Tel: 510-732-9229, and Fax: 510-670-0589; Distributed by Simpson Lawrence Ltd., 218-228 Edmiston Drive, Glasgow, G51 2YT, United Kingdom, Tel: 0141-427-5331. Fax: 0141-427-5419.

A MINI PORTABLE LEADLINE

For less than $5, you can prevent an embarrassing night aground, navigate through rock-strewn channels without touching bottom, or snuggle into an alongside berth knowing you have 6 inches (15.2cm) of water under your keel and your rudder, even if there is a sloping pile of rocks jutting out from shore. The secret? A miniature leadline stored in your dinghy. We made ours from an 8-ounce fishing-line sinker plus 20 feet (6.1m) of 3/16-inch braided line. At the one-fathom point, there is a single figure-eight knot; at two fathoms, two knots, etc. When our anchorage is at all close-feeling, we get into the dinghy and use the leadline to sound around the boat to be sure a change of wind will not put us on top of a shoal patch or a coral head. In more than one instance, this has led us to set an extra anchor to keep us free of an underwater obstruction.

The portable leadline lives in the storage compartment under the forward thwart of our dinghy, so it is handy when we want to check a narrow passage or an alongside berth. When you are exploring rocky areas such as Scotland's Outer Hebrides or Norway's inshore passages, it pays to tow the dinghy ready for use as an escort vessel. Rather than charging in and using your keel as a depth sounder, heave-to, let one crew row the dinghy to sound the passage ahead, then proceed safely and surely along the sounded course.

ALL-IN-ONE BOARDING PLATFORM, FENDERBOARD, BOARDING LADDER, AND PORTABLE SWIM GRID

Peter Bailey was worried about getting guests, boxes of provisions, and jerry jugs on board his 47-foot (14.3m) cutter when it lay at anchor, so he came to us at our tiny boatyard in New Zealand. Together, he and Larry

Figure 26-2. *Boarding platform.*

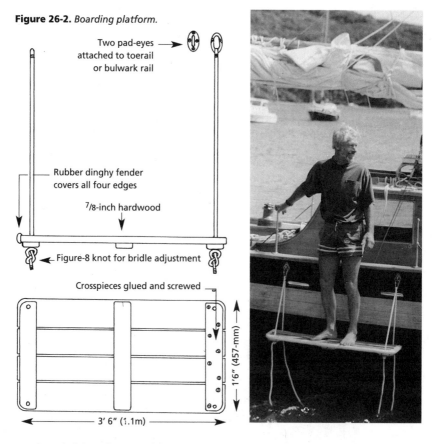

Two pad-eyes → attached to toerail or bulwark rail

Rubber dinghy fender covers all four edges

⁷/8-inch hardwood

Figure-8 knot for bridle adjustment

Crosspieces glued and screwed

1'6" (457-mm)

3' 6" (1.1m)

produced this solution. (Fig. 26-2). Peter used the platform for two charter sessions and said it solved problems he hadn't known existed!

Strongly built of teak slats, fastened with number 10 x 1½-inch bronze flathead screws, then edged all around with either rubber bumper material or Gunnelguard, the platform is hung on ⁷/16-inch- diameter three-strand polyester line. The two attachment points on the toerail or bulwark should be strong pad-eyes secured in place with at least four screws each. Peter's platform was positioned near the running backstays so the boarding crew (and guests) had a strong handhold for the step from platform to deck.

Since the platform is hanging on rope bridles, it will swing out of the way if the shoreboat misjudges the approach. The fendering protects both the mothership and the dinghy from damage. It is far easier to hold onto than a stern boarding platform on a reverse-transom boat. Add a few fenders and it becomes a fenderboard; lash it from the quay to your stern and it becomes a boarding ladder. If you have a two-tiered stern pulpit, you could even design it to become a seat for use underway. That solves the problem of finding a good storage space for this handy item.

MOVABLE SOLAR PANELS

We first chose to use flexible solar panels because they were less bulky and could be stored away quickly. The absence of a metal frame meant less chance of damaging the boat or ourselves when we worked around the panels. Then Bernard Moitessier showed us another benefit that doubled their usefulness. He had added an extension cord to his panels so that he could move them up to the foredeck when he was headed west through the tradewinds in the afternoon. This kept the panels out of the shadow of the mainsail. In the morning they could go aft, again in the full rays of the sun. Because of their flexibility and movability, we find that two panels, though rated at only 1.1 amps each, provide us sufficient power to cover all of our usage, even in the less sunny areas of Europe.
Our panels come from United Solar Systems. USA
Tel: 800-397-2083, Fax: 619-625-2083.

CHAPTER

27

JOURNEYMAN: WORKBENCHES, TOOL STORAGE

Long before Lin and I met, my grandfather was inadvertently steering me toward the life we lead today. Earl Marshall was a journeyman. He traveled and worked all over North America and could build anything – bridges, wharves, ships, houses. Earl even designed and built one of the first lightweight, all aluminum house trailers, which he then used on-site at his construction jobs. I was totally impressed with my grandfather's sharp wit, vast physical strength, and generous spirit, plus his ability to move to wherever the jobs happened to be. He was always able to find employment, even in the 1930s depression years.

When I was about 16, I asked him why he and my grandmother seemed so happy compared to everyone else. Earl explained, "Larry, the only way to beat the system is to take time off to do the things you want to do." Passionate travelers and Bible missionaries, my grandparents worked hard all summer around Vancouver, then, amid envious mutterings from our family, took "time off" and headed south for the sunbelt to spread God's word.

My grandparents weren't the only people feasting on the grapes of personal freedom. The Pacific Northwest had an abundant supply of journeymen. As I looked around, I found many of them were sailing people. People like Allen Farrell, a shipwright who, with his wife, Sharie, built several boats named *Wind Song*. Together they worked right on the beach, using a chainsaw and hand tools to cut up fir and cedar logs that had floated free from the southbound log booms. With little fanfare, the two of them would then sail off into the South Pacific on their latest creation, using their skills (and chainsaw) to earn their way.

John Guzzwell was building 20-foot 6-inch (6.3m) *Trekka* in his mother's single-car garage near where I, as a 17-year-old, was rebuilding my first 8-foot (2.4m) plywood catboat. At 6 feet 4 inches, John was a decidedly large man and we were all surprised when he stowed his tools in that tiny boat and took off to earn as he explored.

Fired by such work-as-you-go success stories, I began dreaming of how to avoid the usual 50 weeks of work each year with only two weeks off. I dreamed of time off to sail to exotic countries, to learn about other cultures, savor the foods, to know the local people and acquire an all-over suntan, with a woman partner at my side to share it all.

It took 10 years from the time I first had this dream to the day when it looked like it might become a reality – 10 years during which I gathered skills, funds, and, fortunately, a partner. Together we finished building a boat, then Lin and I set off with high hopes in 1969, bound for Mexico on board mighty *Seraffyn*, our Lyle Hess-designed cutter.

As we sailed south, we devised a scheme we hoped would mix a bit of business with lots of pleasure. We scheduled our cruising goals so we would arrive in ports hosting the finales of international ocean races a week or two before the raceboats arrived. First we would volunteer for the welcoming committee. That way we could personally greet the arriving sailors and be included in some great fiestas. And that would put us in a good position to help with any repairs or maybe to deliver a raceboat back to the United States. At the end of the Los Angeles-to-Acapulco race, it looked like our scheme would work. We got the offer of a delivery. But two days before we were supposed to take over, her crew had a mishap. The boat dragged anchor and, sadly, became a total loss.

This sent us back to plan B, the one we have found most dependable over the years. Lin and I let it be known among the fleet of overseas cruising boats in Acapulco Bay that *Seraffyn*, the floating toolbox, was open for business and that I was ready to caulk and pay deck seams, fix toerails, splice rigging. That did the trick. A few days later, we sailed over and tied alongside *Simoon*, a 36-foot (11m) ketch. I built a 14-inch-by-16-inch teak hatch through her bridge deck directly into her icebox/refrigerator. This insulated hatch let the owner load ice and get out a beer without going below decks. The owner invited all of his cruising friends over to admire his new idea, and soon Lin and I had enough work to refill our cruising kitty. Several weeks later, we semi-retired to a quiet cove south of Acapulco Bay and anchored near magnificent cliff-hanging houses. Then we rowed ashore to celebrate with a seafood extravaganza at the edge of the moonlit bay. The waiter sensed our elated mood and whispered, "The president of Mexico lives just where your boat is anchored. He comes to eat here and uses this same windowfront table." As soon as that waiter left, I whispered to Lin, "Not too bad for a couple of sailing bums; looks like our scheme is working!"

As we sailed onward, I learned our journeyman's life had other benefits beyond the sheer sense of freedom. It let us know the boatbuilders and people we worked with as real friends, to understand their likes and dislikes, the politics and problems, the whole bouillabaisse of local life. And, as a bonus, I learned new boatbuilding skills, clever ideas and tricks that I have since put to use in our life afloat.

Several months after we sailed from Acapulco, when our funds were running low, I was offered the job of removing the rotten plywood bulkhead on a 48-foot (14.6m) Costa Rican sportfishing boat owned by an American. Through this job, I came to know the crew at Sammy Manley's shipyard in Punta Arenas, Costa Rica. Fernando – the foreman, builder, and designer of the 72-foot (22m) shrimp trawlers that were being built from keel up and launched every four months from this yard – was a 38-year-old Costa Rican with no formal schooling. He could not read or write, yet he created strong, handsome trawlers that drew naval architects from as far away as Louisiana. These architects could not figure out why Fernando's trawlers were always two knots faster than their newest, best American designs of the same length, powered with the identical Caterpillar engines.

Fernando taught me about getting on with the job without waiting for perfect timber, perfect weather, perfect tools. The only timber he could get for the $2^1/2$-inch-thick planking was full of moisture. He knew the planks would dry out and leave wide seams that would be difficult to caulk if the boat was not finished off quickly. So Fernando and his team used a two-stage planking system. First the crew lined out and fit every other plank. This done, they went on to deck work. Two or three months later, when the deckhouses were almost finished, the crew fitted the intermediate, or shutter, planks. By this time, the hull planking as well as the boards for the intermediate spaces had dried in the tropical wind and sun. Each intermediate plank was spiled and trimmed $1/16$-inch wider than the plank gap. Then, starting at the stem, the crew drove the plank into place, using a block of wood and a big hammer. The seams, all even and tight on the inside, could be caulked immediately. The boat was then painted and launched within a few days, before any further shrinking could occur.

It was here at Sammy Manley's that I learned to get a bucket of sand and a long-handled bristle brush ready before our boat was hauled out of the water for bottom painting. Dip the brush in the sand as you scrub off and you end up with a wet-sanded bottom, ready for paint.

Several months later, when we sailed away, our pockets were full of cruising funds and our heads were crammed with new boatbuilding tricks. During the years that followed, we earned a lot of our cruising funds this way as we worked in boatyards in 30 different ports and 11 different countries. We also learned some basic truths we think could help you if you are considering a life as a journeyman. Skilled, productive boat workers, especially those with a variety of talents, are in demand worldwide. But to make it all work, you have to have low operating costs and low overhead (i.e., a modest-size boat, modest living standards) and you must be flexible – not only about the type of work you are willing to do, but also with your cruising schedule.

So what are the secrets to finding jobs along the way? Possibly the most important is to keep your boat looking smart, so it interests and impresses the people you meet. Even better, cruise in a self-built boat, one that will show potential customers exactly what kind of work you do – a floating business card, so to speak.

Whenever possible, try to look for work in developed countries, ones with strong currencies and a tradition of boatbuilding and sailing. If you earn U.S. dollars in Florida, they will buy a lot of tacos and beans in Mexico. If you earn Norwegian kroner at Norwegian wages, despite Norway's relatively high living costs, you still come away with lots to spend in Spain. If you cannot always choose the best country as far as wages go, try to work for owners of boats from developed countries, as I did in Costa Rica at Sammy Manley's yard.

Try to be in the right place at the right time. We either look for race situations, such as we did in Acapulco, or we plan our annual haulout for at least three or four weeks before the normal spring rush in a place where lots of cruising boats and charter boats congregate. By the time *Taleisin* is glowing with fresh paint, we are almost always offered some work, since the boatyard is approaching its busiest season. The yard manager has seen our boat-work skills, our work habits. If we are offered work, we can live on our boat tied alongside the same yard. This schedule works well, because three or four months later, when we have a nice bit of cash, we also have our own boat refitted and ready to go. If we had delayed the work on our own boat until after earning our funds, we'd probably have been too restless to do our own fit-out as well. This same principle can serve you well if you arrive before a wooden-boat festival, or a major local regatta such as the Sydney-Hobart race or Antigua Week.

These regattas give you several chances for work – as a journeyman, fitting out for the race or regatta start, or as a delivery team to bring the boat back, or, if things go wrong, to repair the boat so it can be returned home.

One of our most lucrative jobs occurred because of a combination of these factors when we were in the Balearic islands. It was the busiest time of the year for delivery teams and yards alike, as the charter fleet began heading for the Caribbean. The owner of a 53-foot (16.2m) ketch was desperate, as no one would move his boat because its upper shrouds were shot, and builders had left out the compression post under the mizzenmast. I got the job on a cost-plus basis since I was there with the tools on board *Seraffyn* – right place, right time. We hauled out the boat, removed some worm damage from the rudder and sternpost, added the necessary compression post, spliced up rigging, and set off with extra crew. We returned four months later, set up with funds for a year and a half of cruising.

In that case, it was definitely having our boat that got us work independent of a local shipyard. But in local shipyards, even if you have your boat as a calling card, you may have some obstacles to overcome. Keep in mind that to local employers, you are an unknown quantity with no local references. You might offer to work for free for three days, no strings attached. If you are subsequently hired, the employer pays you for the trial period. Or you can work on a contract basis. The employer has far less to lose if you do this than if you work by the hour. He only has to pay when the job is completed to the agreed specifications. A lot of boatyard owners like this plan, since they don't have to figure out labor costs. They simply take your contract price, add materials costs plus a percentage for profits, and submit this bid to the customer.

Contract work has benefits for you also. If you work extra hard, or put in longer hours by working through breaks, or if you stay an hour longer to glue up a part for the next day's job, the extra efforts will benefit you directly. Furthermore, the locals will not grumble and say you are breaking union rules. Instead, they'll probably shrug their shoulders and say, "Well, he's working for himself. I'd do the same in his shoes."

Figuring out bids for contracts is interesting, though it can be fraught with possible bombshells. Through the years, we have come close to even – losing on a few bids and gaining on a few, but almost always earning more than we would have if we had worked 40 hours a week at a good hourly wage. The system we have come to use – after doing contract work not only as we cruised around the world but also at our own boatyard – is as follows. I carefully figure out how to do the job and calculate how many hours the job should take to reach the agreed specifications. Since I have learned that, like most builders, I think I am more efficient and faster than I am, I have my business partner (Lin) go over the job step by step with me to see if I have overlooked something. When we agree on the man-hours, she calmly doubles them, multiplies by what we want to earn per hour, and, amazingly, almost all of our bids have been accepted. I then work like hell to prove to Lin that I could have done the job in less than her doubled calculations. But – I rarely do.

Contract jobs mean we rarely get involved in short, piece-meal jobs such as putting a few screws in a toerail, then going over to install a cleat on the next boat, and then on to a third job on the far side of the yard – all in the same morning. Jobs like that are a hassle, because each takes less than an hour, but it is hard to bill people for all of the time you spend getting tools ready and cleaning up. Nor do we get involved in long-duration boatbuilding projects. We prefer contract jobs we can complete in two days to two months. We find it is easier to get and keep temporary work permits this way, as we do not threaten the livelihood of local people. Furthermore, we get itchy feet and begin scratching to satisfy our sailing passions after a few months in any one place.

At spring refit time, you may find it is best to work at an hourly wage, to work long hours and over weekends. Help the yard owner over this often-hectic period and he will probably be willing to find longer-term work if you need it when things slow down.

In many countries with union workers, your willingness to work overtime or at odd hours on a contract basis can help the yard get extra jobs, jobs that could go to you. In Poole, England, a fishing-boat skipper came in and asked to have a quote for an outside steering station. The skipper was very concerned when he asked, "How long to fit up, then; how long do you need to keep my boat? Them whitefish aren't half running!" We decided to work until 4 a.m. so the fisherman could catch the next day's tide and the fish. Soon we learned he had spread the word by ship's radio: "Quick-turnaround shipwright work at Cobb's Quay." This extra business made us popular with the boatyard owner and also topped up our cruising kitty.

If you are ready and willing to use hand tools for small repair jobs, you can also pick up work more easily. Most of us automatically think of using our favorite power tools. But without them, many jobs can be completed more quickly and cost-effectively. You don't have to bring the boat alongside the shipyard dock, nor do you need to run halfway across the yard to reset a circuit breaker. There are no extension cords to lay out,

no plug adapters or fuses to sort out. Furthermore, you eliminate the serious danger of working on or near the water with high-voltage electricity (240 volts in most countries outside the United States). Cut costs on these small jobs and you'll please the shipyard manager, because he can keep his regular crew working uninterrupted on his larger bread-and-butter jobs.

You can also pick up good freelance jobs on boats out at anchor if you think "hand power" instead of "electric power." The owner of a 46-foot (14m) yacht in New Zealand was devastated when a local yard estimated almost $1,900 to remove his mast so they could repair the top, where rot had started in a wire covering wood spline. I quoted $400 to do the same job, using hand tools and my bosun's chair. I used a brace and screwdriver bit to remove fittings that were in the way, then chiseled out the damaged area and set a spline in place with glue and screws. The two of us spent only about six hours on the job. (Lin on deck to be "gofer.")

Once you get jobs – either in boatyards or out at anchor – a very important rule is, don't ego-trip on the customer's boat using his money. The key to customer satisfaction is to match the existing construction methods so that the new parts blend right into the existing work. This is important if you are doing woodwork, sailmaking, electrical wiring or rigging. One winter in Gibraltar, I was asked to make two new bookshelves for a French production yacht. The existing shelves were what I would call "cheap-and-cheerful" construction, made from varnished mahogany and fastened with chrome screws and cupped washers. I groaned inwardly and made the new ones so they matched the old ones, with only slightly better varnishwork, and the owner was delighted. He paid instantly, then hired me for more work, more additions to complement and add value to his boat.

Several potential journeymen have asked us about work visas in foreign ports. It has been our experience over the past several decades that the employer will almost always sort out the problem. A simple call to the immigration people will usually get a temporary work permit. This was true in New Zealand, Australia (Sydney), South Africa, and Norway – just a few of the countries where we have visited and worked. Where there are more formal requirements, some cruisers have gotten around the problem by signing on temporarily as crew of the foreign-flagged vessel they will work on. They then are paid as a ship's carpenter. In other cases, where the job is small such as the one I did on *Simoon*, the local authorities will turn a blind eye, since it would be difficult to prove you are doing anything other than helping out a cruising friend.

This is only a sampling of the truths we have learned about getting and doing jobs along the way. But underlying this is an all-important financial fact. If you are considering becoming a journeyman, earning-as-you-cruise, you must make a careful decision about the size of boat you wish to own. No matter how skilled you are, as a visiting craftsman you will not be able to earn enough in a few months to be free to cruise for several more – unless you are conservative when you choose the boat and you are careful about its operating and maintenance costs. If you have a 45- or 50-foot boat and the maintenance takes two or three months a year, and you then have to work five or six months to earn enough to cover your boat and cruising overhead, you won't have much time free to cruise. We have met numerous shipwrights, sailmakers, and other craftsmen who choose to have boats large enough to carry a complete workshop. One had a lathe and heavy-duty welding gear set up with a high-output generator, another had two sailmaker's sewing machines. Sadly, these folks did little cruising, because they found themselves struggling to pay for the high costs associated with their large, workshop-laden boats. On the other hand, I have seen literally dozens of cruisers on small boats, boats under 35 feet, working for three to four months, sailing for seven or eight, and caring for their boat during a two- or three-week haulout period just before they set to work as journeymen. Remember – if you are doing work that requires heavy-duty machinery, you probably will be working in a shipyard, where you can arrange to use their shop and their equipment.

Think "simplicity" on your own boat, in your own life, and consider not only the precious time you will have to spend doing what "you want to do" but also what you can learn along the way. I know the time I have spent in boatyards worldwide has taught me different ways to approach each job. Some of the solutions I have seen have been wonderful, some truly awful. The jobs I have been offered have covered the same range – from rebuilding a 23-foot (7m) plywood runabout in Gibraltar to researching (then building) an exact-replica interior in an all-teak, 1882 Fife-designed cutter in Australia; from pouring several tons of lead directly onto the existing keel of a 60-foot (18.3m) high-tech raceboat to create an improved windward foil shape, to bolting on the bilge keels for a fishingboat. These jobs have ranged from dead easy to challenging in the extreme. But the important thing was, each one helped us achieve the goal inspired by my grandparents. We gained time off to do what we wanted – which, stated simply, was to go off sailing and adventuring together.

Tools and Tool Storage for a Journeyman

Tools comfort me. I would love to carry every tool I own on board. But when Lin and I set off on *Seraffyn*, we had only 6 cubic feet of locker space to dedicate specifically to tools. Yet I carried enough to earn our way for 11 years. (Lin claims my extra tools kept sneaking into her food-storage lockers. I deny this – she offered to put them there.) Then we moved onto *Taleisin*, with her fitted workbench and 21 cubic feet of dedicated tool-storage space. Although I had more room, I carried a smaller selection of my heavy-duty boatbuilding tools than I had on *Seraffyn*. In shoreside storage, I left my adze, two large slicks, and several wood block planes, as I found I had rarely used them. But I did carry a larger selection of power tools, extra bronze fastenings, and more metalworking tools.

The tools listed in Figure 27-1 are generally the same as you would expect any shipwright to own on shore but a few deserve special mention.

Figure 27-1. LARRY's TOOLS

This list includes the majority of tools I carry, but I have not listed the small items, such as punches and gauges, which fit in the corners and edges of trays.

JOURNEYMAN'S TOOLS

PLANES (all cast iron)

Smoothing 9"

Rabbet 12"

Block 6"

Snub-nosed rabbet 4"

CHISELS

Set of 10 from $1/8$" to $1^3/4$"

2" Slick (slicer)

3 Gouges – $3/8$" $1/2$" $3/4$"

Wing dividers (scribe)

Marking gauge

Bevel gauge

SAWS

Handsaw 26"

Bench 14"

Dovetail 10"

Coping $6^3/4$"

OTHER

Brace and bits $1/4$" to 1"

Expansion bit $7/8$" to 3"

Hand drill – two-speed with $1/2$" chuck
  fits $1/16$ to $1/2$" drills

Countersinks (fuller)

Taper-point drills to bore for screws
  and wood plugs to fit #4 to #18
  screws

Matching wood-plug cutters from $1/4$"
  to $1^1/4$"

(These screw tools work in most countries, though occasionally I have to borrow a metric wood-plug cutter.)

$1/2$" drill

Orbital sander (uses $1/2$ sheet of
  sandpaper)

Belt sander 3" x 21"

▶

Laminate trimming router	Rigging vise up to $1/2"$ wire
Step-up transformer 110 V <-> 240 volt	Sail-repair tools and rigging kit
100' 110V Extension (drop) cords	Ball peen hammer, claw hammer, 4-lb. drilling hammer
3-way plug outlet	Assorted screwdrivers
Coarse and fine taps and dies $1/8"$ to $3/4"$ *(Occasionally I buy or borrow metric or Whitworth (English) taps or dies.)*	*(I prefer square-shanked ones, which accept a wrench)*
4 x 2" C-clamps	Files – assorted round, half round, rattail, and miniature file set
4 x Light-duty 10" long adjustable clamps	Hacksaw – 12" keyhole hacksaw
Propane soldering heating torch with 20' of hose for this (a special regulator fits into *Taleisin's* on-deck propane tank).	Pliers, Vise-Grips, regular, water pump (channel lock)
	Adjustable wrenches: 18", 12", 10", 8", 4"
	Pipe wrench 14"
Small, refuelable propane torch and hot knife for electrical connections or for sailmaking (Weller by *Cooper Tools, P.O. Box 728, APEX, NC 27502 USA*)	Impact tool for removing screws
	Combination spanners – $3/8"$ to 1"
	Socket set
	Sharpening stone
Sailmaking dies for sewn liners – 4 sizes	12' and 100' tape measures

The laminate trimming router originally made by Stanley is now sold by Robert Bosch & Co. of Chicago; it's especially helpful, as it can be used to radius the corners of joinery already fitted into place – deckbeams, carlins, bulkhead trim. Fit and install it, then come along with this router and radius the corners all at one go.

I use the router along with a special pattern-maker's file I was first shown in 1966 by Ted Howard, a well-known California boatbuilder. The Nicholson #50 patternmaker's file has teeth set in a random pattern, not in straight rows so you can file across the end-grain of hardwoods without chipping off the sharp corners. Use this file once and you will never be without one. It's available from Jamestown Distributors, tel: 800-423-0030, fax: 800-423-0542.

The $1/2$-hp, variable-speed forward and reversing heavy-duty power drill I carry is made by the Robert Bosch Company of Chicago (Model 1025VSR; tel: 1-800-301-8255 ext. 3300, fax: 773-481-7213). This is not the more widely known German Bosch company. This drill has an extra-small body only 9 inches (22.9cm) long. It will fit into small spaces between frames and floor timbers, and into a smaller toolbox than a normal heavy-duty $1/2$-inch drill. I use it not only as a drill but also as a screwdriver, and for tapping threads into metal. To create a screwdriver bit that works well yet keeps me from overtightening or breaking screws, I have cut the end off a round-shanked screwdriver. (I used a bench grinder to do this, as screwdrivers are made of hardened steel, which is almost impossible to cut with a hacksaw). I then tighten this round bit in the Jacobs chuck with just enough tension so that it will slip and rotate before it breaks the screw. I use this same trick with taps when I am cutting threads into metal.

Although our two-speed hand drill is pretty common, I have adapted it so it can be used with all of the twist drills I carry by removing the original $3/8$-inch chuck and replacing it with a $1/2$-inch Jacobs chuck, complete with chuck key. (A machine shop had to cut special threads to do this conversion.)

The vise we use on *Taleisin* is carriage-bolted to the workbench so I can remove it easily when I accept a job ashore, or even when we are doing a refit on *Taleisin* in a shipyard. I can then either build a temporary workbench or borrow a shipyard bench, drill three appropriate holes, and have my own vise. To protect the vise (and the sails that live near it) from rust, I first had it copper-plated, then nickel-plated. This finish seems to last for six or seven years. I also replaced the steel handle (the hardest part of the vise to keep rust-free) with a piece of $1/2$-inch silicon-bronze round stock. The vise is a standard 4-inch metalworker's vise, to which I have added two sets of protective jaws – one made of copper, the other made of $1/4$-inch plywood to turn it into a nondenominational wood/metal working vise.

The most important tip I can pass on to anyone who wants to protect their tools from the ravages of salt air and life on a boat is to store them in heavy-duty plastic tool boxes. The ones I use are made by Flambeau (other companies make similar ones). They are lightweight, tough plastic, don't leak in the rain, don't dent or stain wood decks, have all stainless-steel fittings, and are strong enough to sit or stand on (see photo page 307). They are lockable and have a strong fold-up carry handle. Mine come with a tool tray with a metal handle, which lifts out and leaves space for larger tools beneath the tray. To keep the tools clean – those I store in the individual boxes and the ones I keep in the sliding tray under the workbench – I use WD-40. Each time I put away my tools, I spray the

---

Figure 27-2. *Toolbox categories*

On board *Taleisin*, our tools are separated into individual boxes as follows:

1. Woodworking tools
2. Metalworking tools
3. Paint and varnish tools and supplies
4. Adhesives, compounds, resins, and fiberglass repair materials
5. Caulking tools, including gun for tubes of paying compound
6. Rigging and sailmaking tools
7. Electric tools
8. 110/240 volt converter, propane burner torch and cords, solder, drop cords, and extra-large crescent wrenches

Cabinet style box: Screws, bolts, small parts, hand drill, and drill index
Tray under workbench: Tools used most regularly
Plastic tube for rod, flat stock, and long drills

whole inside of the box or tray with this light oil. When I need to use the tool, it is absolutely rust-free and needs only a light wipe with a rag. I have tools we have carried since 1969, tools that were old before we set sail, and they are in grand condition because of this box-and-spray storage regime.

To organize the tools efficiently, I have eight different boxes, each dedicated to a separate category of tools, as shown in Figure 27-2. Job start-up time seems to be reduced dramatically if all the tools you need for one type of job are in one box. To store long items, such as extended drills, a 3-foot straightedge ruler, and bronze rod or flat stock, I use a 5-foot-long, 3-inch-diameter plastic water pipe with removable plastic end plugs. This, too, I spray with WD-40 before I close it for storage alongside the bilge stringer in the lazarette.

A Journeyman's Workbench

The most successful workbenches we have seen on small sailing craft have two things in common. First, they are well secured and solid, with a vise in place ready to hold a piece of wood or a bolt while you cut off a bit. Second, they have a sliding tray or drawer directly under the bench for easy access to the tools you use most often. If this tray is directly below the vise, it serves a second purpose, as mentioned in the previous chapter. If you open the tray and put a rag or towel across it while you use your

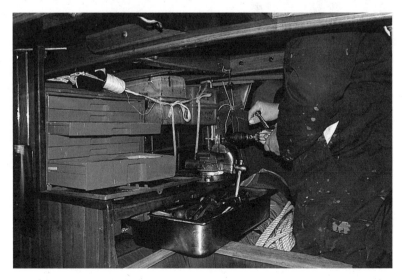

Figure 27-3. *Two possible workbench solutions.*

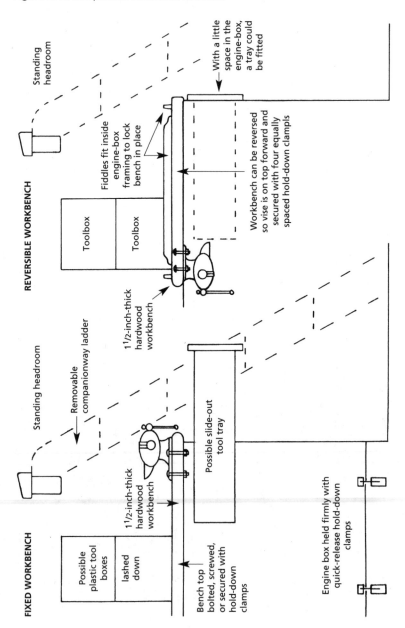

Figure 27-4. *Two possible fo'c's'le workbenches.*

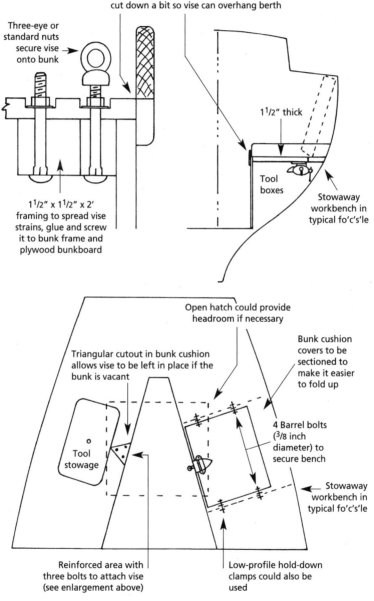

In each case, the bunk front will have to be cut down a bit so vise can overhang berth

Three-eye or standard nuts secure vise onto bunk

1¹/₂″ thick

1¹/₂″ x 1¹/₂″ x 2′ framing to spread vise strains, glue and screw it to bunk frame and plywood bunkboard

Tool boxes

Stowaway workbench in typical fo'c's'le

Open hatch could provide headroom if necessary

Triangular cutout in bunk cushion allows vise to be left in place if the bunk is vacant

Bunk cushion covers to be sectioned to make it easier to fold up

Tool stowage

4 Barrel bolts (³/₈ inch diameter) to secure bench

Stowaway workbench in typical fo'c's'le

Reinforced area with three bolts to attach vise (see enlargement above)

Low-profile hold-down clamps could also be used

hacksaw or drill, the shavings will collect on the towel for easy disposal instead of ending up in the bilges.

What size of boat do you need to find space for one of the bench arrangements shown in the Figure 27-3? We have one on 29-foot 6-inch (9m) *Taleisin* and have seen a workbench fitted into the interior of a boat only 24 feet (7.3m) long. Do you need a workbench to cruise successfully or to earn your cruising funds as a journeyman? No. We managed without one for 11 successful years aboard *Seraffyn*. But now that we have one, we find it indispensable – not only for maintaining our own boat but also for times when we do modest-size jobs on other people's boats. They can tie right alongside and I get straight to work on my own workbench. No need to find a marina berth in which to work, no need to transport tools back and forth or to lock them up ashore.

As you look at your boat's interior and consider where to put a workbench, remember that it could fit anywhere you can stand up (Figs. 27-3, 27-4). If, to get standing headroom, you must place it under an opening hatch as we have done, be sure you choose a hatch, that can be protected easily with a rain or sun awning. Also, if you plan to store all of your tools at or near the workbench, consider their weight and offset this weight on the opposite side of the boat. Otherwise, you could end up with an annoying list to port or starboard.

A small but important final item you'll need in order to make the workbench area less threatening to the homemaker of the crew is a compact, 12V, hand-held, automotive-type vacuum cleaner. Add a 20-foot-long cord so it can reach anywhere on the boat to clean up the journeyman's shavings.

CHAPTER
28
VARNISH,
AS IN
VARNISHWORK

M y mother was careful to explain, "Lin, politics and religion are two subjects to be avoided at any but the most intimate gatherings if you want to keep the peace." But when I flew from her nest, I found myself in a completely new environment because I became involved with a charter yacht skipper. Her words lost their meaning in a world where religion and politics rarely were mentioned. Instead, I came to paraphrase her warning; the two subjects to be avoided in the waterfront fraternity were anchors and varnish work.

Say, "I like Captain's Choice varnish" to a yacht skipper and he would counter, "Loses its gloss too fast; wouldn't use anything but Superspar." Say you liked to get a thick coat on twice a year and his crew would give a knowing look and retort, "Two or three thin coats last better." I listened to a hundred conversations start this way, only to deteriorate as brand names led to brush preferences and then name-calling – until finally there was angry silence. The only thing I've ever been able to get two good varnishers to agree on is: There is a good reason it is called varnishwork. It is *work*, work of the most frustrating kind because there always seems to be some new way to foul it up.

I had never seen a can of varnish until I met Larry. As we built our eventual floating home, he taught me, "Make sure the wood is perfectly clean, no finger prints, no pencil marks or scratches across the grain. Final-sand with 150-grit paper, dust it with a brush, and slap on a first coat, thinned 20 percent with turps. Don't be too fussy, just make sure you cover it all. Wait a day or two, sand, then varnish, until you've got four coats. When you've got four coats, when you are ready to put on the fifth coat, you can start to be particular about dust and runs, because inside the boat, that should be the last coat of varnish you put on for five or 10 years." At his urging, I tried several brands of varnish until I found one with which I was comfortable. In my innocence, I chose the cheapest natural spar varnish I could find, because every penny we saved meant one more penny for timber or sails. With the luck of the innocent, the Man of War varnish, in its shiny red can, is one I'd choose again today.

So I set boldly to work, economy-sized gallon of varnish on one hand, the whole interior of a 24-foot hull on the other. I inspected and dusted every inch of that empty hull, cleaned the only brush we owned, held my breath, and started. The fresh mahogany burst into a deep red blush as I applied each stroke. The white oak turned to a buttery glow. I was entranced by the transformation as I varnished from the sheer of the newly planked hull toward the bilge which we planned to paint a gleaming white. I was so entranced that I didn't notice the coffee can full of varnish I'd perched on a butt block farther along the hull. I let out a scream as it tumbled, varnish cascading across half a dozen frames down the planking, across the floor timbers, and through the limber holes toward the sump of the bilge. "Larry, help me!!! What do I do now?" I yelled. I started to cry as I looked at the mess I'd made of his beautiful woodwork.

Larry poked his head over the sheer, his expression almost panicked. "You all right?" he asked. I pointed below me. His expression flashed from concern through thought to solution in under two seconds. "Guess we're going to have varnished bilges," he said. "Call me when you've spread that varnish and I'll bring you some more."

So, like many female partners of a boatbuilding team, with zero carpentry skills, I became almost a full-time varnisher. Unlike many of my compatriots, I came to enjoy the task, even the sanding it entailed. It was a perfect contrast to the work I did as an accountant and later behind a typewriter. My imagination could fly to the far corners of the earth as I sanded, or as each stroke of the varnish brush brought up another beautiful grain pattern in the wood – like a living thing beneath my hands.

I had a dozen catastrophes as I worked my way through 10 gallons of varnish. Larry had to snip strands of my almost-waist-length hair close to my scalp because I'd sat up under a freshly varnished deckbeam and didn't notice the mess until three hours later, when it was dry. After that, I learned to wear a scarf. A neighbor's cat had a mouse-chase through a new coat of varnish in the forepeak. Lyle Hess, *Seraffyn's* designer, arrived one morning to find me in tears because the entire main cabin had gone milky when a heavy afternoon fog rolled through our canvas-covered shed soon after I'd applied what was to have been the final coat. "Just let it dry for a week," he assured me. "Then do it again. You'll be amazed at what a fine finish you'll get." He was right, too.

As *Seraffyn* progressed, my varnishwork began to get almost as many compliments as Larry's woodwork. I began to forget that the varnished bilges people praised were only the result of an accident. Then one day, an old pro whose varnishwork gave him the right to criticize said, "Varnish sure hides more sins than paint does. But if you want your cabinetry and deck varnish to look good, you ought to get some decent brushes." So I skimped on our grocery money, skipped ice creams, then marched into the marine store. "Give me two Grumbacher brushes," I said. "These really good badger-hair ones are half the price," the salesman said. But I had to have the best, and, went home cradling my treasures.

It may have been the brushes, it may have been as Dennis Conner said, that I now had "no excuse to lose," but my varnish spread more smoothly, I had fewer brush marks, fewer loose bristles. Twenty years later, those brushes were half an inch shorter, worn by the building and maintenance of our two cruising boats plus dozens of jobs on other yachts, so I asked my mother to buy me a new set. (By this time, a set had grown to consist of four brushes.) "I sure hope these are what you ordered," she sighed as we rendezvoused in New Zealand. I gladly paid her as she said, "I don't believe it. They cost more than two good dinners out." But with the smugness of a true boat nut, I could answer, "But they last a hundred times longer."

The ownership of those fine brushes did lead to a new round of controversy in the politico-religious circle of yacht varnishers with whom I hung out as we finished *Seraffyn*. "Clean them seven times in turps, then wash them in brush cleaner. Suds them in warm water and liquid dish soap, rinse extra well, then shape the bristles and hang them in a warm, dust-free room to dry," an artist type admonished me. "No," a boatbuilder said, "just stick them in motor oil right after you use them; clean them in kerosene next time you want to varnish." I compromised, and to save money only rinsed them three times after I varnished. I then hung them suspended in a jar of kerosene. Larry laughed at my concerns. He also swept his workbench an hour later and filled my perfectly clean brushes and kerosene with a cup of mahogany sawdust. I glowered at him as I fought to get every last fleck of dust out of the bristles. Then I hid my jar and its precious cargo on the top shelf of my pantry, far from any invading dust.

After going a week without varnishing, I reached for my brushes and came up against another horror. A gummy, slimy, yellow film had formed all over their bristles. (Years later, I learned this was residue from the varnish, and six or seven kerosene rinses would have prevented it, as would wrapping the brushes in brown paper before suspending them.) But to save on the expense of kerosene or thinners, which I have found I could use interchangeably, I began tending my brushes as carefully as some homemakers tend their potted plants, checking the color of the thinner every day, admonishing Larry to change it if I had to be away overnight. If I had to be away for more than a week, I dried and saturated the brushes in 30-weight oil and wrapped them in aluminum foil.

It wasn't until we'd been cruising for a year that I realized I had become a varnish fanatic. The loan of a marina berth in northern Mexico gave us free access to fresh water for the first time in nine months, so we emptied *Seraffyn* completely. Larry helped me to sand the whole inside of the deckhouse, which had only received four coats of varnish before we moved on board. Once the mahogany was flatted to a perfect sanded tone, we hosed and scrubbed every inch of the boat so she'd be dust-free (and, incidentally salt-free) for the "perfect" varnish job on these highly visible surfaces – surfaces that I and every varnish critic who came aboard stared at as we sat having drinks.

"It's you who want the perfect job," Larry said. "So you lay the varnish on." I hitched my bikini bottom to a more comfortable position and tightened the rubber band on my unruly pony tail. Brush, spread, inspect, move quickly so there are no lap marks, watch the lower edges of the portlights for any possible sags. I concentrated for all I was worth, sweat forming on my forehead as I worked.

Larry sat down on the cabin sill, cocking his head to look along the cabin side, "You've got a holiday here," he said, pointing to a spot 4 feet from where I was working. I rushed to stroke it out. "There's another one here: you are putting it on too thin," he said.

"There is not a holiday," I growled as I continued brushing. "It's so big it's more like a summer vacation than a holiday," Larry answered. He climbed into the cabin and pointed at yet another thin area. I barely held my temper until I reached the natural stopping place beside a cabin cornerpost. "You're such a smart-ass, you do the other side. See if you can do any better in this glary light."

I watched him like a hawk: "You've got a sag there." He reached back and stroked it away. "You missed a run there: that one looks more like a lace curtain," I taunted.

"We want protection, not perfection. Better too thick than too thin," he mumbled as he worked to get a good job in that hot cabin. But I didn't let go, and neither did he until we were standing on the dock yelling at each other. I don't know how long we stood there being furious, but all of a sudden Larry began to laugh. "We sure are lucky if the only thing we have to fight about is a coat of varnish." He was right, and through the years, our varnish methods seem to have almost reversed, until a few months ago we shared the same dinghy and he varnished one side of *Taleisin's* transom while I did the other. It was a tricky job, trying to meet behind the rudder to catch each other's brushstroke, yet not capsize. When we went back out to see the results the next morning, the varnish glowed beautifully. But if you looked along the transom with the sun behind you and your face within a foot of the surface, you could see a holiday on Larry's side, a sag or two on mine.

It was after I'd used another 17 gallons of varnish as we built *Taleisin*, after Larry had accused me of enjoying varnishing better than sailing, that I met the ultimate varnish freak. I was scrubbing the decks as we lay alongside the San Diego Yacht Club docks. A tall, slim man asked, "What brand of gloss you use?" Soon Bob and I were exchanging varnish gospel over a pot of tea. "I charge double the going rate around here and I'm booked full time," he said. "When I'm doing an interior, I use 320-grit for the final sanding. I vacuum the boat stem to stern, then I close every

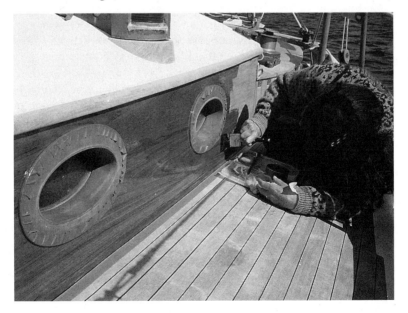

hatch, stuff the ventilators with dust-free rags, and use a tack rag on every inch of the boat – not just the surfaces I plan to varnish, but the floors, counters, and overhead. I squeeze out of the boat and wash down the decks late that evening. Next morning, I come back early, while it's still and the dew holds down any dust. I strip off my clothes in the cockpit, slide inside through the smallest opening possible, turn on the stereo, pour my varnish, take my brushes from the airtight container I use, tack the whole boat again, and varnish to a perfect dust-free gloss finish." As he waved his cup of tea, his eyes sparkled. I could imagine him getting high as a kite on solvent fumes as he sang to the strains of Puccini and varnished in the nude inside his private cave.

It has been 32 years and at least 50 gallons since I first met a varnish brush, and I've had almost every catastrophe there is. Larry walked across two freshly varnished hatches when he came back from a shower on shore. Pea-size hailstones driven by 75-knot winds put 150 BB-size dents through the varnish on the forward side of our mast. Unexpected rain squalls have left their mark, the man on the next boat in the shipyard emptied his vacuum bag upwind of our newly varnished transom. I still get panicky when I am faced with a portlight-studded cabin side, still hum as I sand and prep, still treat my brushes like rare potted plants. And I still have to work hard to hold my tongue when I meet a new initiate to varnishing and hear him or her extol the virtues of a varnish I know is less than perfect. Last week, I finally got an absolutely perfect varnish coat, with a finish like molten glass, not a speck of dust. The skylight looked so magnificent in the dust-free shop that I hated to carry it out and sit it on the boat. So Larry volunteered, handling the hatch with two soft towels to keep from smudging the brilliant glow. He set it in place, stepped back, admired my work, then said, "Looks perfect, almost too good for an intermediate coat." I started to flare, then laughed; he was right. Six months from now, I'll have to take sandpaper to that smooth but sun-battered surface and confirm once again that there is a reason it is called varnishwork.

Tips for a Voyaging Varnisher

Some people love gardening, spending most of their spare hours enhancing the approaches to their home with well-tended shrubs and flowers. In a way, we are like them. We enjoy the distinction that varnish gives to a boat, the personality it lends. We also enjoy the work that goes into keeping it looking good. But we know that the absolute simplicity of our boat makes this pleasure possible. Without mechanical or electrical maintenance to do, there is little else to take up our boat-care time other than routine checks on rig and sails plus varnishwork. Even so, as we voyage through different climates and ever-changing situations, we have had to learn some special tricks to make this maintenance easy. The most important ones may be helpful to all those who want the glow of varnish on the exterior of their boat.

1. Don't stain any exterior wood before varnishing. It will be difficult later to match up any scratches or scuffs.

2. Whenever possible, choose teak for exterior varnish surfaces. It does not stain or change color when it is exposed to dampness, and light sanding will blend scratches back into the rest of the surface. (To make sure your teak holds varnish well, use 100-grit sandpaper before the first coat. We have had superb results this way, better bonding even than with mahogany or oaks.)

3. Avoid varnishing horizontal surfaces or heavy-wear areas on the exterior of your boat. Vertical surfaces hold varnish better. A mast is less work to keep varnished than 2-inch-wide full-length toerails.

4. Radius wood corners well under all exterior varnishwork. We use at least a 1/2-inch radius (like your middle finger) wherever possible, a 1-inch radius on hatch edges, and a 2-inch radius on boomkin corners.

5. Avoid varnishing small pieces of exterior trim, such as grabrails or cabin trim. Many woods can safely be left bare. Besides, sanding, taping and cutting in takes far more time on these small pieces than on wide surfaces such as hatches.

6. Keep a varnish touch-up kit handy. A paste bottle with a brush attached inside the top works well. Use a rubber band to attach a few pieces of sandpaper so it can be kept handy to cover any scratches you see before they get wet and turn black. Feather in the scratch and sand 1 inch beyond the bare wood; touch up and leave a border of sanded wood so you remember where the scratch was. Sand and touch up two or three times. Then, next time you varnish the whole surface, your patch will blend right in and have full-strength protection.

7. Don't waste time by using any sandpaper finer than 180-grit on exterior work, 220 in the interior. A good varnish will cover the scratches left by these grades of paper. Finer paper will not give you the

mechanically bonding grooves your varnish needs to hold well in rough conditions.

8. Try disposable foam brushes if you are so inclined, but remember that you cannot buy them in many places other than the United States and some European countries, so it might pay to learn to use bristle brushes also.

9. Avoid epoxy undercoats or polyurethane varnishes for exterior work – or for surfaces that might experience temperatures over 40°C, 98°F – as these coatings are heat-sensitive, and scraping them back can be very hard work. (Natural varnish can withstand direct contact with temperatures as high as 160°F.) Also, if they get dented or scratched, it is hard to feather them out so you can then apply touch-up coats.

10. In areas with air traffic or air pollution, varnish the same day that you sand. Otherwise, the waste fuel spewed out by air traffic can leave a fine coating of oil that will keep your varnish from bonding. Newport Beach, California, on the approaches to Orange County – John Wayne Airport – is famous for this problem.

11. If at all possible, do your varnishwork while you lie at anchor. You will get far less dust this way.

12. Don't varnish after 3 p.m., even in the tropics. Dew can start falling as soon as the sun is behind the horizon. It will flat out your work.

13. Create shade over any horizontal surfaces you plan to varnish in the tropics. Otherwise, you will tend to get orange-peel-like areas where surface varnish has dried faster than the varnish under it.

14. If you see any fine lines radiating along the surface of older varnishwork, sand and varnish immediately. This is the first sign of crazing, and if you leave it even a week or two, you may have to strip the whole surface back to bare wood. If you cannot varnish immediately, cover the area with soft canvas until you can.

15. Set up a regular varnish schedule and stick to it as closely as possible. Ours is as follows:

TROPICS OR SUBTROPICS

Mast vertical surface, spruce – once a year (tops of spreaders are covered with sheet copper)

Transom, vertical surface, teak – every five months

Cabin sides, vertical, teak – twice a year
Hatches, horizontal, teak -every four months
Bowsprit and boomkin, horizontal, spruce – every four months
Tiller, locust, stored under sail cover when at anchor – once a year
Touch-up patrol – once monthly, more often if racing or sailing a lot

16. If you sand well between coats and redo varnish before it crazes deeply, there is no need ever to scrape back to bare wood. *Taleisin's* teak hatches have not been scraped in 14 years of use, yet they look almost new.

17. Remember that it is always an intermediate coat, so a flaw, a scratch, or even a good ding caused by using the boat will be gone and forgotten a few months from now.

18. Don't come to my boat looking for a perfect varnish job. Surprisingly, people do not inspect every varnish surface on your boat for runs, sags, brush marks. They look at the overall appearance, and if they do not see any black marks, if the general appearance of the varnish is that of a well-cared-for, loved boat, they'll say, "Great varnishwork." I can show you all the flaws on the inside of our cabin sides, yet everyone says, "Oh" and "Aah" when they look at them. I might note that I did not invite that ultimate varnish freak from San Diego down below; we shared our tea in the cockpit.

AFTERWORD
TEN QUESTIONS

A great Native American chief was preparing to testify at a formal court hearing late in the last century. When the bailiff said, "Do you swear to tell the truth...," the chief answered, "I cannot tell the truth; I can only tell you what I know."

In early 1997, we presented seminars in the United Kingdom, the United States and New Zealand and spoke with more than 5,000 potential cruisers. When we returned to *Taleisin* in southwest England to voyage north to Scotland, a cruising friend, Tom Linskey, now an editor at *Sail* magazine, suggested we jot down a list of the 10 questions we'd been asked most frequently. He published this list, asking readers to let him know if they were interested in the answers. Hundreds of readers responded. Our answers to these questions in many ways sum up much of what we have tried to show in this book. They may not be everyone's idea of "the truth." We can only, as that wise man said, tell what we know, gathered from our experience of some 30 years of voyaging, of feeling amazingly free yet enjoyably challenged as we visited 66 countries under sail, earning as we cruised.

But first, some background to help you understand our perspective. Long before Larry began building our first cruising boat, 24-foot 4-inch *Seraffyn*, his course had been set by his grandparents, two very satisfying and satisfied folks who lived simply and modestly, working only six months each year and traveling the rest on land. Their axiom was: "The only way to beat the system is to take time off to do what you want to do." Their corollary to this was: "If everyone else does it, look at it with suspicion." Or to put this in a modern context, the pressures of societal rules all lead people toward a central, "normal" way of thinking. By being willing to accept the consequences of being different, you can break free to do what you want. Only after Larry and I had worked and saved to build *Seraffyn* did we begin to understand his grandparents' corollary, since we found no one encouraged people to go off cruising. Your employer doesn't want you to leave. Your parents don't want to worry about your being "out there." The local boatyard owner, local boatbuilder, and marine store owners don't want to lose a customer. Your friends are worried they'll miss you, or maybe they'll resent hearing about how much fun you are having in Mexico while they grind through another pile of papers and fight another blizzard-swept winter day. Other voyagers may be concerned that you will dilute their sense of accomplishment or add to the crowd in their favorite anchorages. And the list goes on.

In every one of the 200-plus letters we have received since these questions were published, there is an implied desire to get out soon, on a realistic budget. So if finances are not your problem, skip questions 1 and 2. We hope these brief answers will give you food for thought and encouragement to follow through.

1. WHAT IS A REASONABLE CRUISING BUDGET FOR SOMEONE WHO ISN'T REALLY RICH?

We have met literally dozens of voyagers on all-inclusive budgets of $800 to $1,200 per month (1995-97). These people did not try to take all of their shoreside comforts with them, accepted a degree of simplicity on board and were self-sufficient and willing to depend mostly on wind and sail power. They did not fly home often and were using boats in the 28-to 37-foot range. They did not spend a lot of their time cruising in company. We came to know two cruising couples on budgets of less than $600 per month – one on a classic 35-footer, the other on a modern 30-footer. Both couples had been out more than five years and considered a meal ashore a luxury, but they felt the restrictions of their budgets were not so tight that they would choose another lifestyle. These couples are cruising in Europe, a relatively expensive area. In the Western Pacific and Indian Ocean, where costs are lower, we met more low-budget sailors. Several surveys of cruising-rally participants mention budgets from $1,900 to $3,000 per month, on boats averaging 40 to 45 feet. But rallies are among the most expensive ways to cruise, and 40-footers are expensive to own and maintain.

2. WHAT SIZE OF BOAT DO I TRULY NEED?

The desire for the physical comfort and prestige represented by a large boat could keep you from ever getting "out there." You do need the capacity to carry really good ground tackle, lots of books, sufficient provisions, and some luxuries. For a young couple eager to be away now, a boat displacing five tons (total loaded to go, cruising weight of 10,000 to 11,000 pounds) is a practical choice; examples are 24-foot 4-inch *Seraffyn*, the Triton 28, Twister 28, 25-foot Folkboats. We've seen dozens of cruisers out in similar boats. For those with more financial resources who want to go now, who want to earn along the way or live well on a limited income, 28 to 32 feet is definitely enough.

As you look at the questions of budget and boat size, keep in mind these points:

A) A cruising life is not a credit-card life. Once you set off, all of your money will be going out and little will be coming in. You have to live modestly and leave a nest egg in the bank for real emergencies.

B) Letting boat size or brand name determine your feeling of personal status will be a serious drawback to realizing your dream. Or – to put it simply – it is better to go in a Chevy than stay home and make payments on a Mercedes Benz.

C) To live on a 28- to 32-foot boat, it is imperative that you be willing to and enjoy limiting your personal possessions. You need to be tidy and look forward to figuring out and implementing clever storage ideas and improvements without always trying to buy solutions.

D) To keep your budget in control and gain mental confidence, learn to repair the gear you have on board. The skill you gain can pay economic dividends by way of requests to repair other people's cruising problems.

3. HOW DO YOU BREAK AWAY FROM SHORESIDE ENTANGLEMENTS?

If you have material possessions that are irreplaceable, it is difficult to go cruising on a limited budget. We had no problem selling our 1948 MG and our favorite skis. But as you acquire that perfect waterfront home, handsome furniture, lovely pets, it becomes very hard to divest. You may be able to store a few things with family, and take a favorite treasure with you, but you will have to pare down your possessions. Our advice: Begin simplifying your life as soon as you begin thinking about going cruising. Look at each material possession as a potential trap and convert as many objects as possible to interest-bearing freedom chips ($). (Larry does occasionally wish we'd stored that MG instead of selling it to buy sails for *Seraffyn*.)

Cutting loose from the entanglements of jobs and people is harder. That is why we suggest easing ties before you sever them. Plan for a sabbatical or a six-month voyage of discovery instead of saying you are selling out, going off forever. Then, if the life fits, you'll have had the time and space to consider how to handle the remaining mooring lines. If, on the other hand, the six-month respite (aka trial run) leaves you fully sated or fully turned off cruising, you can easily return home. You set a goal, accomplished it, and probably didn't fall behind on any career ladder. You may even be ahead, because you returned with fresh ideas, new insights. That was our strategy, and it's the one we still use today, even though people probably see us as the eternal gypsies. When we set off, we said, "We have the money to sail to Mexico for six months." Only because we found work along the way did we continue for the next "six months" and onward, not once saying we were headed around the world. Today we still avoid specifying long-term plans. Doing that risks failure. For if you announce, "I am going around the world," and then come home early from a great year of sailing in Mexico, having changed your circumnavigation plans, friends and family inevitably will ask "Why didn't you sail around the world?"

4. WHAT ABOUT MEDICAL INSURANCE?

Cruising seems to be far healthier and safer than most lifestyles onshore: more fresh air, more natural exercise, fewer germ-filled rooms, less risk of road accidents, and little long-term nagging stress. Furthermore, excellent medical care is available in most countries at about half of U.S. prices. For these and other reasons, we and the majority of cruisers do not carry medical insurance. We have only known one cruising family who found that medical costs ate away their cruising reserves, and we therefore feel the risk is justified for younger voyagers. For older sailors who feel the odds may be adding up, there are several reputable-appearing companies that offer long-term travelers' insurance with coverage of medical evacuation costs. Three whose policies we have looked at include:

International Health Insurance Danmark A/C
8 Delagegade
1261 Copenhagen, Denmark
Tel: 45-3315-3099, Fax: 45-3332-2560

Health Care Group – Private Patient Plan
International Insurance Dept.
Phillips House, Crescent Road
Tonbridge, Kent, TN1 1BJ, United Kingdom
Tel: 44-1892-512345, Fax: 44-1892-51514

American Pioneer Life Insurance Company
Hemisphere Health Plan, Blue Water Insurance Inc.
725 North 1A1, Suite E-201
Jupiter, FL33477, USA
Tel: 1-561-743-3442 or 1-800-866-8906

Coverage for one person aged 50 to 59, providing $500,000 in medical expenses of all types at your choice of facilities worldwide, would cost approximately $950 to $1,300 per year, if you are willing to carry an excess (deductible) of $5,000.

5. HOW DO I MEET A PARTNER WHO WANTS TO GO CRUISING?

A) Get out and get involved where other sailors gather; get a part-time job in the boating service industry, such as in a sail loft, marina office, West Marine store; take a charter organized for single cruisers; spend your holidays in ports where cruisers prepare their boats for ocean passages – San Diego, La Paz (Baja California), Gibraltar, Panama, Tahiti.

MALE-SPECIFIC. Join a dinghy or small-boat sailing club, because few women currently own bigger boats. Work with sailing schools and offer your boat for learn-to-sail or cruise situations; make it obvious that women are welcome. Join a camping or hiking club; women who enjoy being out-of-doors are likely to enjoy cruising. Post a notice at the local hospital: We don't know why, but half of the long-term cruising women we know are or were nurses.

FEMALE-SPECIFIC. Put up a notice at a yacht club or sailing club, offering to share expenses and help prepare boats in exchange for some sailing. I met Larry when I was looking for an 8-foot sailing dinghy. Just talking to the people selling boats will introduce you to the sailing crowd.

B) Advertise. We know of several cruising couples who met this way. But make sure your ad is neither too specific nor threatening. Here's a politically correct ad:

> Looking for 2 or 3 crew to join me on my 33-footer for a daysail or weekend of exploring under sail – possible longer voyage in the works.

Politically incorrect:

> Single, fun-loving, under 35, slim, athletic crew wanted for endless voyage into sunset.

The latter ad sounds too much like you are looking for an "escort." Remember that you are looking for a real person as a cruising partner, not a figment of your imagination.

6. WHAT ARE OUR CHANCES OF RUNNING INTO A REALLY BAD STORM?

If you make an effort to cruise along coastlines with lots of easy-to-enter harbors, avoid cyclone-prone areas during (and a month either side of) cyclone season, and monitor the weather, it is possible to sail for years without running into a really bad storm. Probably the odds are 1 in 100. Once you set off down an inhospitable coastline, though, or across oceans, you must be prepared to face gales and storms. When we cruised in middle latitudes, we spent less than 3 percent of our time in winds above 30 knots – for a 3-in-100 chance. As soon as we began venturing on passages above 40°N and below 40°S, when we delivered boats during off-seasons, the averages went up to 6 percent – or a 6-in-100 chance of hitting really bad weather. Only once did we sustain damage in a storm; only once did we see our mast shoved below the waves: when we broke our own rules and foolishly chose to run in a late autumn storm in the Baltic (56°N) rather than heave-to.

7. CAN YOU STILL HAVE PERSONAL ENCOUNTERS WITH LOCALS OR ARE THERE TOO MANY PEOPLE OUT CRUISING?

It may be easier now to have these encounters than it was when we first set off. But – to make these encounters happen, you have to be willing to go off on your own, to choose less-traveled routes or anchorages (even along the main cruising tracks), to slow down and give yourself time to get to know local people.

8. WHAT ABOUT PIRATES AND GUNS?

Our solution is to avoid them both. Avoid pirates by staying away from infected areas – the ones known for wars, revolutions, or drug-running. If you do this, you will not need guns at sea.

Avoid unfriendly countries.

Avoid guns in friendly countries – you won't need firearms. To cope with a burglar boarding your boat, keep pepper spray or mace next to your bunk. This is far easier for an unskilled person to use in close quarters, and it will not severely damage the intruder if he happens to be a drunken cruiser mistakenly boarding the wrong boat to look for someone he met on shore. This weapon will most likely control the problem, not kill it.

During our cruising life, we have seen many problems caused by guns on board: skipper shoots girlfriend in the lung; intruder kills skipper using skipper's gun; innocent couple spends 10 months in jail because their gun was similar to a murder weapon. We have never heard of any case where a gun, especially a handgun, solved a problem.

9. HOW DO THE TWO OF YOU STAY HAPPY TOGETHER AFTER 30 YEARS IN SUCH A SMALL SPACE?

Believe us, we have occasional moments of stress that boil over into super-heated domestic arguments. Usually they are caused by outside problems – business, weather, port fever, relatives – that seem insolvable because we can't fix them by writing a check, grabbing a hammer and nails, or rowing out another anchor. These events occurred when we were living on *Seraffyn*, when we lived on shore in a house, when we were on large boats during deliveries. The space or lack of it doesn't do anything to solve or prevent these outside frustrations. But in some ways, our boat herself has cut down on reasons to disagree. Because of our lower overheads, we do not have the stress of being in constant debt and since we are self-employed, we don't worry about losing our jobs. These problems seem to spark the biggest flare-ups among our shoreside friends. We also have common goals and enough time to talk about solutions to the problems that bother us. Without the shield of friends and families being close by (and without the pressures they can exert), we need to support each other far more than we would otherwise. Living closely together, we have come to admire each other's totally different but complementary skills, and we have learned to accept each other's foibles and goof-ups. Our life seems to be getting better each year as we gain more control over our domestic and business affairs.

It is, however, a misconception to think we "live" in a small space. We live on a big ocean in a wide-open world. When we are anchored in the tropics, we are in a 360-degree swimming pool we don't have to maintain. It is when you are tied up in a marina during inclement weather that even the biggest cruising boat begins to feel restrictive. This is where one of the extra advantages of a smaller, more affordable boat comes into play. It gives us the excuse, plus the spare funds, to rent a furnished cottage on shore every few years so we can savor life as part of a local village. This is so much easier than carrying groceries out to the end of a marina dock on a windswept, cold, rainy day. Furthermore, it gives us a chance to spruce up the interior of the boat.

To us, living on a cruising boat is about going places, and being able to spend time off the boat and out in the middle of the countries we visit, just as much as it is lolling in lovely tropical anchorages, joining in a local sailing race, or drinking warm beer in a cool Cornish pub!

10. WHAT ARE YOUR FAVORITE PLACES TO CRUISE?

For sheer cruising pleasure, give us a protected, island-dotted coastline with a variety of small villages, deserted anchorages, and an occasional town – places like the Gulf Islands of Canada, Baja's Gulf of California, New Zealand's North Island, Isla Grande in Brazil, the southeast coast of Norway or Finland.

But our two most memorable destinations were places we'd never have been able to savor if we hadn't had a sailing turtle shell to take us there and make it financially practical to stay for a while and get to know the local people: Poland in the early 1970s and South Africa in the mid-1990s. In both cases, excursions into the hinterlands left indelible impressions of the amazing political changes, wild history, intimate "people experiences," plus stunning vistas. (Next time we meet up, ask us about the seven wondrous months we spent exploring off-road through five southern African countries in a four-wheel-drive Nissan camper-truck we kitted out using the tools we carried on *Taleisin*.)

ONE FINAL PIECE OF ADVICE

Any cruise – whether a trip from your home harbor to an offshore island a day's sail away or a three-to-six-month voyage to Mexico or the Bahamas – can be labled a real cruise. Each one is a learning experience that can bring its own satisfactions. In fact, when we look back at actual sailing experiences, some of the short passages have brought the greatest satisfactions. Sure, it was wonderful to sail successfully up and across the Atlantic from Brazil to Ireland, but it was the daysailing and exploring along the 200 miles of rivers and islands of the "old country" that we remember with the most pleasure. Plan your first overnighter now – do it in the boat you have, even if it is not the perfect heavy-duty cruiser. Try to get out on the water in as many different boats as you can. Then, when the time is right, you'll have the background to help make longer cruises seem far less daunting.

APPENDIX

This information, prepared by Peter French, a British independent financial adviser (IFA), may give you food for thought, no matter what your country's tax rules may be.

Overview of the Financial Implications of Setting Sail into the Sunset

Every year, a few hundred more people decide to cut adrift from the environment of work and living in a house, intending to fulfil their dream of cruising wherever the fancy takes them. Some of the people who make this bold decision will be retired with very comfortable investment and/or pension incomes living on large yachts with all modern conveniences. Others may be young and hoping to earn money doing casual work on the way when in ports of call. Many have a dream of yacht charter income from taking paying passengers on day trips or longer voyages. I have found that in most cases, people intending to make this break do not think through the financial implications of their actions and frequently fail to seek the necessary financial advice to ensure that they avoid all the pitfalls that can occur.

Generally, I believe that the wealthier and older the sailaways, the greater risk that exists of making serious financial errors. The more money you have at the outset of the voyage, the greater the potential losses through not planning your finances correctly.

DOMICILE AND NATIONALITY CONSIDERATIONS

Many of the matters that need careful consideration will be the same, regardless of the nationality of the yachtsman. However, because tax regimes vary greatly according to country of residence, nationality, and domicile, advice from an independent financial adviser (IFA), accountant, tax expert, or lawyer could be essential, well before the decision is made to depart. (**Note:** We would avoid going directly to government bureaucrats for this information, as they will almost always suggest the most conservative interpretation of any given tax situation. – Lin Pardey.)

I have written this particularly from the United Kingdom point of view, but the issues raised are likely to be similar for all nationalities. Governments in Britain in particular are notorious for constantly moving the positions of the financial goalposts. For this reason, you need to be aware of the changes announced at annual budgets in March, unless as a UK citizen, you have cut adrift from the implications of UK domicile.

The term *domicile* refers to the country to which you are most attached or would treat as your real home. It is not the same as nationality or residence.

Domicile definitions and the effect on tax liability will vary considerably, according to your country of birth and residence. Everyone will have domicile somewhere but not necessarily residence, as your boat can be treated as your residence, wherever it is. Again, this can affect tax liability. The name of the game obviously is to use the system to ensure that you pay as little tax on your investments and other income as possible, both during and after your voyage.

ALWAYS ACT LEGALLY

It is important to work within the system that affects you, rather than fight it. Citizens of the U.S. will be aware of the system of worldwide tax liability regardless of where you live and earn your money. Other countries are now operating similar regimes that are much harsher in their effect than the very liberal tax regime currently operating in the UK or New Zealand, where those living outside the UK enjoy potential tax advantages at the moment. (These are referred to later.) Tax evasion is illegal almost everywhere. Tax avoidance is legal everywhere, and one may arrange one's financial affairs to minimise tax payable under the law.

It is important to ensure the legality of your financial arrangements well before leaving, and to have some understanding of the tax laws relating to any country that you may be visiting for anything more than a six month stay, especially if you intend to undertake any remunerative activity during that stay. Your yacht could be confiscated by tax authorities who believe that you may have breached their rules.

YOUR PENSION – THE COST OF TAKING EARLY RETIREMENT

For many people, a pension is likely to be the largest asset capable of producing income. Generally, the pension income can be drawn from the age of 50 in Britain, but different rules apply elsewhere.

It is a near certainty that wherever you live, the earlier you take your pension benefits, the less you will receive as income. This is clearly because you are investing less into the plan and then potentially drawing the benefits for a much longer term. In the case of some occupational pension schemes, early retirement might reduce the pension payable by 6 percent per annum, for every year before normal retirement date. Thus, retire at 50 instead of 60 and your potential pension income could be reduced by 60 percent!

TAKE ADVICE WELL BEFORE RETIREMENT

Wherever you are, you should take advice about pension matters from an independent financial adviser (IFA) at least a year before setting off. The UK pension regime allows for 25 percent or more of the pension fund to be taken as tax-free cash for a personal pension. Occupational schemes work out tax-free cash on a different formula. The income from the pension will be liable to income tax deducted at up to 40 percent. However, if you are resident in another country, it is sometimes possible to have the income from the pension taxable in your new country of residence, which may be at lower rates. If sailing, however, and having no residence, this is not possible, and UK tax is payable out of the pension income before you receive it.

However, for those of you who are UK residents with a pension fund of £350,000 or more, or are likely to receive a pension of £30,000 or more per annum, there is a way of paying far less tax and enjoying a far better pension from your fund, provided that you comply with a number of procedures. It is possible to receive the proceeds of a UK pension at very low tax rates via an offshore facility; unfortunately, this interesting route is little understood by most pension advisers.

Double-taxation arrangements existing between the UK and other countries can affect you and pension planning very beneficially. This tax advantage is an opportunity of great significance for the early retiree who is going to be sailing away and not taking up new residence anywhere in the foreseeable future.

In the UK, it is important to consider the option of taking a transfer value from an occupational pension scheme into a personal pension plan and then drawing upon this plan for income while in retirement. This is particularly the case where life expectancy is limited or where the spouse is much younger than the pensioner, especially if early retirement is being taken.

LIVING ABROAD – ESPECIALLY RELEVANT TO UK CITIZENS

If you are UK, domiciled, but nonresident, then all income apart from perhaps pension income (read the above most carefully) may be received free of UK tax. (U.S. citizens may not be so fortunate.) To achieve this status, nonresident UK citizens will need to spend at least a whole year outside the UK, but up to 90 days spent in the UK as a visitor annually would not necessarily prejudice this tax-free status.

It would be wise to use an offshore tax haven, such as the UK Channel Islands or Isle of Man, for the management of your assets, such as investments and deposit interest in banks.

It is better to dispose of property, but should you retain it, it is wise to let it on lease and place it under management control. Net rent income in the UK will be subject to tax at the standard rate (23 percent).

Do not retain a UK bank account other than for the conduct of management of a property investment, which will need to be looked after by a managing agent.

For UK citizens leaving behind any assets that might be subject to income tax at source, it will be necessary to convince the Inland Revenue that you have definitely left the UK for a long period if they are to agree to permit you to draw your income from investments free of tax . They may be quite reluctant to agree.

Many UK citizens will have invested their savings in Personal Equity Plans (PEPs). They will not be able to continue adding to the PEP, but they may leave the plans in place and draw from them after they have ceased to be resident.

RETIREMENT RELIEF. If selling a business in the UK, provided you are over 50, you may obtain retirement relief from capital-gains tax on sale of your business, on the first £250,000 of gains. The next £500,000 is subject to tax at 20 percent. The budget of March 1998, however, has created a new regime which is to be phased in, whereby, profit from assets held in a business for 10 years will be subject to a capital gains tax of 10 percent and it seems likely that there will be no limit on the amount of gains. For the next five years, the old regime for taxation of retirement sales of business assets will run in tandem with the new regime. It is very clear that any person who is retiring at age 50 plus and disposing of a business would do well to consider disposing of it before the 5th April 1999, especially if the assets being sold have been held for at least 10 years.

You may however escape capital-gains tax altogether regardless of the type of asset and how long you have held it and whether or not it is a retirement sale, by leaving the country before April 5th, and then negotiating the sale of your business, or shares in it, or any other assets, while abroad. However, the budget of 1998 has reduced the value of this loophole as it will be necessary for you to remain outside the UK for five years for residency purposes. If you return before the five years you will be liable for the tax on your return.

You should ensure that you have cut all ties with the UK including disposing of any residential property that you could use for your own residential purposes before leaving the UK. Proceeds of sale should be removed from the UK and placed in a suitable tax haven for investment. While non-resident in the UK you are restricted to a total of 60 days in the UK per annum over a five years period.

DISPOSAL OF ASSETS, INCLUDING STOCKS, SHARES, AND COLLECTIVE INVESTMENTS

Dispose of all assets on which capital gains may occur, after you have left Britain. Take advice in your own country, if you are not British domiciled. Those who are neither UK resident or domiciled, and living on boats, may be able to make use of tax havens but U.S. citizens may have difficulties and anyway are liable to tax on earnings worldwide (after quite generous tax-free allowances). (Note: U.S. taxpayers who have proven they have bona-fide nonresidence, i.e., have physically been outside the U.S. for more than 510 days, are eligible for $70,000 of earnings tax-free in certain cases. – Lin Pardey.)

Offshore investment management can be tax-efficient for U.S. citizens, but it is necessary to examine the U.S. tax laws in this matter. UK rules indicate that three years abroad establishes nonresident status, but one full year *working* abroad will establish this status. Working as a charter skipper can be acceptable!

TAX RETURNS

It is advisable to inform the Inland Revenue or your tax authority that you are leaving your country of residence and establish the rules that exist for those who are leaving their country of normal residence. Arrange to pay tax due so as to avoid nasty shocks on your return. You should be able to prove the actual day when you left the country. For UK citizens, retention of any financial connection with the UK, including ownership of assets in the UK, may prejudice avoidance of inheritance tax if this is desired and another place of domicile of choice is the target. U.S. citizens and some others, such as green-card holders who are likely to wish to reside in the U.S. later on, need to file annual tax returns for tax, regardless of where they live. Failure to do so can cause loss of U.S. residency right.

TAX ABROAD

You should be aware that if you stay longer than 180 days in any one country, care needs to be taken because you may be liable to that country's income tax and maybe capital-gains tax. Some countries provide for acquisition of residential status and tax liability after a shorter period. *Find out before overstaying your welcome.* As long as you keep moving, you have no residential status and its attendant liability for tax, and therefore no income tax to pay (except those from countries applying worldwide tax liability). Thus, your investment income should attract no tax at all.

DEATH TAXES, CONSEQUENCES OF DOMICILE. While keeping moving to avoid residential status and therefore liability to income tax, domicile as such cannot be avoided. Quite simply, you have to be domiciled somewhere. When you die, if you are a UK-domiciled person and your assets are worth more than the Inheritance-Tax (IHT) threshold, your estate will be subject to inheritance tax at 40 percent on all assets apart from what you leave to a surviving spouse.

You can achieve relief from this risk of tax liability after death by applying for residence in a place where such taxes do not exist. The Isle of Man and the Channel Islands are examples, but Jersey is effectively closed to newcomers. Guernsey is fine, but you will need a residence there which is likely to cost £300,000, as it must be on what they call the Open Property Register. The cost of property on Alderney is far cheaper. The Isle of Man is also ideal. All three places have no capital-gains tax, no inheritance tax, and a 20 percent maximum income-tax rate. The benefits of transferring residence and becoming classified as working in the Isle of Man, may have some considerable benefits for many people intending to eventually depart from the UK to either sail away living on their boats, or who wish to eventually take up residence abroad.

One warning, however, about the Channel Islands. There are restrictions over the discretion which you have over instructions in a will for distribution of your estate. You could escape this consequence of Guernsey or Alderney domicile by placing your non-property assets in an Isle of Man Trust to act as custodian of your assets and investment certificates. The trust can provide for the beneficiaries to be those whom you specify.

For your estate to successfully avoid IHT, you will need to be away from the UK for at least three tax years, sever all business and property connections, and buy a burial plot in your new domicile.

WHERE THERE IS A WILL...

It is important to write a will, taking legal advice as to where it is likely to be the subject of probate.

Equalising of estates for husband and wife may be sensible if UK probate is likely. Two inheritance-tax bands will then be available. Each can leave half to children. However, it is quite acceptable at the moment to set up an Isle of Man Trust, with named beneficiaries, to include all children and grandchildren (born or unborn). The assets placed in this trust can be written as a single-premium life-assurance bond. If you live for seven years, the gift to that trust will then be outside your estate for the purposes of UK IHT liability. Meanwhile, you can still draw income at a rate of, say, 5 percent per annum from the bond to help finance your voyage. On your death, the surviving spouse may benefit, and after that your family.

USE AN INDEPENDENT ADVISER FOR INVESTMENT MANAGEMENT

An independent financial adviser (IFA) can assist with the investment of assets in a suitable tax haven. However, you should request an indication of the cost of this service, as offshore-investment services can be expensive. If the cost of setting up and running a portfolio reduces the investment returns by more than 1.8 percent per annum over a 10-year investment term, then question it. You need security, good investment returns, and low charges.

The illustrations which are now required to be provided to investors in the UK who invest in Unit Trusts, do show the true high cost of management of your investments by this route. Certainly the costs are likely to be higher than the alternative available of using a discretionary fund manager to look after your money. UK-based advisers are sure to have a minimum level of qualification, as all financial advisers are individually registered with a government regulator since mid-1998. In most other countries, there are very few, if any, controls on the activities of financial advisers. However, not all advisers fully understand or specialise in offshore investments and tax implications, so it is necessary to establish that they do specialize in this activity.

FUND MANAGEMENT FOR YOUR MONEY TO PROVIDE INCOME

I believe that most people who wish to sail away do not wish to be constantly concerned about the day-to-day performance of the stock markets or take undue risk with their money. This means there is all the more reason to suggest that most people will be best advised to ask an Independent Financial Adviser to use a discretionary fund management service to manage their money so as to provide a secure income. The cost is quite modest where over £100,000 is invested and is likely to be lower than investing in collective investments such as Unit Trusts and OEICS or, as the Americans term them, mutual funds. Account will be taken of tax situation, risk acceptance attitude, income requirements and changing investment opportunities while you are sailing. Arrangements to place assets in trust in, say, Jersey or the Isle of Man, can be arranged by the adviser. The fund management may well be operated from the City of London where vast sums are successfully managed. However, the stock holdings can be actually held outside the UK in a tax haven. The advantage of this approach is that UK financial advisers are well regulated and subject to individual registration with the Financial Services Authority who will regulate their activities. They all have to be qualified to a minimum standard and excellent investor protection and compensation schemes operate in the UK, the Isle of Man and the Channel Islands, with many giant UK financial institutions in the UK providing investor protection guarantees which apply to funds held in the offshore tax havens. Such a combination of security factors is not available elsewhere.

ACCESS TO LIQUID FUNDS. A suitable bank-account arrangement will provide credit-card and instant access to money anywhere, with accounts designated in any desired currency. It would seem that a Visa card is overall the most useful, but Mastercard/Eurocard and American Express are also very widely accepted. For ready cash, U.S. dollars is the most readily accepted cash anywhere. It must be worthwhile keeping some money as US$ AMEX traveler's cheques; they are very safe and if lost can be replaced and are acceptable anywhere.

TRAVEL AND LIFE ASSURANCE

If you choose to have insurance to pay for medical treatment, a worldwide plan is needed. If you are domiciled in the EU, while traveling in European Union countries, then obtain an E111 form from your local post office. This will give low-cost emergency medical treatment anywhere in the EU.

You might consider life assurance to pay a sum to a surviving partner were either partner to die on the trip. Remember that one consequence of early retirement is that any occupational life assurance will be lost. I believe that you should also arrange coverage against consequences of a critical illness while away. Such a plan can pay a lump sum on diagnosis of many very serious illnesses, such as cancer, heart trouble, or total and permanent disability. This could help to get you and your boat back home and pay for costs. If such plans are in place before intending to leave home, then the terms of the insurance are in place, but if you arrange the insurance with the trip in mind, it must be stated on the proposal, and the cost will increase. Again, it is best to take independent advice on the most suitable protection contracts.

AN ADDITIONAL MATTER ABOUT BOAT PURCHASE

If you are a resident of the EU and purchasing a boat, it will be subject to value-added tax (VAT). In the UK, VAT is 17.5 percent of the purchase price; it's similar throughout the EU. There is, however, a VAT concession within the EU which will allow a person who fully intends to take a boat outside of EU territorial waters to purchase a boat without paying VAT.

However, it may be better to take delivery in, say, Guernsey, where there is no VAT, and then sail off, leaving the countries of the EU altogether. On your return to the European Union countries, you will be liable to pay VAT in the country of entry at a rate operating in that country. Once tax is paid, the boat can be moved to any country in the EU without tax problems.

It is decidedly risky owning a boat built after 1985, that is used within EU waters, unless you can prove that VAT has been paid on it. (**Note:** Current EU regulations allow non-EU citizens to cruise within the EU for up to a year, with a further year's extension in most cases. Many countries, such as Scandinavian ones and Spain and Ireland, are quite generous in interpreting these regulations as long as you prove you are a bona-fide cruiser and do not become noticeably employed. – Lin Pardey.)

Foreigners staying in the U.S. or Australia for more than half a year are also at risk of paying massive taxes, even if their boat has had tax paid elsewhere. Greece is well known for its revenue-raising ability by this method, plus massive penalties for not volunteering to pay the tax. The application of the tax rules does seem to vary with veracity, according to where you are in Europe.

Customs booklet No 8 from HM Customs in Dover (UK) should provide most of the answers; however, I would advise anyone with a boat on which tax has not been paid to seek advice from the tax authorities in the country that they intend to visit within the EU, preferably before landing, and obtain the necessary confirmation and permits to allow them a tax-free visit.

DO NOT LEAVE IT TOO LATE

You need good health and strength to enjoy cruising. After a career, sitting in an office or traveling on airliners, sailing every day may seem like hard work. Allow for the fact that one day you may want a home ashore again. Grandchildren and declining years may beckon you home again, so the financial planning program must allow for all eventualities, even when home is the sailor, home from the sea.

This information is believed correct at the time of writing and is provided in the light of the writer's understanding of United Kingdom taxation. Changes in tax legislation may affect the above adversely, and no liability can be accepted for individual consequences of acting on any of the information provided. It is essential that individual advice be obtained from professional advisers who can advise on financial, legal, and accounting matters with individual circumstances taken into account.

Peter R. French is an Independent Financial Adviser and Partner in Troy French and Partners, based in Wimbledon, London. Tel: 044-181-879-0802. E-Mail: troyfrench@cableinet.co.uk. Unfortunately, Peter says, "As my wife does not share my passion for sailing, I will not be sailing off to the sun."

INDEX